Discontented Discourses

Feminism / Textual Intervention / Psychoanalysis

EDITED BY

MARLEEN S. BARR

AND RICHARD FELDSTEIN

UNIVERSITY OF ILLINOIS PRESS

URBANA AND CHICAGO

Permission to reprint "For Hélène Cixous," by
Ursula K. Le Guin, is gratefully acknowledged.

Library of Congress Cataloging-in-Publication Data

Discontented discourses: feminism/textual intervention/psychoanalysis
/ edited by Marleen S. Barr and Richard Feldstein.
p.   cm.
Includes index.
ISBN 0-252-01562-2 (cloth : alk. paper). ISBN 0-252-06023-7 (paper : alk. paper)
1. Feminism in literature. 2. Feminism and literature. 3. Women in literature. 4. Women
and literature. 5. Psychoanalysis and literature. 6. Women and psychoanalysis.
7. Literature, Modern—Women authors—History and criticism. I. Barr, Marleen S.
II. Feldstein, Richard.

PN56.F46D57 1989
809'.93352042—dc19   88-11943
                                                                     CIP

CONTENTS

Sexuality: The Misrepresented Woman

SECTION III
Theory and Disruption

Reading: The Revisionary Woman

Influence: The Vital Woman

Ursula Le Guin

Ursula Le Guin

For Hélène Cixous
"Je suis là où ça parle"

I'm there where
it's talking
where that speaks I
am in that talking place
                    where

That says
my being is
            where
my being there
is speaking
am I
            And so
laughing
in a stone ear

(1986)

Introduction

MARLEEN S. BARR

The antagonism between feminism and psychoanalysis is well known. Jane Gallop's *The Daughter's Seduction: Feminism and Psychoanalysis*, for example, addresses the problem of the feminist psychoanalytic critic whose theoretical stance is derived from the disruptive relationship between the two disciplines. Gallop, a mediator between French feminism and French psychoanalysis, sets up textual interventions to create "exchanges" between these opposing discourses. *Discontented Discourses: Feminism/ Textual Intervention/Psychoanalysis* benefits from Gallop's exchanges. The theorists who participate in this collection use feminism and psychoanalysis as a mediative tool to intervene between their own position and an opposing discourse. They call upon psycho-feminism itself to create exchanges between other belligerent perspectives. In each of the essays presented here, feminism and psychoanalysis intercede to mediate between a patriarchal discourse (named by each chapter's title) and a feminist discourse (named by each chapter's subtitle).

The volume presents broadened perspectives encompassing related issues that impact upon feminism and psychoanalysis. Seen from these altered perspectives, feminism and psychoanalysis serve other objectives, intrude to act as mediators of other, diverse methodologies. In terms of Ursula Le Guin's poem "For Hélène Cixous," this anthology is positioned in "the talking place," the site of Gallop's exchange, the space where feminism and psychoanalysis speak to each other, where laughter resounds "in a stone ear."

Helena Michie's opening essay discusses the unrelated Other woman who stands outside the family and disrupts the familial metaphor. Michie explains that while discord between sister and father fuels feminist practice, a harmonious mother/daughter relationship reproduces feminist psychoanalytic discourse. These metaphors become problematic when the

1

sister and mother delimit feminist discourse, which is both helped and hindered by the familial metaphor.

Michie shows that this familial metaphor—the disruption of the Oedipal triangle "from the space between father and daughter to the space(s) between sisters"—fails to incorporate "the Other woman" within the feminist family. She intervenes, disturbing the familial metaphor by viewing it, from a feminist perspective, as an ineffectual go-between: "What about the woman who is not one of this family, the 'other woman' who comes from outside to disrupt the home? It is this Other woman who concerns me here; it is she in her many guises for whom this paper attempts to make room."

Her detailed discussion of three essays written by feminist sister/mothers (Catharine Stimpson's "Feminism and Feminist Criticism" and Jane Gallop's "The Monster in the Mirror: The Feminist Critic's Psychoanalysis," and "Annie Leclerc Writing a Letter, with Vermeer") undermines "the very familial metaphor that Harold Bloom suggests is the basis of all re(mis)reading." Michie continues, "[t]o begin to acknowledge the possibility of the Other Woman one must work through the texts of other women; to move outside the family is to chart the places made accessible by its idiom."

Terry Brown discusses the problematic psychoanalytic familial metaphor by voicing her dissatisfaction with the father/daughter relationship. According to Brown, the feminist psychoanalytic critic mediates between feminism and psychoanalysis by progressing from familial estrangement to a feminist activism and alliance. The family becomes a metaphor to explain the position of psychoanalytic feminists in the romance between two feuding disciplines. Like Cordelia, psychoanalytic feminists find themselves "acting as 'daughters' who must speak in their 'father's' terms in order to stake out a place for themselves in the psychoanalytic kingdom." Brown views Juliet Mitchell's defense of Freud as representing the ambivalent relationship between feminism and psychoanalysis. This observation leads her to confront her own position in relation to Norman N. Holland. Instead of being a dutiful daughter who complacently applies Holland's ideas about identity theory to her own female experiences, Brown positions herself as the Other woman who intervenes to disrupt Holland's notion of identity theory. She responds to Holland by asking, "[H]ow can I be a woman without being only a woman?" When Brown becomes the Other woman, she questions the predictable psychoanalytic metaphorical role of the family. She intercedes, calling for new mediative metaphors, "an other way of thinking, one which transcends the predictable structures of triads and diads, and the hegemonic institutions of family and academy." Brown, who turns toward Lacanian psychoanalytic theory after demonstrating that identity theory leaves her no theoretical means to understand personal truths, might appropriately share Michie's conclusion. She disconnects herself from the language of identity theory by becoming a female Other who calls wholeness an "alien, even alienating, concept."

While Michie and Brown propose alternatives to the familial metaphor, Caughie and Salvaggio offer alternatives to gender constructions. They argue that discourse personified as an androgynous voice challenges the notion of discourse personified as either a masculine or feminine voice. Caughie exposes how certain feminists have appropriated Virginia Woolf's *Orlando* by making Woolf "the acclaimed Mother of Us All." Salvaggio exposes the masculine appropriation of science which leads to the negative feminization of literature. They both argue that the female "Other" is in truth a misunderstood feminine component which is improperly situated within specific texts.

Caughie believes that a faulty feminist rhetorical position has been attributed to *Orlando,* that Orlando's sexual identity is referentially misunderstood: "In promoting Virginia Woolf's *Orlando* as a feminist work, feminist critics have picked the right text, but for the wrong reasons. *Orlando* works as a feminist text not because of what it says about sexual identity, but because of what it manages not to say." She calls upon Lacanian readings by Jane Gallop and Shoshana Felman to support her argument.

Salvaggio shows that, like the misguided feminist appropriation of *Orlando,* the relationship between literature and science is referentially misunderstood. She believes that the discontent between science and literature can be assuaged through a psychoanalytic model of gender reconfiguration: "What is ultimately at stake here is a reconfiguration, in psychoanalytic terms, of the relationship between the masculine and the feminine. This reconfiguration would not invert the positions occupied by science and literature, masculine and feminine . . . but instead allows us to reposition ourselves so that we can respond to phenomena . . . in ways other than those that privilege one discourse over another, one sex over another." Feminist psychoanalytic theory interposes itself between literature and science and informs Salvaggio's notion that science may not continue to adhere to a masculine mode and literature is free to redefine its value system.

Salvaggio's "case of two cultures" posits a simultaneous or, in Caughie's terms, a "double discourse" for literature and science. This double discourse originates when particular discursive systems act according to the abrupt shifts from masculine to feminine in *Orlando*. Salvaggio explains: "particular discursive systems—which we know as science, as literature, and as psychoanalysis—have themselves assumed the characteristics of specific genders and have behaved according to their gendered identities." Caughie touches upon Salvaggio's point about gender and meaning: "The androgyne threatens meaning by breaking down those oppositions that allow us to make meaningful distinctions." Salvaggio concludes that rather than providing a means to circumvent gendered discourse, psychoanalysis enables us to reconstruct discourse and identity.

Salvaggio's points regarding the rhetorical repositioning of literature and science seem to be reflected by Caughie's statement about the face of scientific, literary, and psychological change: "[O]ne cannot locate innate sexual traits or essential literary values in the face of changing attitudes, conventions, and paradigms (whether scientific, literary, or psychological), one must continually posit and undermine, affirm and doubt." Salvaggio and Caughie assert the need to look at what language does in a particular text and context before satisfying the impulse to construct rhetorical references to the feminine. Backed by feminist psychoanalytic theory, they intervene to quell this impulse. They insist that when discourse is understood as a rhetorical split between female and male, feminists should not automatically appropriate the referential woman.

Barr and Feldstein are concerned with another area of representational configurations of male and female: humor from a feminist point of view. Feldstein's feminist psychoanalytic stance intervenes in the pictorial and lexical text of Woody Allen's films to discuss their displaced representation of women. His analysis seeks to expose Allen's tendency to locate women on the margins of comedy. In Barr's essay, a comic feminist utopia insists upon women's humor and women's empowerment. By intervening to bring a feminist reading of Sigmund Freud and Norman N. Holland to bear upon Gerd Brantenberg's *Egalia's Daughters,* Barr describes a specifically feminist humor. Feldstein argues that women are marginalized in a narcissistic cinema; Barr argues that women have been denied the chance to laugh with a humor of their own.

Feldstein states that "[l]ike Allen, most of his critics have ignored his repeated representation of women as supplementary commodities in a patriarchal system of exchange, refusing to acknowledge what privilege the writer/director/protagonist retained for himself and what significance he bestowed on his female protagonists." It is only in his eighth film, *Love and Death,* that Allen permits a woman to share the narrative privilege he has wielded from the beginning of his career. Further, "representation of women who are no longer the image of . . . [Allen's] eye and the

4

unacknowledged support of his system" only become central to Allen's narrative in a serious film, *Interiors.* As the absence of humor allows a female phallic figure to act as a self-referential stand-in for director Allen, the presence of feminist humor allows Brantenberg's Egalian women to act as stand-ins for powerful patriarchal men. Feldstein's reading of Allen's filmic discourse raises our insights about its humor to a level of feminist consciousness immediately presented in Brantenberg's text. Feldstein shows that the displacement of funny women in Allen's films reflects Allen's ambivalence toward women. Barr's reading of *Egalia's Daughters* reveals that patriarchy's displacement of feminist humor is yet another social suppression of women.

Barr concludes that "*Egalia's Daughters* is important because instead of simply functioning as a predictable sex-role reversal utopia it acts as a catalyst to encourage the untapped and unpredictable power of women's shared laughter. It shows that rather than having patriarchy construct women's identity, laughter can help women to avoid complacently accepting demeaning identity constructions." The Egalian woman is a displaced laugher. She functions as an empowering force for women, a corrective to Allen's displaced representation of the female comedian.

Feldstein points to a scene in *What's Up, Tigerlily?* where a shipment of women is described as a shipment of meat. *Egalia's Daughters* speaks to this scene by laughing at male anatomy and imagining new psychological constructions of body images. Barr points out that *Egalia's Daughters* confronts the patriarchal notion of woman's proper place during the sex act. Feldstein stresses that Allen's "repetition of phallocentric examples reveals a misogyny that repeatedly depicts his female protagonists as those who complement the Bond hero by masquerading themselves as the mimicked objects of male desire." Barr and Feldstein rely upon feminism and psychoanalysis to further their understanding of what constitutes a specifically feminist humor, a humor in which jokes do not misrepresent and distort depictions of women.

Judith Roof and Victoria Frenkel Harris move the second section's focus upon representation and distortion from a specifically female humor to a specifically female sexuality. They explore distorted representations of women and posit correctives to such distortions. When discussing Robert Bly's *Loving a Woman in Two Worlds,* Harris addresses issues regarding the distorted representation of women which are also raised by Feldstein, Barr, and Roof: "When [in Bly's volume] . . . an actual woman appears, she often retains the position typifying patriarchal portraits of woman; specifically, the object for the subject, man. . . . Though *Loving a Woman* is Bly's most overtly sexual volume, no female sexuality is articulated."

Roof seems to respond to Harris by arguing that literature incorrectly represents lesbian sexuality by defining it in terms of dominant, phallic sexuality. Literary versions of lesbian sexuality become distorted, or misrepresented. Roof intervenes to suggest a metaphorical corrective to these distortions: Virginia Woolf's image of the match in the crocus. Woolf's image informs Roof's discussion of "the difficulty of locating the place of lesbian sexuality in relation to the requisite visibility of a phallocentric system of representation." She insists upon the visibility of true lesbian sexuality by taking issue with male writers who superimpose the phallus as a means to represent lesbian sexuality: "The representation of lesbians . . . is for the benefit of the phallocracy, reinforcing phallic presence and attesting to its privilege. In this way, a great threat is turned to a great reassurance; a crisis becomes a cure." She intervenes in the male writers' texts to unmask the misrepresented nature of this reassurance and cure. She also intervenes in the texts of women writers who are "faced with the difficulty of representing perceptions unaccounted for in a phallic economy in terms of that economy." For Roof, Woolf's match in the crocus can mediate between misrepresentations of lesbian sexuality and the truth of that sexuality: "Like female genitalia . . . the match in the crocus hides the source of light, reveals its radiance, and simultaneously expresses its own inexpressibility."

With words applicable to Roof's concerns, Harris comments upon women's misrepresented insignificance in the patriarchal sexual signifying system: "[D]iscourse which addresses sexuality by marginalizing female sexuality is both distorted and ideologically consistent with a patriarchy that inscribes a superior male whose biologic economy becomes metonymic of central organization, logocentrism, monotheism, and rationalism." While Roof directs her points to the prose of various male and female writers, Harris addresses the relationship between patriarchy and the poetry of Bly and Adrienne Rich. The woman presented in *Loving a Woman* exemplifies Roof's notion of misrepresented female sexuality. Harris describes Bly's image as "trivialized, existing as an object of the masculine gaze, a female of essence whose gap accommodates a fetishized penis." Harris, in the manner of Roof, interposes a perspective designed to correct a distorted literary discourse "which addresses sexuality by marginalizing female sexuality." Rich's "Diving into the Wreck" functions as Harris's version of the match in the crocus, what Harris views as the salvaging of that which remains from patriarchal destruction. Roof and Harris define the male gaze as a misrepresented depiction of female sexuality. They reveal a new sense of radiant light illuminating an accurate representation of women's sexual experiences.

6

Roof's and Harris's new light is followed by Elizabeth Hirsh's and Christine Di Stefano's new ways of reading particular "isms." Hirsh views H. D. as a disruptive reviser of Modernism. Di Stefano views the (m)other as a disruptive reviser of John Stuart Mill's liberalism. This chapter asserts that both H. D. and the (m)other disrupt feminism. Hirsh states that H. D.— who enjoyed having her nude body become the focus of the camera's eye—"liked being an Image." Di Stefano states that evoking the image of the (m)other has both positive and "distinctive anti-feminist implications." Hirsh reveals H. D.'s missing proper image by bringing feminism and psychoanalysis to bear upon the poet as well as upon post-structuralist theory. Di Stefano reveals the (m)other's missing proper image through a psychoanalysis of Mill's liberalism and contemporary political theory.

Hirsh indicates that "in connection with the work and reputation of H. D., . . . feminist issues are implicated in this conflict about Modernism [Imagism's Image] through their implication in the problematic of the Image, whose dimensions feminism and psychoanalysis have been redefining." After arguing that Joseph Riddel's Lacanian reading of H. D. succeeds by pulling out her feminist eyes, Hirsh proposes that H. D. should be read in terms of Irigaray rather than Lacan. This alternative reading reveals that H. D. splits the "Image of Imagism, responds with a 'hieroglyphic' text that . . . reinterprets the Image in light of psychoanalysis, as a mode of hermeneutic veiling that restores the centrality of reading, and . . . prefers the pleasurable illusion of a feminine presence over the desire for knowledge." This rereading creates a pseudospace in literature by female Modernists in which Woman appears and leads to a revision of Modernism.

Hirsh's notion that rereading H. D. is analogous to Irigaray's "elsewhere of vision" seems to address Di Stefano's rereading of Mill and political theory. By locating the (m)other in Mill's texts, Di Stefano considers the elsewhere of vision of the (m)other in Mill and suggests revisions of political theory. According to Di Stefano, rereading political theory "in the name of the (m)other reveals and disrupts . . . patterned privileging of masculine experience and meaning." Her interventions within Mill's texts disrupt his liberalism by revealing that "in the case of the political and feminist theory of . . . Mill, the (m)other suggests that those terms [human need, desire, and achievement] are more specifically masculine than human." As Di Stefano posits that particular terms are more specifically masculine than human, Hirsh argues that the term "Imagiste" is more masculine than specifically applicable to H. D.: "H. D. has been accorded a certain place in the history of literature—but only insofar as she exemplifies, perfectly, . . . a certain *theory* of the Image, which is not her own. . . . H. D. was no theorist, only an example of and for a theory, an image . . . offered in evidence of a male-authored truth." H. D. is an at once absent and present disruptive referent created by Pound. Hirsh's H. D. is analogous to Di Stefano's (m)other "of masculine projection and exclusion, simultaneously present and absent, [who] serves as an unacknowledged referent of meaning within masculine discourse . . . she threatens to decenter and undermine the very discourse that has created her." H. D. and the (m)other find their images as respective psychoanalytic intermediaries between feminism and Modernism and between feminism and political theory. They are revisionary referents for rereading masculine discourse.

Hirsh and Di Stefano engage in unauthorized reading practices when they scrutinize masculinist texts with new feminist eyes. The (m)other's presence reveals that the working-class people and the women in Mill's discourse "must make themselves over in the image of the liberal Everyman in order to benefit from the promise of liberalism." H. D., in turn, must make herself over in the image of Pound's "Imagiste" in order to benefit from becoming the exemplar of Modernism. H. D. must deny parts of herself to become an exceptional woman in a Modernist culture that privileges masculinist discourses. In Di Stefano's words, "the exceptional woman, within the terms set by Mill, is also effectively transsexed and regendered. For the terms of her exceptional talent and drive are masculine terms." Di Stefano's comment describes Hirsh's H. D., the exceptional woman, the Imagiste, the nontheoretician who becomes an exemplar for theory, the female who becomes Pound's exemplar of the masculine subject. Di Stefano continues: "Without the (m)other, however, there is no masculine subject. He must have her. And so he does." Hirsh and Di Stefano both describe how the masculine subject appropriates the Woman. It must have her. It does have her—until feminist theorists reread, revise Woman's place in male discourse, intervene to assert that (in the words of Hirsh quoting filmmaker Peter Gidal) " '*images* of women' can never be 'images of *women*.' "

While Hirsh and Di Stefano disrupt theory through a process of rereading, Herr and Ragland-Sullivan disrupt theory by rethinking patriarchal influence. These four critics all seek what Herr, echoing Nietzsche and Fredric Jameson, calls "a release from the prison house of a patriarchal language." Ragland-Sullivan explains how her essay on Dora—and, indirectly, how Herr's consideration of anxiety—locate this release through an analysis of influence: "Humans are, then, the only cultural animals whose distinctive feature at the level of meaning is that they speak. When Lacan labels the Symbolic father the dead father, he means that any societal order defines human subjects and positions them in reference to lineage. The Real is linked to the Name(s)-of-the-father as they give meaning to biological parts encoded for *sens* within a context of *jouissance* speaking to one person." Both Herr and Ragland-Sullivan focus upon how women speak in a societal order that defines female subjects in reference to male lineage, to encoded meaning within an imposed context where the Name(s)-of-the-father are binding agents. Herr charts the influence of a male literary lineage as it both displays and portrays anxiety before considering Hélène Cixous's *Angst* and Lucia Joyce's life as responses to patriarchal encoded meaning. By viewing Lucia's life and Cixous's art within the context of patriarchal social order, Herr critiques Harold Bloom's concept of the anxiety of influence; she also presents a startling interpretation of Lucia's insanity as a by-product of her father's creativity. Ragland-Sullivan presents a new reading of Freud's analysis of Dora by posing a question about the case in Lacanian terms. "What did Dora want?" Ragland-Sullivan's incorporation of Lacan's influence within her own psychoanalytic perspective functions as a textual intervention which gives Dora a voice in the imposed context of patriarchal psychoanalytic lineage. The presentation of Dora and the protagonist of *Angst* within this chapter can be understood according to Herr's explanation of Cixous's term "the Vital woman": "The success of Cixous's endeavor [*Angst*] . . . finds witness in the book's epigraph: 'to the Vital woman, to whom this text did not know it would lead.' . . . The Vital woman, as Cixous would have it, finds her true self beyond the words—or at least in the emptiness between the last one written and the word that will follow." Much as Dora's unconscious desire is located between Ragland-Sullivan's intervention with the influence of Freud and Lacan, so, in the manner of Cixous, Herr and Ragland-Sullivan locate their own critical spaces in a place beyond a patriarchal use of language.

Herr enables the texts of *Angst* and Lucia's life to intervene within a line of literary primogeniture which includes Dickens, Freud, Joyce, and Barthelme. She mediates between feminism and psychoanalysis to clear space for new feminist paths and influences: Lucia's and Cixous's experiences emphasize "that the determinants of anxiety are enormously complex, dialectical, linguistic, and interpersonal. . . . The hope is that coming to terms with fiction that interrogates the prevailing masculinist models of behavior, experience, and response may produce alternative patterns of interaction and hence paths for personal and social development. Such feminist paths might sidetrack the obvious fill-in-the-blank model of male structures . . . in favor of a tolerance of emptiness as the site at which something new may begin to take shape." She charts the intrusive nature of patriarchal influences to clear a space for a new understanding of Lucia—

and, by implication, Dora. Further, when Herr proposes that Cixous's *Angst* is a new feminist scion of anxiety's patriarchal literary lineage, she alludes to her own—and Ragland-Sullivan's—enterprise: "What Cixous attempts is a fictional escape from the chain of influence that breeds anxiety—or at least a feminist intervention that refuses mere passive acceptance of the Father's Name and authority. Her narrative constantly bears witness to Joyce's presence . . . but . . . also insists on its own agenda of meanings." Herr and Ragland-Sullivan attempt to depict psychoanalysis as a means of mediating anxiety. Their feminist interventions bear witness to patriarchal tradition and insist upon establishing their own agenda of meanings—a voice and place for women (such as Dora and Lucia) within or, ideally, beyond patriarchal tradition.

Ragland-Sullivan views Dora as a symptom-ridden woman whose *raison d'être* resides in the emptiness of her words: "Lacan, like Freud, takes . . . [Dora's] symptoms to be metaphors; indicative of something else. . . . Kate Mele credits the editors [of *In Dora's Case*] for . . . wisely suggesting that 'there is no conclusion to Freud's story of Dora.' " Metaphors, not directly articulated symptoms, result in the absence of words with which to continue Freud's story of Dora. Ragland-Sullivan intervenes in the space opened by this absence to articulate the following proposal: "the feminist attention to Dora's plight—reminiscent of woman's lot . . . would take up the issue of the clinic as a place where individual, singular, suffering persons go with some degree of hope that psychic pain can be attenuated there." She fills a newly opened space by mediating between feminist theory and psychoanalytic clinical practice, by incorporating Freud and Lacan within endlessly opening new spaces: "Dora's case will be reinterpreted far into the future, for the case is a paradigm whose value lies in the large problematic it opens. Not only is Dora symbolic of the turn Freud made in taking women's symptoms seriously, she is also representative of Lacan's argument that Woman is, moreover, man's Symptom." Hence, like Herr, Ragland-Sullivan uses the influence of patriarchal tradition to blaze a new feminist path for her female subject

Herr intervenes to rethink the nature of anxiety as experienced by a female subject living within a patriarchal system. Ragland-Sullivan intervenes to place the feminine within the "dead" father's influence regarding the psychoanalytic structure of hysteria. She states that "[o]ne reading of these identifications [in Dora's dream testimonial] would support Lacan's view of a hysterical structure as vacillating between female models and unconsciously impotent—and thereby powerful—fathers." For Ragland-Sullivan, "silence or excessive talking become similar ways to use the voice in a quest whose aim is to deny or to know one's worth (ego) and one's desire." This questing voice allows a woman to know her worth—and allows her to become a Vital woman who locates her desire beyond the alienated words of the Other. Thus, as Herr explains that "Cixous had both come to terms with one of her fictional fathers, James Joyce, and found a place for Lacanian psychoanalysis within her own theorizing about female subjectivity," Ragland-Sullivan comes to terms with one of her psychoanalytic fathers, Freud, and derives her own theorizing from Lacanian psychoanalysis.

Ragland-Sullivan arrives at her conclusion regarding Dora's case by mediating between her own theorizing and Lacan's influence. This mediation takes the form of a textual intervention and corrective to certain feminist interpretations of Dora's case: "[B]y ignoring the scope of Lacan's theories and the precision of their formulation, and by blaming psychoanalysis and patriarchy for Dora's plight (her symptoms), I would suggest that certain feminist arguments miss the larger issue." Ragland-Sullivan places Dora within a space opened by her own application of Lacanian theory, which corrects what she views as some flawed feminist readings. Further, instead of pitting Freud against feminism, she attributes the failure of some psychoanalytic theory to neo-Freudianism. Both Freudian and feminist readings of Dora's case "still leave something to be desired." For Ragland-Sullivan, then, the best answers to questions raised by this case are provided by a Lacanian revisionism which acts as a corrective to the influence of ego psychology and essentialist feminisms. During the process of finding these answers, Ragland-Sullivan concludes that "Woman is not the object of psychoanalytic study but psychoanalysis *is* the discourse mode opened up by Lacan's idea that Woman is man's symptom." According to Ragland-Sullivan's argument, "the parties would not be psychoanalysts versus feminists, nor psychoanalysis and feminism, but the psychoanalytic feminist dialectic itself."

At the conclusion of Ragland-Sullivan's essay, this "psychoanalytic feminist dialectic itself" becomes isolated from the Freudian model and synonymous with the juxtaposition of her own theorizing with Lacan's theorizing. Further, when Ragland-Sullivan's final sentence locates psychoanalysis within the realm of praxis, she makes it possible for psychoanalysis to be controlled by Woman: "In this scenario psychoanalysis becomes the tool of Woman, and not the reverse." Ragland-Sullivan's textual intervention, her understanding of Lacanian theory which gives Woman the ability to use psychoanalysis, is a mediation which moves beyond the critical anxiety caused by "psychoanalysts versus feminists" and "psychoanalysis and feminism." After rejecting ego psychoanalytic and essentialist feminist interpretations, Ragland-Sullivan posits that psychoanalysis itself can be a means to achieve feminist ends. Her intervention casts out the conjunctions "and" and "versus" from their role as mediative links between "psychoanalysis" and "feminism." In the empty space situated within praxis and opened by moving beyond these conjunctions, Ragland-Sullivan establishes a coexistent relationship between "feminism" and "psychoanalysis," a feminist psychoanalysis born from her vital appropriation of Lacanian theory.

As Ragland-Sullivan indicates, feminist psychoanalysis displaces and replaces patriarchal psychoanalysis. Herr speaks to this point when commenting about *Angst*: "Cixous's story-without-a-father shows us a daughter who insists on saying it all." Feminist psychoanalysis is a daughter born of two mothers—feminist theory and psychoanalysis itself—and this hybrid discourse insists on trying to say it all. Herr's continuing remarks about *Angst* provide further commentary upon the voice of feminist psychoanalysis: "What seems to me significant . . . is the father's utter absence and the utterance that replaces him. Culture is thus rewritten from the daughter's point of view. . . . Her potentially freed subjectivity is, as yet, rendered mostly through silence. . . . [T]he loss of self occasioned by the interaction of female readers and patriarchal texts transforms identity into a state beyond a language that has become, for these readers, synonymous with suffering and anxiety." Within the essays presented in *Discontented Discourses,* the psychoanalytic feminist dialectic is the utterance which would replace the absent, often discredited, patriarchal psychoanalysis itself.

This anthology represents a gesture toward ending Woman's silence and realizing the potential of her freed subjectivity. It presents the transformations formulated by feminist readers who intervene to locate patriarchal texts within a vital position beyond alienated language. For these readers, this vital state becomes synonymous with locating Woman's desire, with ending Woman's suffering and anxiety. According to Le Guin's poem, the patriarchal critical establishment can no longer respond to what Woman has to say with "a stone ear."

SECTION I

Language and Disconnection

Not One of the Family:
The Repression of the Other
Woman in Feminist Theory

HELENA MICHIE

Feminism has come to occupy a contradictory place with regard to the family and to the familial drama at the heart of all psychoanalytic and some sociological accounts of gender. Accused by their critics of being antifamily, feminists have become, in the idiom that will be explored here, home-wreckers. Certainly the dominant metaphors of feminist critiques of society are familial in origin; the world "patriarchy" itself, familiarly ensconced at the center of the feminist lexicon, locates power in literal and metaphorical fatherhood and defines the family as the scene, if not the source, of women's oppression.

There is within feminism, however, a mirror tendency to reclaim the family and to reproduce it in altered form. The figural response to patriarchy is the "sisterhood" invoked as its challenge. The attack, then, comes from within the family, and from within the structuring metaphor that makes intimacy the place of conflict. It is by displacing that conflict generationally, by circumventing the mother and projecting aggression onto a historical, diachronic process, that feminists appropriate for themselves and their sisters the power of teleology and of progress. The struggle of *many* sisters with a *single* father is no simple reenactment of the Oedipal triangle, as it is almost inevitably construed. Criticized repeatedly for its ahistoricism, its synchronicity, and its isolationist insistence on the single child, the Oedipal conflict is disrupted although not dismembered by the introduction of politics and community as they enter onto the familial stage embodied severally as "sisters."

Sisterhood projects a series of daughters who usurp the function and privilege of the father by reproducing themselves. In choosing sisterhood over daughterhood, feminists have turned their gaze horizontally and have chosen—or tried to choose—to mirror each other and not the father. The axis of symmetry, the mirror of likeness upon which the Oedipal triangle is based, moves, then, from the space between father and daughter to the space(s) between sisters. Perhaps more important, feminist disruption of the symmetry to which the traditional Oedipal triangle accedes mixes the dominant metaphor, renders ungrammatical the word of the father, and exposes the faulty syntax of what Jacques Lacan calls his Law. It is important, however, that syntax, word, and language remain familial matters; the new grammar is still the grammar of the family.

If the clash between sister and father produces the rhetorical energy that fuels feminist practice, it is the relation between the mother and the daughter that has become the locus of the reproduction of feminist psychoanalytic discourse. For American object-relation theorists like Nancy Chodorow as well as neo-Lacanians like Hélène Cixous and Luce Irigaray, it is the problematic bond between mother and daughter that produces language, identity, and a provisional notion of "self" in the little girl. Feminists have, largely, turned their gaze from the Oedipal triangle to the pre-Oedipal period in which the girl struggles with her likeness and unlikeness to her mother before her entrance into and her inscription within the law of the father.

For a variety of historical and political reasons which I will not go into here, feminist literary theorists have followed psychoanalysis in recentering their inquiry around the mother.[1] While very early feminist theorists like Kate Millett struggled with the words of literary and academic fathers, more recent critics and theorists on both sides of the Atlantic have begun to turn their attention to maternal figures, maternal discourse. This discourse has taken many forms and has both figured in and figured almost all major feminist projects. Canonical revision has, for example, frequently been articulated as a search for foremothers; feminist post-structuralists have looked for the place of the mother in producing the *jouissance* that for critics from Roland Barthes to Jacques Derrida in turn produces and disseminates meaning, desire, and language; linguistic theorists have scanned literature and language for marks of *écriture féminine*, the mother tongue, what Cixous so famously refers to as "white ink . . . good mother's milk." Perhaps more fundamentally, motherhood and the maternal body have been seen as the location of language and self, the place where the female subject and the female narrative "I" are produced and reproduced.

16

As feminist discourse converges on the mother and the sister, it begins to problematize its own central metaphors. Most feminist theorists now acknowledge on some level at least the ambivalence of the mother-daughter relation, the painful tension in the female subject between love and matrophobia, likeness and unlikeness, the need for nurture and the need for separation.[2] Jane Gallop has explored the often-bitter rivalry between sisters for the love of the father, and increasingly, for self-love.[3]

Although theorists locate the causes of tension and rivalry differently—Chodorow, for example, sees matrophobia as a production of patriarchal familial relations, while Gallop seems to see it as an inevitable component of the growth of both mother and daughter—the mother-daughter relation is invoked as much to dramatize and problematize notions of the female self as it is to produce an integrated and integrative notion of female selfhood. No matter how problematized, metaphors of sisterhood and motherhood remain central to the feminist project. "Sister" and "mother" become the vessels that contain, shape, and delimit feminist discourse just as the family as it is now construed contains and shapes the roles and bodies of "real" mothers and sisters.

What about the woman who is not one of this family, the "other woman" who comes from outside to disrupt the home? It is this Other woman who concerns me here; it is she in her many guises for whom this paper attempts to make room. In popular parlance the Other woman is the mistress, the rival, the sexual threat. She is, however, Other in other senses: she is the third-world woman, the lesbian, the antifeminist, the one who is excluded from or resists the embrace of Oedipal sisterhood. While this paper cannot hope to deal effectively with all Other women, cannot even hope to name them since it is the nature of otherness to resist incorporation even by the act of naming, it is the beginning of an exploration of what lies outside what Gallop has called "the pitfall of familial thinking."[4]

The "Other Woman" is a phrase, a name, a non-name, that is beginning to surface in feminist writing and thinking. It finds a place in a veritable litany of popular and academic book titles. To name a few: the best-selling novel, *Other Women* by Lisa Alther, about the relationship between a female psychologist and a lesbian patient; *The Other Woman: Stories of Two Women and a Man,* an anthology of short stories edited by Susan Koppelman; *The New Other Woman,* by Laurel Richardson, a sociological study of single women who have affairs with married men, and of course, Luce Irigaray's critique of the phallogocentrism of Western metaphysics, *Speculum of the Other Woman.* The very similarity of the titles hints at a problem central to feminist perceptions of otherness; these titles, hardly other to each other, at once name the other woman and insert her into familiar sexual tropes.

Feminist unease with otherness lurks behind issues of title and entitlement; all four of these texts, in their different ways, can be read as strategies to control otherness, either by its displacement or removal from the speaking subject—the female structuring "I"—or by the incorporation of the other into the family, into sameness. An example of the first rhetorical strategy, *The New Other Woman,* opens, remarkably, with a statement about the author's motives in writing the book that is at once personal and disjunctive. The very first sentence invokes the familiar, improbable fiction of the "friend" who makes possible so many confessional moments: "A friend had been an Other Woman for almost two decades. . . . Her experience was the initial impetus to do the research leading to this book."[5] Literally true or not, the explanation of the book's inception as a response to the situation of a "friend" has the rhetorical effect of projecting otherness onto the life and the body of the other, of establishing a boundary between self and other that is rigorously maintained by sociosexual law, by, in other words, the law that produces and maintains the family. The Other woman, exiled from the family, provides a convenient and articulable space for the exile of otherness. All that is troubling, adulterous, troublingly adulterous within the family and within the wife can be impersonated by the Other woman.

Speculum of the Other Woman employs an opposite strategy by naming otherness between women only to reproduce it in its more familiar context of heterosexual difference. The "Other" of the title, in both French and English, would seem to modify "Woman" and to hint at the presence of at least two women, other in some sense to each other. In her only discussion of otherness as a category, however—which significantly and tantalizingly takes place in the course of her critique of Freud on female homosexuality—women's sexual identity becomes a matter of identity between women, lesbianism becomes a form of autoeroticism, and women's relations with each other, in the absence of men, become, quite explicitly, the relation of like to like, same to same. While she begins her critique by problematizing the words "like" and "same" by setting them off in quotation marks—"That a woman might desire a woman 'like' herself, someone of the 'same' sex, that she might also have auto- and homosexual appetites, is simply incomprehensible to Freud, and indeed inadmissible"—the quotation marks, those marks of difference, disappear as "same" and "like" get absorbed into the text and into the undifferentiating and capacious trope of sisterhood: "Yet what exhilarating pleasure it is to be partnered with someone like oneself. With a sister, in everyday terms."[6] Sisterhood as "everyday" term, as the infinitely iterated rhetorical move, surfaces here to erase difference between women and to close down its possible orthographic location between ironic quotation marks. Irigaray mirrors Richardson in her need to delimit otherness; like all mirrors, perhaps more vividly like all specula, *Speculum* both reproduces and inverts what it reflects.

If these mirror strategies for the containment of female otherness surface at crucial moments in Richardson and Irigaray, they serve as structures for three important texts of feminist criticism which this paper will discuss in some detail: Catharine Stimpson's "Feminism and Feminist Criticism" and two essays by Jane Gallop—"The Monster in the Mirror: The Feminist Critic's Psychoanalysis" and "Annie Leclerc Writing a Letter, with Vermeer." In examining how these texts simultaneously are and are not about the Other woman, how they make textual space for her entrance onto the scene of feminist criticism and close it off, I necessarily become absorbed by and into the texts of Other women as I absorb them into my paradigms. I hope throughout the process of these close readings of texts of my feminist sisters/mothers to disrupt the very familial metaphor that Harold Bloom suggests is the basis of all re(mis)-reading. To begin to acknowledge the possibility of the Other woman one must work through the texts of other women; to move outside the family is to chart the places made accessible by its idiom. I begin with Catharine Stimpson, who in her role as creator and first editor of *Signs* clearly occupies the place of mother in American feminist critical discourse, and with Jane Gallop, who repeatedly and disingenuously figures herself as daughter, sister, and rival in the field of psychoanalytic and feminist criticism.

Catharine Stimpson's essay is, on first reading, a triumph of the family of feminism, of a marriage not only as its title suggests between feminism and feminist criticism, but between and among a polyphony of feminist voices and enterprises. It summarizes, for an indulgent but perhaps uninformed public, the multiple projects of feminism. As a review essay it promises synthesis and integration. In describing feminism as a "mosaic" of women's voices, it comfortably subsumes differences among feminisms and feminists into a structuring metaphor that sees pattern and beauty in difference. More problematically, perhaps unconsciously, the essay seems at the same time to be a deconstruction of the mosaic, an exploration of the Otherness(es) within feminism. The specter of the Other in what at first reading seems to be a manifesto of pluralist coherence makes its entrances into her text through a series of linguistic slips and shifts. From her invocation of *Jean* Foucault, to whom she refers as "the other Foucault," to her concluding account of the rape of a colleague, another woman at her university, the other is simultaneously invoked and kept at bay.

On the surface, the essay's function is to integrate otherness, to make it other than other through a systematic dialectical pluralism that sympathetically includes and mediates among a number of disparate voices. It is also meticulously integrative on a rhetorical level, moving with ease from the personal to the academic to the political and refusing to see any rupture between them. Some of the most successful integrative moments in this essay are its numerous lists, which move lyrically among categories of feminist experience. In describing what she calls the contemporary feminist aesthetic she deliberately mixes genres and styles: "The new woman's culture self-consciously produces a feminist aesthetic that reconciles the flavorful gratuitousness of style with the imperatives of ideology. It appears in posters; clothing, such as T-shirts; demonstrations (those in Italy have a special elegance, verve, and theatricality); fine arts; films, and texts that experiment with a voice both personal and collective, that alludes to ricotta and Adrienne Rich, wool and Virginia Woolf, the domestic and the public."[7] Separated only by semicolons, the objects that make up these lists flow naturally into each other; they are litanies of inclusion, testaments to the graceful ease of feminist bridge-building. They promise a continuum, a seamless fabric: the mosaic naturalized and made fluid. This survey of feminist topography knows and inhabits all spaces, moving with equal freedom from the public world of demonstrations to the private world of wool, from England to (parenthetically) Italy.

The alliteration of the final list-within-a list "ricotta . . . Rich" "wool . . . Woolf" adds to the incantatory quality of prose based on the most liquid of metonymies and free associative techniques. The movement from ricotta to Rich undermines the potential grammatical impasse of the proper name, while the transmutation of wool into Woolf makes even the canon a matter of feminist weaving. Stimpson's parentheses absorb and contain difference, the foreign, in an expansive and expanding political syntax.

The larger structure of the essay repeats and amplifies the structure of the lists; there is an exhilarating sense of motion throughout as Stimpson moves with ease from topic to topic, from allusion to allusion. The authority of logic, of phallogocentrism, has been replaced with the enabling authority of experience. The essay's assured experiential voice moves with ease from paragraphs about Emily Dickinson to a Yale University computer program named Boris, to the New Testament, to Gertrude Stein. The structure of the essay, like that of the lists, proclaims that within feminism there is no Other, or rather that Otherness can be enveloped in feminism's fertile and nurturant embrace.

It would seem that the fluidity which marks the structure of the essay extends to its pronominal shifts. Apparently untroubled by the pain Monique Wittig and other feminist theorists have reproduced in the engendering of their female narrative "I"s and "she's," Stimpson begins with a historically situated "she": "In 1861, Emily Dickinson cut one of her shard-like poems about language," and moves immediately in the second paragraph to the academically forbidden narrative "I." Indeed, the "she" and the "I" come together in the act of producing the mosiac which structures this essay: "I place Emily Dickinson as the first inlay in the mosaic of my argument to the power of women writers. . . . I do not want to subordinate criticism to feminism, complexities of analysis to the severities of ideology. Neither do I wish to subordinate feminism to criticism. Rather, I seek a 'dialectical mediation between them' " (p. 272). Stimpson, in demonstrating her power to "place," has created a place for the "I" and the "she," the contemporary feminist and the nineteenth-century female poet, to create together. The "I," however, subsumes the "she" in creating both metaphor and mosaic. Like Derrida's "choreographies" of gender, Stimpson's mosaic both disguises and foregrounds the agent and her/his agency; a mosaic, like a dance, is an arrangement of seemingly spontaneous gestures and pieces.

It is not only women who have a place in Stimpson's mosaic. The embedded quotation in the passage just cited—"dialectical mediation between them"—represents the voice of a male, Marxist critic. Stimpson need not have depended on a footnote here; the term "dialectic" is common enough. The quotation marks, like the parentheses around Stimpson's earlier sentence about Italian demonstrations, serve precisely as marks of incorporation. Something foreign, something outside the nuclear family of Anglo-American feminism has been swallowed but left undigested as a testament to the power of feminist inclusion.

If the essay opens with a choreography of positions, of voices, to borrow from Stimpson's remarks about Emily Dickinson, "at once monolithic and polyphonic," it closes with an attempt to simplify and personalize these voices. In the last paragraph of the essay, the "I" reappears for the first time; the paragraph is worth quoting in full:

I began with a quotation. I wish to end with a difficult anecdote. I was thinking about feminist criticism one night as I was driving home from my university work. On either side of the highway's twelve lanes were oil refineries, with great curved pipes and round towers. I smelled industrial fumes. I saw no green, except for paint and neon signs. Earlier that day, after a meeting, a woman colleague had told me

21

about an experience. She had been raped, at knife-point, in her car, with her son watching. She was in her late twenties, her son only six. She was no Leda, the rapist no swan. To remember that story, to keep it as a fire within consciousness and political will, is the feminism in feminist criticism. Such a memory is a base of our use of language, no matter how skeptical we might be of language's referential power, as feminist criticism annuls powerful cultural arrangements, anneals again the materials of history, and reclaims language's push of joy.

By self-consciously calling attention to the narrative framing of her essay, Stimpson prepared us for both symmetry and teleology. The line "I wish to end with a difficult anecdote" simultaneously reminds us of the quotation with which the piece begins and promises us a change of direction, a movement inward that runs counter to symmetry, perhaps even to coherence. The "I" in "I wish to end" prepares us for its vulnerability; for the first time something is "difficult."

Significantly the "I" is one which both does and does not appear; it announces a violent opening-up (in the sense of both rape and discourse) that does and does not happen. The essay has set itself up for the rape of the author, for the personal to overwhelm the critical, for the "I" that has "placed" Dickinson to lose all control and distance. At the beginning of the paragraph we are made aware for the first time of the narrator's body. "I was thinking ... I smelled ... I saw" is both familiar in its integrative movement from thinking to smelling, the intellectual to the sensual, and radically defamiliarizing in its announcement of the presence of the body. Catharine Stimpson's body is the last piece of the mosaic to fall into place. We are prepared to move inward, to violate it, to share its violation, to be moved by it, to move below the surface of the mosaic. At this moment, tentatively embodied by the difficult, the vulnerable narrative "I," we are presented suddenly with a "she." She is the Other woman.

The words "a woman colleague" appear uneasily to us as the narrative "I," reassuring even in its vulnerability—we do, after all, know that the "I" survived, wrote, and is writing—disappears. "She had ... she was ... she was" become the sinister mirror burden of a song that began "I was thinking ... I smelled ... I saw." The Other woman appears only briefly; she is raped and vanishes. We only know that she is Other, that "she was no Leda." We do not know who she is except that she is not Catharine Stimpson, not Leda. The answer to the question, "Who is this other woman?" does not of course lie in her name or in any facts about her life before or after the rape. What interests me here is who she is not, and how who she is not allows her painful entrance into Stimpson's lyrical text.

The power of Stimpson's feminism depends on the somewhat problematic power of the tropes of analogy and metonymy at work within this final, moving, paragraph. The author remembers the story of the rape of her colleague when she, like her colleague at the time of the rape, is in a car. Stimpson's body positions itself in an act of rememberance and re-creation, at the wheel of her car. The author's body, in not being raped as she drives, simultaneously alludes to the body of the woman colleague and allows her the safety to speak for her colleague; the text becomes a witnessing by someone whose speech is made possible because she was not a witness in the usual sense. The "real" witness, the colleague's little boy, cannot speak here of this nightmare amplification and deformation of the primal scene; Stimpson substitutes for the little boy as she substitutes for his mother. The family idiom of feminism allows her to speak what for the family is unspeakable.

On one level, of course, this "difficult" personal/impersonal anecdote acts as a displacement, a way of mediating terror, an attempt to incorporate even the ultimate Otherness of rape into feminist discourse. The Other woman and her body become a test case for the integrative "I," for the warmly integrative yet respectful phrase "woman colleague." The strangely inappropriate phrase "push of joy" that ends this paragraph and this essay brings us back to the beginning where Stimpson quotes the same line from Dickinson. It is too much to say that the rape, through the triumphantly rhetorical ending, has become "a push of joy," that feminist language has been produced by the rape in the act of reproducing it. It is not too much to say that otherness appears briefly, violently, only to be "reclaimed" by feminism and its language.

It might at this point be useful to recall the beginning of Stimpson's essay, the opening invocation of Dickinson, whose name was the first to be placed in the mosaic. Running counter to the dominant metaphors of connection and coherence is a more troubling set of images that have to do with cutting, pain, and violence. "In 1861 Emily Dickinson cut one of her shard-like poems about language." Dickinson's voice, then, is not easily or unambiguously placed; her poems are "shards"—perhaps bits of mosaic broken into sharpness. Dickinson's voice severs connections even in the act of making them. In this context, Dickinson, the heroine in the romance of literary foremothers who constitute the feminist narrative of literary history, becomes herself Other, not only to the series of editors who tried to remove her shardlike dashes, not only to the patriarchy that kept her imprisoned in her father's house, but to the women who read her, identify her, identify *with* her, write about her, and try to "place" her.

Dickinson joins the colleague whose rape disrupts but is accommodated by the end of this essay to construct a frame that belies the body of Stimpson's argument; both colleague and literary foremother hint at the presence of otherness within the family, be it biological, academic, or literary. If the shardlike frame of Stimpson's essay implicitly undercuts its pronouncements of unity in diversity, the ending of Gallop's "The Monster in the Mirror" explicitly forces us to reread them with a view toward the crevices, cracks, and dislocations that signal the presence of the Other woman. Making familiar a rhetorical closing move out of the family, Gallop repeats in "Monster" the structural strategics of *The Daughter's Seduction*. In *Daughter*, Gallop moves chapter by chapter through the family as she discusses the daughter's struggles with and against her father, her mother, and her sister/rival. The final chapter disturbs the symmetry and intimacy of family relations by invoking otherness within the home in the person of the governess. "Monster" also turns toward the Other woman, offering her the last word. The Other woman of "Monster" is the woman of color, the third-world woman. In a paragraph visually separated from the body of her essay, Gallop concludes with a brief appreciation of Gayatri Spivak's "French Feminism in an International Frame":

> I see a connection between the problem I am pursuing and Spivak's critique of Western feminist theory. She argues that Western elite feminism can only project onto Third World Women. As an antidote to such narcissistic projection, she advocates a new question for feminism to ask. That antidotal question seems equally appropriate to the dilemma I have traced here . . . so I will close with Spivak's words: "However unfeasible and inefficient it may sound, I see no way to avoid insisting that there is a simultaneous other focus: not merely who am I? but who is the Other woman?"[8]

By quoting the Other woman on Otherness, Gallop would seem, in so far as this is possible, to be resisting the domestication of Otherness. She has not only given Spivak the last word, she has given her the last question— and it is one which Gallop will not try to answer. By placing a blank space between the body of the essay and the paragraph in which Spivak's words appear, she refuses the temptation to deny or absorb Otherness; she is, in effect, acknowledging the blank spaces between the pieces in Stimpson's mosaic. This gesture that closes but does not end the debate on Otherness is a gesture toward other answers, the answers of Other women.

Something happens, however, in the move from "Monster" to "Annie Leclerc"; the quotation from Spivak appears in identical form, but this time within the body of the essay. The appearance of the same Other woman in identical guise familiarizes her, makes her part of the family, makes her a Gallop. In quoting something she has already used, Gallop is now, in effect, quoting herself.

In "Annie Leclerc" Gallop structures a critique of the two covers of the *Critical Inquiry* special issue, *Writing and Sexual Difference,* much as I have structured my critique of Stimpson's two framing paragraphs. She looks first at the apparent sexual symmetry between the paintings reproduced on the two covers: "Together they compose a particularly well-articulated illustration of 'writing and sexual difference.' The woman is writing a letter, the man a book. Women write letters—personal, intimate, in relation; men write books—universal, public, in general circulation. The man in the picture is in fact Erasmus, father of our humanist tradition; the woman without a name. In the man's background: books. The woman sits against floral wallpaper."[9] In and between these covers, then, oppositeness, Otherness, will be defined as sexual difference. *Writing and Sexual Difference* will find its place within that difference, between the two covers that represent Man and Woman. The space between these covers is also, however, the space between marital, familial covers; it is a space defined, like heterosexual marriage, as the space between a man and a woman, a place of and constituted by their difference. There is certainly conflict in *Writing and Sexual Difference,* just as there are "differences" in the best-regulated marriage, but the paintings on the covers stand like sentinels to contain difference in its allocated, safe space "between" the sexes.

Gallop's article moves out of this safe space and text into another, more troubling text illustrated by a perhaps even more troubling painting: Annie Leclerc's "La Lettre d'amour," an extended love letter to another woman, and the painting to which the text consistently refers—Vermeer's "Lady Writing a Letter and Her Maidservant." In the painting, a woman is handing a (love?) letter to her maid.

The last five pages of Gallop's article perform an elaborate reading of the painting through Leclerc's text. Gallop's analysis focuses both implicitly and explicitly on the question of the otherness of the maidservant, on the otherness produced by class difference and reproduced as sexual desire in Leclerc's piece. Otherness also permeates the structure of Gallop's essay, which moves metonymically from *Writing and Sexual Difference* and the paintings which frame it to "Lettre d'amour," to the painting, to the Other woman within its frame.

25

Gallop preserves throughout the sexual dimension of Otherness, its challenge to heterosexual love and to what heterosexuality construes as "sexual difference." She reads Leclerc's desire for the other woman as it is problematized by class difference: "[Leclerc] contemplates the difference between these women [in the painting] and rather than feeling guilt at this difference, rather than feeling pity, she feels desire. She writes 'I love the woman servant . . . oh no, not out of pity, not because I would take up the noble mantle of redressers of wrongs . . . but because I want to touch her, to take her hands, to bury my head in her chest, to smother her cheeks and neck with kisses" (111). Difference, recast, produces desire; class becomes an erotic, a "sexual" difference. The maidservant in the painting, seen through a series of mediating concentric circles, frames, texts, comes to embody desire and the absences and lacks which constitute it.

The concentric nature of this article's textuality repeats itself in the topography of its sexuality. After discussing the possible "problems" with Leclerc's desire for the servant ("there is a long phallic tradition of desire for those with less power and privilege"), Gallop inserts herself and her own desires into the text—parenthetically: "Despite these problems I have with Leclerc's desire for the maid (an erotic attraction to women of another class which I share, I should add), I think it is valuable as a powerful account of just that sort of desire" (111). Gallop places herself last in a chain of desirers who through a series of differences announce their attractions to the maid. Like the woman colleague in Stimpson's essay, Gallop appears only briefly, parenthetically, near the end of the essay. Gallop's entrance into the text as a narrative "I" simultaneously confirms the maidservant's otherness, her position as object to a telescopic series of readers and desirers, and announces Gallop's own otherness to her text. Gallop becomes, then, her own sexually disruptive, parenthetically contained Other. Her intrusion into this multiple scene of desire marks her, sets her off in the very act of identifying with Leclerc, with Vermeer, and with the maid. The "should" of the doubly parenthetical "I should add," foregrounds the problematics of textual self-insertion as effectively as Stimpson's announcement that the closing anecdote of her text will be "difficult." There is coercion in Gallop's "should" that is itself difficult, hard to locate. Who is telling Gallop to confess? Perhaps it is the prescriptive teleology of feminist discourse that demands that a place be made for the "I" and for its (her) desires. Like Stimpson, Gallop promises an "I" only to give us a "she"; like Stimpson the "she" is subsumed under the signature of the "I" as the Other woman becomes other than Other.

Gallop ends this essay, which explores sexual difference as a space between women, with a fragment of the quotation from Spivak with which she ended "Monster" and which she has already placed so securely in the body of this essay. She ends with the "necessarily double and no less urgent questions of feminism: 'not merely who am I? But who is the other woman?' " By repeating Spivak's questions at the end of the essay, Gallop obviously underscores their centrality. By making them central, by placing them in, as it were, her mosaic, she is denying that they are Other. By ending two essays with the words of the same Other woman, she is rendering Spivak's words familiar and welcoming her into the family. The mirror that so frighteningly replicates women in "Monster" is held up to Spivak's face. In looking over Spivak's shoulder, Gallop sees Jane Gallop. The question, "who is the Other woman" transforms itself on the surface of the mirror into the questionable statement "The Other Woman is myself." Gallop's essay, like many rhetorical and political gestures that begin as explorations of Otherness, ends by absorbing Otherness into an increasingly capacious notion of self. It is this capacious and hungry self—most benignly embodied in the metaphor of sisterhood—that feminists must learn to recognize so that they can ultimately recognize the face outside the mirror: the face of the Other woman.

Notes

1. For a review of recent theoretical explorations of the mother-daughter bond see Marianne Hirsch, "Mothers and Daughters," *Signs* 7, no. 1 (1981), 200–222.
2. Luce Irigaray inscribes the maternal/filial dilemma orthographically by coining the word "in-difference" to describe both the (inevitable?) split between mother and daughter and their non-difference (lack of differentiation). Both underlie surface "indifference." See Luce Irigaray, "When Our Lips Speak Together," *Signs* 6, no. 1 (1983), 71.
3. Jane Gallop, *The Daughter's Seduction* (Ithaca: Cornell Univ. Press, 1982), chap. 5.
4. Gallop, *Daughter's Seduction*, p. xv.
5. Laurel Richardson, *The New Other Woman* (New York: Macmillan, 1985), p. ix.
6. Luce Irigaray, *Speculum of the Other Woman*, trans. Gillian C. Gill (Ithaca: Cornell Univ. Press, 1985), pp. 101, 103.
7. Catharine R. Stimpson, "Feminism and Feminist Criticism," *Massachusetts Review*, 24, no. 2 (1983), 275.

8. Jane Gallop, "The Monster in the Mirror: The Feminist Critic's Psychoanalysis," delivered for the first time at the English Institute, Cambridge, Mass., September, 1983.
9. Jane Gallop, "Annie Leclerc Writing a Letter, with Vermeer," *October,* Summer, 1985, pp. 104, 107.

Feminism and Psychoanalysis, a Family Affair?

TERRY BROWN

Lear: ... What shall you say to draw
A third more opulent than your sister? Speak.
Cordelia: Nothing, my lord.

Cordelia's defiant response to her father's demand dramatizes the dilemma that each feminine subject has in relation to a patriarchal discourse. It is a dilemma that has preoccupied virtually every post-structuralist feminist in recent years: how can a woman "answer" the partriarchy in its terms without relinquishing her own identity as a woman? If a person comes into subjectivity by entering into a symbolic order of language, how can a woman come into subjectivity *as a woman* in a language that is a reflection of masculine desire? Teresa de Lauretis asks, "How does one write as a woman?" (10). Juliet Mitchell places the question within the context of the clinic: "If language is phallocentric, what is a woman patient doing when she is speaking? What is a woman analyst doing when she is listening and speaking back?" (*Women: The Longest Revolution* 288). When the question—are you a woman?—is put directly to Luce Irigaray, she tries to answer from a position in which being and subjectivity have been deconstructed: " 'I' am not 'I,' I *am* not, I am not *one*." Irigaray, in other words, attempts to answer outside the phallocentric economy of the question in order to keep from being identified as a masculine subject by speaking a masculine discourse.[1]

In Shakespeare's dramatized version of the dilemma, Cordelia, as a feminine subject, like Irigaray, tries to confound the patrocentric economy of competition and measurement by refusing to speak in its terms. "What shall Cordelia speak?" she asks. "Love, and be silent." Cordelia refuses to identify with her father, unlike her sisters Regan and Goneril, who identify with him by imitating his discourse which speaks of love as a system of weights and balances. But Cordelia will pay with her life for her silence, her refusal to enter into the symbolic order that her father's

29

discourse exemplifies, just as a human subject pays with her ability (not willingness) to speak—psychosis—for her unconscious decision not to enter into the symbolic order of language.

Cordelia's dilemma, then, may metaphorize the unconscious psychic choice that the feminine subject as a daughter makes when she negotiates her way into subjectivity through an alienating language, the language of her father. While many psychoanalytic feminists have been theorizing this unconscious psychic negotiation, they have ironically found themselves in a position similar to the one they have been theorizing. Cordelia's dilemma, in other words, also serves as a metaphor for the difficult place in which some psychoanalytic feminists have found themselves in relation to psychoanalysis—as "daughters" who must speak in their "father's" terms in order to stake out a place for themselves in the psychoanalytic kingdom.

With the recent alliance between feminism and psychoanalysis, feminist theorists often rely on family metaphors—particularly the father-daughter metaphor—in describing their relationship to psychoanalysis. Given the historically uneasy relations between feminism and psychoanalysis, the Oedipal narrative about how a child struggles with desire and hostility toward its parents has become an appropriate metaphor for each discipline to explain its connection with the other.[2] This family metaphor is appropriate because the family structure is the one fundamental structure which reconstitutes itself every time two human subjects try to communicate, given the fact that we come to subjecthood in relation to a mother and a father. Jane Gallop's "daughter's seduction" constitutes perhaps the most celebrated and controversial example of the feminist critic's use of Freud's family romance as a metaphor for the network of desire that comprises the relationship between psychoanalysis and feminism.

Perhaps it is the very "familiarity," the intimacy, of the father-daughter metaphor which makes it so difficult for some critics to accept. However expressive this intimate metaphor may be, many feminists, psychoanalytic and nonpsychoanalytic, fear that describing feminism as a daughter in relation to psychoanalysis, its father, forces them into a role of submissiveness that they have been striving to escape.[3] Nina Baym, a nonpsychoanalytic (even *anti*-psychoanalytic) feminist, complains that some feminists have elevated the bad guys, Freud and Lacan, to dubious positions of authority. She says: "We are most 'daddy's girl' when we seek—as Jane Gallop not long ago expressed it—to seduce him. Our attempt to seduce him—or our compliance with his attempt to seduce *us*—guarantees his authority" (52). Gallop, of course, is speaking metaphorically when she compares the relationship between feminism and psychoanalysis to that between a father and a daughter. Even more important, the metaphor itself does not make us, as feminists, submissive guarantors of psychoanalytic authority. Rather, the metaphor reflects the real anxiety that some psychoanalytic feminists feel in this controversial relationship. Instead of rejecting the metaphor because it is too intimate, or because it seems to place feminists in a vulnerable position, a position from which we have been struggling to escape, we have to ask why this intimacy makes us uneasy. Why is the daughter necessarily considered to be submissive in relation to the father? What real truth about the relationship between feminism and psychoanalysis does the metaphor reveal? We can use this metaphor to make the strange familiar, by figuring the strange—that is, feminism and psychoanalysis—in terms of the *famili*ar—the family narrative.

In trying to understand the contours of this narrative spoken by feminism and psychoanalysis, we might consider some notable psychoanalytic critics who both consciously and unconsciously place themselves in such a triangular, Oedipal relationship to other theorists. I am especially interested in the way that psychoanalystic feminists such as Juliet Mitchell and Jane Gallop perceive themselves in this family romance between two "subjects," two theories, and the way in which they recognize and expose their position in that romance. My intention here is to lead myself—and other feminist psychoanalytic critics—to some tolerable perception of our position in this family romance. Let me begin with the father-daughter dynamic, a dynamic that has served as one of the most important metaphors for describing feminism's relationship to psychoanalysis, and a dynamic that is complicated by a knot of power exchange called "transference." Once we understand the father-daughter dynamic we may eventually understand a suspiciously absent dynamic in this family metaphor—the dynamic between mother and daughter.

The position in which Juliet Mitchell places herself, a position which many feminists have criticized, is symptomatic of the difficulty that most psychoanalytic feminists encounter when they practice their theories. Mitchell's career as a psychoanalytic feminist, in fact, might be considered a microcosmic symbol of the process that some feminists in the last decade and a half have followed in coming to terms with psychoanalysis. In 1971, Mitchell published *Woman's Estate,* a forceful political history of the women's liberation movement and a book which established her as a prominent political feminist. Then, three years later, she published *Psychoanalysis and Feminism: Freud, Reich, Laing, and Women,* a book which, because of its dutiful reading of Freud, prompted many feminists to question the sincerity and direction of Mitchell's feminism. Most recently, in 1984, Mitchell published a collection of her essays, *Women:*

The Longest Revolution, which reconciles the two sides of her career, bringing her interest in psychoanalysis and her interest in feminism together in a balanced, unified statement. My point is that, like Juliet Mitchell, psychoanalytic feminists struggle with the same problem of identification, and that Mitchell's defense of psychoanalysis in *Psychoanalysis and Feminism* is emblematic of this difficulty.

While Mitchell claims that she is trying to engage feminism in a dialogue with psychoanalysis, the dialogue becomes a monologue as Mitchell speaks entirely for psychoanalysis, failing to give feminism a significant voice in the conversation. It is this one-sidedness of Mitchell's study that has provoked feminists such as Nancy Chodorow, who complains that Mitchell's "otherwise provocative and important discussion includes a zealous defense of every claim Freud makes. She implies that all have equal empirical and methodological status and are always valid. Therefore (I think unfortunately) she has sometimes failed to convince others, since she often seems another apologist for Freud's misogyny and patriarchal distortions" (141). But while Mitchell's defense of Freud may appear too obedient, it is important at least historically insofar as it attempts to engage feminism in a dialogue with psychoanalysis (an achievement which I suspect was in part responsible for the attention and interest with which Chodorow's *The Reproduction of Mothering* was received five years after Mitchell's book was published). Despite its problems, Mitchell's book may mark the moment in the history of the relationship between these subjects when feminism begins to speak to psychoanalysis in "familiar" terms.

Why does Mitchell feel compelled to silence feminism in this important conversation with psychoanalysis? Jane Gallop argues that Mitchell wants to transcend the feminism that she engages, and that she wants to distance herself from the feminists she criticizes—de Beauvoir, Friedan, and Millett—while she engages their ideas in a dialogue with Freud's theories. Gallop says, "she is locked into an exchange with those whom she is trying to transcend. Hence she is most forcefully lucid in criticizing these her interlocutors, and weakest in synthesizing a version of Freud that goes outside the limits of that conversation" (*Daughter's Seduction* 5). Mitchell's problem may not be that she cannot "transcend" the terms of her exchange, but that she refuses to see, or simply cannot see, that her own identity is intricately linked to both psychoanalysis and feminism. Her position, in other words, is already within the terms of her exchange—she is already Freud's daughter.

Pushing Gallop's schema to its limits, Mitchell's attempt to recuperate Freudian theory might become a gesture that arises out of penis envy, an attempt to look like, or identify with, the father by espousing his (phallic) ideas. Here we reach the limitations of the father-daughter metaphor. For applying the same method that Gallop uses to describe Irigaray's relationship to Lacan, we arrive at absurd conclusions about Mitchell's desire for a penis which will give her value. Mitchell's defense of Freud nonetheless illustrates what Gallop describes as the "father's seduction," the "vicious circle" of seduction in which the daughter, however complicit, feels trapped. As the story goes, the daughter desires value, so she desires her father's penis, which will give her value (the penis being the most significant symbol of power and value in a patriarchal culture). Since the father cannot give in to the disordered and dangerous desire of the incestuous relation, he refuses to seduce her with his penis, seducing her with his law instead. The daughter submits to the law in order to please her father, in order to seduce him by doing his bidding (*Daughter's Seduction* 70–71). In desiring to do Freud's bidding, Juliet Mitchell is seduced by father Freud and his "law": she may not actually espouse his phallocentric theory, yet she identifies with the agent—the father—who has spoken those terms.

This vicious circle of desire and seduction depends on the fundamental "fact of transference" in which the daughter perceives the father as the subject who knows, the subject who has the value that she desires. According to one of several definitions of transference, the relationship between the subject and her parents is reconstituted in the relationship between her and her analyst, her teacher, or even her lover. In other words, the transference occurs between two subjects when one is presumed to possess authority, or power, over the other. It is also important that this transferential relationship is steeped in "instinctual ambivalence" because the subject transfers both affectionate and hostile feelings onto the subject presumed to know. If transference becomes a liability in any relationship where the other is presumed to know, then Freud's seduction of Mitchell, and her ambivalent compliance, would have been predictable—perhaps inevitable. Unlike some feminists who criticize Mitchell for her defense of Freud, I would like to suggest that her defense is not only symptomatic of the effects of transference but also symbolic of the difficult position that feminists find themselves in with respect to psychoanalysis. I am not surprised, then, when I find myself, as a student of feminism and psychoanalysis, in a similar transferential relationship with another analyst-father-teacher, Norman N. Holland.

When I began studying "under" Norman Holland over two years ago, I was swept away—"seduced"—by his theory about how our human identity shapes the texts we read. In general, identity theory holds that every human subject perceives the world according to his or her own, unique "identity theme"—a personal style of encountering the world and reacting to it. Holland explains identity theory using the metaphor of the feedback loop, in which the mind acts as a sort of thermostat, testing the outside world, then adjusting itself in response to environmental stimuli. According to this model, every human identity tests and adjusts to the outside world in unique ways, given the variables—biological and cultural—that affect the way in which the mind processes the stimuli (*The I* 112–14).

I accepted Holland's theory without questioning its assumptions (just as Mitchell unquestioningly defends Freud), and I became a dutiful daughter by reading and writing according to father Holland's reader-response theory—his "law." I applied Holland's idea that we "transact" texts, that we read according to our own individual defenses, expectations, and fantasies, to my own approach to teaching and research. In my teaching, I now explore more readily and with more respect the various emotional responses that the text elicits in my students, encouraging them to express their associations in order that they might understand their own patterns of responses, or "identity themes." In my research, for instance, I have argued in one project that teaching styles are as personal as fingerprints: the transaction between teacher and students is analogous to the transaction between reader and text. In a different manner, I have also employed Holland's reader-response theory by self-consciously admitting that my way of reading, say, one of Keats's odes, is determined by my identity theme, a theme I discovered in a self-exploratory seminar with Holland.[4]

In that seminar I learned that because the power exchange between my real father and myself has been crucial to the development of my identity, I tend to read texts aware of such exchange between imaginary and symbolic fathers and daughters—as I do here in this essay. Thus I confront imaginary and symbolic fathers rather in the manner that Cordelia confronts Lear—resisting, often defiantly, assimilation into their economy and discourse. I learned in Holland's seminar that insofar as my identity is defined by my unconscious positioning with respect to "the father," I am not at all certain about my identity as a woman. And in that seminar I uncovered a fragment of my desire—my "identity theme" in Holland's terms—which I phrased not as a sentence or declaration about my being but as a question: "How can I be a woman without being only a woman?"

It will not surprise any reader-response critic that my question, my identity theme, is a version of the question that I hear post-structuralist feminists asking about feminine subjectivity. What does it mean to be a woman in patriarchy? feminist theorists have been asking. What value does the patriarchy ascribe to woman, to women? And how does this value affect the psychosexual development of a feminine subject? I believe that my question of desire reflects the split subjectivity of woman that de Lauretis theorizes in her book *Alice Doesn't,* when she distinguishes between "woman" as a "fictional construct, a distillate from diverse but congruent discourses dominant in Western cultures" and between "women" as "real historical beings who cannot as yet be defined outside of those discursive formations" (5). In a sense, my identity theme expresses a psychic dilemma that I have experienced as a woman, a real historical being, confronting a discursive construct that mythologizes woman as "only a woman."

Holland's identity theory and method ironically allowed me to uncover at least one question in my desire, but it left me without a means to begin to answer that question, or even explain it psychoanalytically. First of all, identity theory posits a "constant core" of the self that is unified, knowable, and representable. For Holland, "identity is a way of putting into words the dialectic of sameness and difference that is a human life." That "putting into words" or representation of identity "leads to two possibilities. How do I represent the wholeness of you? How do I represent the wholeness of me?" (*The I* 36). When I confronted these questions that are fundamental to Holland's theory, I discovered that I could not state anything certain about the "wholeness" of my identity since wholeness of being is an alien, even alienating, concept for me. The notion of framing the complexities of a human identity—my own or someone else's—in a sentence or two seemed too imperialistic. I began to feel like the narrator of one of Grace Paley's stories who shuns plot because, she says, "everyone, real or invented, deserves the open destiny of life" (36).[5] I felt uncomfortable forcing my identity or the identity of another into unified statements that seem to foreclose any possibility of change.

My own question of desire—how can I be a woman without being only a woman?—reflects a splitting of subjectivity into two perplexing pieces: woman/only a woman. Thus, the idea of a "constant core" of identity as Holland has explained it seems too unified to describe accurately my experience and desire. Since studying with Holland, my question of desire has taken me to another theory of psychoanalysis, a theory which "feels right" to me because it does not posit a whole, knowable, and representable self. As Ellie Ragland-Sullivan says, "The whole of a life story can never be recovered within a Lacanian purview, indeed never exists in 'full' form at any time or in any place" ("Dora and the Name-of-the-Father" 216). Lacanian psychoanalysis has helped me understand that my question of desire is one that reflects a hysteric's discourse and a hysterical structuration of the unconscious. The question "how can I be a woman without being only a woman" is a version of the hysteric's question "am I a man or am I a woman?"

In the course of my discipleship to Holland, I eventually realized that I could not be both a good daughter to father Holland and the kind of feminist that I wanted to be at the same time without some careful psychological negotiations on my part. I therefore distanced myself from that identification with "the father," and tried to identify instead with some other, feminine and feminist figure (risking the transference once again, only this time in relation to a woman). I mention this transferential relationship because I want to point out the dilemma that feminists face as daughters of paternal psychoanalytic critics. It is, of course, a dilemma that most female graduate students face, considering the fact that most mentors, graduate research professors, are male, despite the fact that, as Carolyn Heilburn has said, "we have begun to produce women mentors in impressive numbers" (283). We seem initially seduced by theories that assimilate us into the masculine realm, and then later we become caught up in the anxiety of having to reclaim our individual identity by extricating ourselves from the subservient position we inevitably assume in that identification. But why must psychoanalysis assume the position of father, the subject supposed to know, and feminism that of seduced and seductive daughter? If we can speak of these disciplines as if they were human subjects (they are, of course, "subjects" in another sense), then I would say that psychoanalysis *wants* to father feminism, to seduce feminism with psychoanalytic discourse, its law—perhaps in order to protect itself from the disordered otherness of feminism. It is no coincidence that this desire of the father, the subject supposed to know, functions as a countertransference in which feminism the daughter influences the father's own unconscious feelings.

When feminist criticism finds itself inscribed within the psychoanalytic discipline at the same time that it resists that inscription, the transferential relationship with the psychoanalytic discipline, the father, becomes charged with desire *and* rejection, compliance *and* contempt on the daughter's side. As feminist psychoanalytic critics we must be aware of this transference, always exposing the law of the father-discipline even as we submit to its language and borrow its terms. In her preface to *Reading Lacan* Jane Gallop proposes an alternative way for feminists to read father-psychoanalysts, and uses her own reading of Lacan as an example. She says that in reading Lacan, she is "attempting to do psychoanalytic reading that includes recognition of transference as it is enacted in the process of reading: that is, readings of the symptomatic effects produced by presumption that the text is the very place 'where meaning and *knowledge* of meaning reside' " (30). But what are these "symptomatic effects"? In my own "reading transference" into the text of my teacher Norman Holland, these effects would seem to include faithful applications of his theory to my research and teaching. Yet even these dutiful responses, while they inevitably accompany transference, at the same time expose the slips and inequities in the father's law. In my "case," I still accept, and even practice, the very fundamental notions of Holland's reader-response theory, while I continue to resist being positioned within its implied hierarchy and, in Holland's own terms, its "major imperialism" ("Twenty-Five Years" 50).

Until now, I have been talking about a relationship between only two terms in the Oedipal triangle—the father and daughter. I am tempted at this point to speculate about the place of the mother in this figurative triangle. Who and where is she when we are discussing the father-daughter relationship between psychoanalysis and feminism? I think that this question might very well lead us to new perceptions of ourselves as psychoanalytic feminists when we rethink our indebtedness to psychoanalysis. Several psychoanalytic feminist critics have tried to recuperate the figure of the mother, especially in their theories about psychoanalysis and literature. Susan Rubin Suleiman discusses the ways in which a writer's narrative emerges out of her desire to recover the mother's body. "The work of art itself," says Suleiman, "stands for the mother's body, destroyed repeatedly in fantasy but restored or 'repaired' in the act of creation" (357). Madelon Sprengnether, for instance, compares the narratives that her young daughter constructs in order to explain the perplexing realities of life to the ways in which literary critics interpret and write criticism out of a similar desire. But such speculations about motherhood can be subtly dangerous, and often offensive to feminist critics who are not mothers. Julia Kristeva's most recent theories about motherhood point to the danger of valorizing motherhood as the duty of every woman. Kristeva calls for a reformulation of a contemporary ethics which "demands the contribution of women. Of women who harbour the desire to reproduce (to have stability). Of women who are available so that our speaking species, which knows it is moral, might withstand death. Of mothers" (185). It is difficult to tell whether or not Kristeva is literally, seriously, promoting a normative vision of womanhood as motherhood, but the ambiguity of her statements about motherhood reflects the problematic of trying to resurrect the lost mother's body in theory and in practice.

If the fate of the mother in Western culture has been to be abandoned, we need to understand the effect of such a fate on real and imaginary daughters. As we continue trying to understand what the mother's absence means as the source of our nostalgic desire to return home to her, we

37

inevitably speculate about what her presence might mean. We might ask of Shakespeare's drama, where is Cordelia's mother? Could her presence, her voice, have offered her daughter some third choice, a third answer to her father's alienating question? Perhaps there is another way to speak as psychoanalytic feminists without either assimilating entirely to the theories of psychoanalytic fathers or answering with a theoretical "Nothing, my lord," then paying the deadly price for such a defiant answer. If the hysterical structure of the unconscious is, as Ellie Ragland-Sullivan explains, "a refusal to exit from the family novel," those of us feminist psychoanalytic critics who imaginarily identify ourselves as daughters imitate the hysteric's unconscious positioning.[6] Once we recognize and understand consciously the effects of our imitating this unconscious position, we can break from the narrow Oedipal frame by positioning ourselves in an other way of thinking, one which transcends the predictable structures of triads and diads, and the hegemonic institutions of family and academy. I suspect that feminist psychoanalytic critics will create other narratives when we renegotiate our present position in a controversial and provocative narrative of desire and influence.

Notes

1. Julia Kristeva places the psychic choice of the feminine subject within a Marxist theoretical frame, asking, "What is there in the psycho-sexual development of a little girl in monotheistic capitalistic society that prepares her for this economy of which the *ecstatic* and the *melancholic* represent the two extremes of the attempt to gain access to the social order?" (148). Hélène Cixous proposes an answer to the dilemma by celebrating a feminine language that subverts the dominant discourse. "Woman must write her self: must write about women and bring women to writing, from which they have been driven away as violently as from their bodies . . ." (875). Woman comes into being, according to Cixous, by writing herself into being in an other language.

2. For instance, in an article which urges psychoanalysis to be more responsive to women, Judith Kegan Gardiner compares feminism and psychoanalysis to a daughter and her mother. "Psychoanalysis must provide a responsible and accurate psychology of women from which psychoanalytic literary criticism can learn," she argues. "A daughter rejects her mother in the Freudian model, when the mother is perceived as defective. If the poor stepdaughter of analytic literary criticism sees her theoretical mother as strong and intact, she will not be afraid to identify with her" (107).

3. Without the disdain that Nina Baym demonstrates toward psychoanalytic feminism, Kristina Straub, borrowing the filial metaphor of the husband-wife re-

lationship, warns about the consequences of the union between feminism and other disciplines (including psychoanalysis): "But it is too easy at this point in history to treat feminist criticism, let alone the feminist critic, as the wife, essential, practical, 'concrete'—and subservient to specifically if unavowedly male purposes and goals."

4. Holland describes the pedagogical method and procedure of his seminar in an article with Murray Schwartz, "The Delphi Seminar."

5. Paley's story, "A Conversation with My Father," is another illustration of the dilemma that female writers, or subjects, have in expressing their own female identity within a male tradition of literature. The narrator of the story confronts her father's traditional view of fiction and tries to justify her subversion of and aversion to that tradition.

6. Quoted from a seminar on "Feminism and Psychoanalysis" conducted by Ragland-Sullivan at the University of Florida, Fall 1987. I am indebted to Ellie Ragland-Sullivan for her teaching of Lacan, and I gratefully dedicate this essay to her.

Works Cited

Baym, Nina. "The Madwoman and Her Languages: Why I Don't Do Feminist Theory." *Tulsa Studies in Women's Literature* 3 (1984): 153–57.

Cixous, Hélène. "The Laugh of the Medusa." *Signs* 1 (1976): 875–93.

Chodorow, Nancy. *The Reproduction of Mothering: Psychoanalysis and the Sociology of Gender.* Berkeley: Univ. of California Press, 1978.

de Lauretis, Teresa. *Alice Doesn't: Feminism, Semiotics, Cinema.* Bloomington: Indiana Univ. Press, 1984.

Gallop, Jane. *The Daughter's Seduction: Feminism and Psychoanalysis.* Ithaca: Cornell Univ. Press, 1982.

———. *Reading Lacan.* Ithaca: Cornell Univ. Press, 1985.

Gardiner, Judith Kegan. "Psychoanalytic Criticism and the Female Reader." *Literature and Psychology* 26 (1976): 100–107.

Heilbrun, Carolyn G. "Presidential Address 1984." *PMLA* 100 (1985): 281–86.

Holland, Norman N. *The I.* New Haven: Yale Univ. Press, 1985.

———. "Transactive Teaching: Cordelia's Death." *College English* 38 (1977): 276.

———. "Twenty-Five Years and Thirty Days." *Psychoanalytic Quarterly* 55 (1986): 23–52.

Holland, Norman N., and Murray Schwartz. "The Delphi Seminar." *College English* 36 (1975): 790.

Kristeva, Julia. "*Stabat Mater.*" In *The Kristeva Reader.* Ed. Toril Moi. New York: Columbia Univ. Press, 1986.

Mitchell, Juliet. *Psychoanalysis and Feminism: Freud, Reich, Laing, and Women.* New York: Vintage, 1974.

———. *Woman's Estate.* New York: Vintage, 1971.

———. *Women: The Longest Revolution.* New York: Pantheon, 1984.

Paley, Grace, "A Conversation with My Father." *Enormous Changes at the Last Minute.* New York: Farrar, Straus, Giroux, 1974.

Ragland-Sullivan, Ellie. "Dora and the Name-of-the-Father." In *Discontented Discourses.* Urbana: Univ. of Illinois Press, 1989.

Sprengnether, Madelon. "Ghost Writing: A Meditation on Literary Criticism as Narrative." In *The Psychoanalytic Study of Literature.* Ed. Joseph Reppen and Maurice Charney. Hillsdale, N.J.: Analytic Press, 1985. 37–49.

Straub, Kristina. "The Wives of the Critics and the Authority of Edith Bunker: Feminism and Literary Theory." Conference on Feminism and Psychoanalysis, Normal, Ill., May 1–3, 1986.

Suleiman, Susan Rubin. "Writing and Motherhood." In *The (M)other Tongue: Essays in Feminist Psychoanalytic Interpretation.* Ed. Shirley Nelson Garner, Claire Kahane, and Madelon Springnether. Ithaca: Cornell Univ. Press, 1985, 352–57.

Virginia Woolf's
Double Discourse

PAMELA L. CAUGHIE

> If human beings were not divided into two biological sexes, there
> would probably be no need for literature. And if literature could truly
> say what the relations between the sexes are, we would doubtless not
> need much of it then either.
>
> BARBARA JOHNSON
> *The Critical Difference* (13)

Written by a feminist (Virginia Woolf), for a bisexual (Vita Sackville-West),
about an androgyne (Orlando), the novel *Orlando* would seem to be the
quintessential feminist text. And that, indeed, is what it is in danger of
becoming, just as Woolf is in danger of becoming the acclaimed Mother
of Us All. In promoting Virginia Woolf's *Orlando* as a feminist work,
feminist critics have picked the right text, but for the wrong reasons.[1]
Orlando works as a feminist text not because of what it says about sexual
identity but because of what it manages not to say; not because of what
it reveals about the relation between the sexes but because of what it does
to that relation; not because its protagonist is androgynous but because
its discourse is duplicitous. With its eponymous character who changes
from a man to a woman halfway through the novel, with its capricious
narrator who at times speaks in the character of Orlando's male biographer
and at others sounds suspiciously like *Orlando*'s female author, this novel
assumes what Jane Gallop calls a "double discourse." This double discourse is one that is oscillating and open, one that "asserts and then
questions," "a text that alternately quotes and comments, exercises and
critiques."[2] By drawing on the Lacanian readings of Jane Gallop and Shoshana Felman, I want to offer a reading of *Orlando* that will explore its
functioning as a feminist text and that will expose many feminist critics'
appropriation of it.

Orlando is a biographical novel about a poet who lives and loves for over three centuries (and who is likely to live and love three more), changing from a man to a woman halfway through the novel, somewhere around the end of the seventeenth century. When discussing this novel, one must begin with this caution: anything you can say about *Orlando* can be used against you. For *Orlando* defies conclusions. The text of *Orlando* is as unstable as the sex of Orlando. The first words of the novel shake our certainty about anything in this text. We read, "He—for there could be no doubt of his sex . . . ," and immediately our doubt is aroused. The emphasis on what should be obvious makes it seem unnatural. The emphasis on an innocent pronoun makes it suspect. This novel abounds in qualifications ("Change was incessant, and change perhaps would never cease"), paradoxes ("the [blank] space is filled to repletion"), and contradictions (the androgyne itself). This sexual and textual indeterminacy links language and identity. As the androgynous Orlando brings the question of sexual identity to the fore, the obtrusive narrator brings the textual language to the fore by intruding to discuss his own art (e.g., 65), to mock his own method (e.g., 266), and to characterize his own readers (73). Orlando is identified with writing throughout: she is read like a book (25); she concludes that she is "only in the process of fabrication" (175); and she writes at her poem through four centuries, borrowing indiscriminately from different literary ages, all the while questioning "What's an 'age,' indeed?" (205).

This novel, then, is a text about writing, about constructing lives, histories, identities, and fictions. Its desire is for expression itself, as Orlando says, for the fulfillment of desire "in whatever form it comes, and may there be more forms, and stranger" (294). This fulfillment of desire, this desire for expression, encourages us to read androgyny not in terms of some innate bisexuality but in terms of the situation of desire, the subject's situation in a signifying chain. One must assume a sexual identity in order to take one's place in language, in order to express anything. Sexual identity is assumed in language; it is, as Felman says, "conditioned by the functioning of language."[3] Woolf brings out the arbitrariness of that identity, the arbitrariness of language itself, through Orlando's switching from one sex to the other, and from one poetic language to another, as well as through the shifting of her own rhetoric in this novel.

Just as Orlando's identity swings from the extreme of conventionality—Orlando as a boy slicing at the swinging Moor's head—to the extreme of eccentricity—Orlando as a woman discovering she has three sons by another woman—so the language of the text shifts from the transparent conventionality of clichés—to put it in a nutshell, by the skin of his teeth—

to the opaque originality of Orlando and her lover Shel's cypher language—Rattigan Glumphoboo. Just as the bombastic masque of the Three Sisters hyperbolizes Orlando's sex change, the self-conscious diction maximizes the language of the text, not just the self-conscious diction of Orlando's extravagant metaphors (he calls his lover a melon, a pineapple, an olive tree, a fox in the snow), but the self-conscious diction of the biographer's narrative as well (he describes Orlando's betrothed as fair, florid, and phlegmatic). Just as the sexual differences are put into confusion ("You're a woman, Shel!" "You're a man, Orlando!"), so are the extremes of rhetoric. For as Woolf reveals by mocking her own "Time Passes" section of *To the Lighthouse,* what is highly original in one context can, in another, be a tedious, grandiloquent way of saying simply "time passed" (*Orlando* 97–98). What is conventional and what is original, what is mainstream and what is marginal change, like Orlando's sex, with time and circumstance. We see that identity is as variable as language, language as vulnerable as identity. Woolf's rhetoric in *Orlando* is no more chaste than is her protagonist.

What this novel expresses, then, is the difficulty of reaching conclusions about identity or language. Both are based on making distinctions, yet these distinctions are not fixed by reference to anything outside them. There is nothing "out there" to measure them against. What Woolf shares with a writer like Lacan is his verbal play meant to undercut his own position as the one presumed to know.[4] What Woolf admires in and shares with writers like Browne, De Quincey, and Montaigne is their willingness to entertain a variety of opinions, their contentment to remain in uncertainties, and their use of qualifying language to avoid "the rash assumptions of human ignorance" ("Montaigne," *The Common Reader* 64). And so, in *Orlando,* "we are now in the region of 'perhaps' and 'appears' " (102). To speak directly and with certainty on any matter is beyond the novelist Woolf as it is beyond the poet Orlando. Desperately seeking the irreducible linguistic episteme, Orlando discovers that one cannot simply say what one means and leave it: "So then he tried saying the grass is green and the sky is blue and so to propitiate the austere spirit of poetry. . . . 'The sky is blue,' he said, 'the grass is green.' Looking up, he saw that on the contrary, the sky is like the veils which a thousand Madonnas have let fall from their hair; and the grass fleets and darkens like a flight of girls fleeing the embraces of hairy satyrs from enchanted woods. 'Upon my word,' he said, . . . 'I don't see that one's more true than another. Both are utterly false' " (101–2).

As Orlando discovers, poetry and nature, language and identity, must be learned together.[5] This is the point of the vacillating rhetoric and the epicene protagonist of Woolf's novel. Orlando's identity, like her poem, is a palimpsest. It is "compounded of many humours," composed of "odds and ends," a "meeting-place of dissemblables" (73, 176). Orlando continually wavers between beliefs, changes or disguises her sex, moves in harmony with and at odds with the times. So too Woolf's novel offers support for differing positions without arguing for any one. She writes: "Society is the most powerful concoction in the world and society has no existence whatsoever" (194); there is not much difference between the sexes, for Orlando remains "fundamentally the same" throughout, and the difference is "one of great profundity" (138, 188); "Clothes are but a symbol of something hid deep beneath," and clothes "wear us," changing "our view of the world and the world's view of us" (187–88). Such oscillations on the thematic and narrative levels of this novel are presented metaphorically in the recurring image of the perpetually swaying arras and in the alternation of light and dark in Orlando's cab ride with Alexander Pope. It is in the midst of all these contrarieties, in the midst of such violent shifts in viewpoint, that Woolf offers her famous androgynous statement, not as a metaphysical or feminist theory, not as a resolution to or a synthesis of contrarieties, but as a way to remain suspended between opposed beliefs: "For here again we come to a dilemma. Different though the sexes are, they intermix. In every human being a vacillation from one sex to the other takes place, and often it is only the clothes that keep the male or female likeness, while underneath the sex is the very opposite of what it is above" (189). Androgyny embodies this oscillation between positions. It figures a basic ambiguity, not only a sexual ambiguity but a textual one as well. Androgyny is a refusal to choose.[6]

And yet so many critics choose androgyny as the appropriate textual strategy or the appropriate sexual identity. In praising Woolf's *Orlando* for its presentation of transsexualism and its theory of androgyny, most critics have tended to take Woolf's statements out of their context in this novel and to cite them as unambiguous truths about sexual identity or modernist-feminist novels. The androgynous Orlando is appropriated as a symbol of the more unified self, or as a resolution to the problem of true self and conventional self. "Androgynous wholeness" is the phrase Sandra Gilbert uses (119, 127). Androgyny becomes a form of self-mastery, a metaphor for the autonomous self, a freedom from history, society, language. Yet such readings fail to grasp the concept of identity in *Orlando* because they fail to attend to its rhetoric.

In *Orlando,* androgyny and transsexualism call into question not just conventional assumptions about sexuality, but, more important, conventional assumptions about language itself. In its rhetorical transports, Woolf's novel challenges the reference theory of meaning. In particular, it questions the notion that words get their meanings from things they refer to; the definition of words and categories by their essential traits; and the isolation of words and statements from their contexts of use in order to interpret them. The point of focusing on the marginal case (e.g., the transsexual) is to reveal the crucial decisions made in the application of a term or in the assumption of an identity. We can see this point most clearly in the famous clothes philosophy passage in Chapter Four, the passage often cited as Woolf's theory of androgyny.

Now a woman and living in the eighteenth century, Orlando in this chapter is becoming acutely aware of her sex as she faces a legal challenge to her property rights, as she parries the advances of the ship's captain and the Archduke, and as she contends with "the coil of skirts about her legs" (153). Initially unchanged by the sex change, or so her biographer tells us, Orlando is now assuming a more feminine nature. Her biographer writes: "The change of clothes had, some philosophers will say, much to do with it. Vain trifles as they seem, . . . they change our view of the world and the world's view of us" (187). According to this philosophy, our identity is as changeable as our apparel. Clothes make the man, or the woman. The difference between men, and between men and women, would seem to be a superficial one. However, the biographer continues: "That is the view of some philosophers and wise ones, but on the whole, we incline to another. The difference between the sexes is, happily, one of great profundity. Clothes are but the symbol of something hid deep beneath. It was a change in Orlando herself that dictated her choice of a woman's dress and a woman's sex" (188). That is, clothes don't *make* the woman, clothes *mark* the woman beneath. But again, the biographer continues, and two sentences later we find the famous androgyny passage cited above: "For here again, we come to a dilemma. Different though the sexes are, they intermix. In every human being a vacillation from one sex to the other takes place, and often it is only the clothes that keep the male or female likeness, while underneath the sex is the very opposite of what it is above," (189).

Placed in its context, this paragraph not only contradicts the earlier assertion that Orlando's sex change had not affected his/her identity, and that other philosophy that says we put on our identity with our clothing, but it also contradicts itself. For the biographer begins by saying that clothes are a symbol of something deep beneath, that is, one's nature or identity, and ends by remarking that often what is deep beneath is the opposite of the clothing above. In other words, the passage asserts both that clothes are natural and fitting and that clothes are arbitrary and deceiving. Such a self-contradiction is not in the least surprising in this particular novel. What is surprising is that in appropriating this statement as Woolf's theory of androgyny, critics pass over the contradictions, accepting the statement at face value, taking the biographer at his word, which is to take his discourse for granted.

If we consider this passage within its eighteenth-century context, we see that Woolf is not arguing for one of two ontological theories—that is, that identity is fixed or it is changeable, that sexual differences are natural or they are learned—but presenting two positions in eighteenth-century thought which come out of a particular conception of language. On the one hand, we have Samuel Johnson's position: thought must be distinguished from rhetoric, the content from the form, the man from his attire. On the other hand, we have Alexander Pope's position: the rhetoric makes the thought, the form and content are inseparable, the man must dress to advantage. On the one hand, clothes are vain trifles and rhetoric is superfluous; on the other hand, clothes are expressive and rhetoric is essential.

But these apparently opposing views are grounded in the same assumptions about language and identity. To speak of rhetoric as either revealing or concealing, to speak of appearance as either natural or contrived, is to set up a false opposition. It is to assume that we can get beyond or beneath the linguistic paradigm, in which rhetorical and sexual differences function. Such assumptions about language and identity imply the possibility of a natural or naked state or status. Thus, when Sandra Gilbert offers us the choice of stripping away "costumes (and selves) to reveal the pure, sexless (or third-sexed) being behind gender and myth" (214–15), she assumes a pure, free ontological essence which we can locate and define prior to its insertion into language, society, culture. Proving the contrary is precisely the point of the vacillating rhetoric and epicene protagonist of Woolf's novel.

In *Orlando,* clothing, identity, and rhetoric are not an ornamentation of something prior, but an orientation to something else. What matters is not what they mask or mark, but what they enable the protagonist or the writer to accomplish. That is, what matters is not the *nature* of the sign, the transsexual, but its position and function within a particular discursive situation. And so, we must attend to the production of the androgynous Orlando, not to her properties.[7] If we return to that clothes philosophy passage, we see that in trying to distinguish the ways in which Orlando has changed with the sex change and how Orlando embodies traits of both sexes, the biographer ends up making stereotypical remarks, for he can make such sexual distinctions only by relying on conventional assumptions about sexual difference. His only recourse, then, is to look at the particular case: "but here we leave the general question [of sexual difference] and note only the odd effect it had on the particular case of Orlando herself" (189). We, too, must attend to the particular case rather than the general category. What we need in order to read this novel is a conceptual model that enables us to discuss the androgyne not in terms of its relation to the self beneath or the world beyond, but in terms of the multiple and shifting relations among signifying systems, such as rhetoric, fashion, gender, and genre.

Thus, we must attend not only to the various relations among changing historical periods and rhetorical styles, but also to the changing sexual metaphors as well. By employing three metaphors for sexual identity in *Orlando*—androgyny, transvestism, and transsexualism—Woolf shows us that there are different ways of talking about identity, different kinds of appropriateness, different functions of language. When we fail to specify the kinds of distinctions we are relying on (as Sandra Gilbert does in equating these metaphors), our conclusions become suspect. Woolf knows all too well that any language she can use is already embroiled in certain conventional assumptions about gender and identity. Her solution, changing metaphors for sexual identity, is less a freedom from a gendered reality than a freedom from referential thinking. Such freedom comes about by a change in our conception of language. What is at issue here is a language that sets up opposing alternatives and one that plays out various relations. Such an epicene novel is possible when different functions of language are tested out rather than one being taken for granted.

The androgyne, as Felman says, is "constituted in ambiguity" and therefore is not representative of any "single signified" (32). The androgyne threatens meaning by breaking down those oppositions that allow us to make meaningful distinctions. It calls attention to and calls into question one way of making meaning, the institution of representation. Androgyny is not a freedom from the tyranny of sex, as Maria DiBattista says, so much as a freedom from the tyranny of reference. The shifting and blurring of sexual identities, like the shifting and blurring of literary genres, periods, and styles, disrupts meaning brought about by fixed polarities, by defined standards, by rigid categories, by "rhetorical hierarchy" (Felman's phrase). Sex and text are rhetorical terms; they function not only according to certain grammatical and syntactical patternings and social norms but also rhetorically and historically. They are constructed according to a particular model of language. To put sexual identity and textual meaning into confusion, as Woolf does in *Orlando*, is to disclose the dependence of sexual traits and literary standards on certain kinds of discourse. Because one cannot locate innate sexual traits or essential literary values in the face of changing attitudes, conventions, and paradigms (whether scientific, literary, or psychological), one must continually posit and undermine, affirm and doubt, "yield and resist" (155). Oscillation is the rhythm of *Orlando;* oscillating exploration is its method.

Far from defeating sexual difference, as many feminist critics claim, *Orlando* enacts it, enshrines it, exploits it, makes a spectacle of it, but as a playful oscillation not a stable opposition. The androgynous self in *Orlando* is a metaphor for the dramatic, the role-playing self. Androgyny is a metaphor for change, for openness, for a self-conscious acting out of intentions. It is not an ideal *type,* but a contextual *response.* Identity is always disguised in *Orlando* not because the "true self" is running around "incognito or incognita as the case might turn out to be" (168) but because identity is a series of roles. And successive roles subvert referential poles (Felman 31). In this sense, *Orlando* presents a Lacanian view of identity. Woolf no more than Lacan tries to *define* female identity, for any identity assumed finally, definitively, essentially will be constraining; any identity deemed authentic, appropriate, natural will be illusory. Yet Orlando does not *transcend* identity any more than Woolf advocates a gender-free reality, as Sandra Gilbert asserts. For one cannot deny the reality of gender or the necessity of identity. "Identity," Gallop writes, "must be continually assumed and immediately called into question" (xii), just as expression must be exercised and at once critiqued. Divesting Orlando of property and patronym, putting her paternity and propriety into question, Woolf does not liberate her identity but refuses the categories by which it is fixed, determined, legalized. *Orlando* "compromises the coherence" of sexuality and textuality (see Felman 31). Its open-endedness, its openness to other literary texts, resists closure and containment, refuses to provide a conclusive and thus an exclusive statement.[8] *Orlando* shows us how sexuality and textuality perform in the world; it does not tell us what they are or what they should be. What Woolf defies in this novel is any attempt to *define* writing or identity by definitive standards to which it conforms or from which it deviates.

In her diary Woolf refers to *Orlando* as her "play side."[9] It refuses to stop the play of speculation with a consistent argument or theory. The play side is concerned with writing as pleasure, not as production. As Woolf wrote in her typescript of "Professions for Women": "When people said to me what is the use of your trying to write? I could say truthfully, I write not for use, but for pleasure" (*Pargiters* 7). When Orlando admires the anonymous writers who built the house of literature, she means those writers who wrote with no practical purpose in mind, whether to protest or to proselytize, but only out of the love of writing. For too long we have downplayed the play side of Virginia Woolf as displayed in such works as *Orlando, A Room of One's Own,* and *Flush.* We have turned her play side into a meaningful representation, into an alternative or an appropriate form. But as Ionesco once cautioned, any established form of expression can become a form of oppression, can become authoritative, can become, in Gallop's words, "a position and a possession." Orlando and Woolf neither reject past aesthetic standards nor prescribe new ones. They take from the literary past what is useful to them, use up standards, dispose of them, and thus expose them as provisional and changeable, disclose their dependence on certain contexts. Enacting a type of discourse rather than codifying one, as Woolf does in *Orlando,* exposes the supposed universality of aesthetic standards of value. By questioning various metaphysical positions, by testing out various narrative strategies, Woolf produces not "stable assumptions" but "contextual associations" (Gallop 64). She disrupts our tendency to see language as the transparent medium of communication; she defies our habit of looking through discourse to representation. It is not that *Orlando's* playful surface has no point to it; its point is its playful surface. It is time this play side of Woolf's writing be accounted for in terms of different conceptions of self, language, and reality—in terms of a dramatic self not an appropriate one, in terms of a performative view of language not a cognitive one, in terms of a rhetorical reality not a referential one.

It is not, then, that the appropriate identity is androgynous, but that the androgyne defies an appropriate, a definable, identity. Androgyny in *Orlando* is not so much a psychosexual category as a rhetorical strategy, less a condition than a motive. Androgyny does not *substitute for* anything; for that would be to fix it, possess it, universalize it. The androgyne defeats the norm, the universal, the stereotype that Woolf feared becoming, as she so often expresses in her diaries: "I will go on adventuring, changing, opening my mind and my eyes, refusing to be stamped and stereotyped" (*A Writer's Diary* 206). The stereotype, says Roland Barthes, is "the word repeated without any magic, any enthusiasm, as though it were natural, as though by some miracle this recurring word were adequate on each occasion for different reasons" (*The Pleasure of the Text* 42) or, I might add, on different occasions for the same reason. To continue with Barthes's terminology, the androgyne, unlike the stereotype or the norm, is neither consistent nor insistent; it is perverse.

By taking the androgynous personality out of its context in this novel, by turning it into an alternative to or a substitute for the conventional character of the traditional novel or for the conventional self of patriarchal society, so many feminist critics run the risk of reducing it to a platitude.[10] They risk turning a text that works to undo norms, stereotypes, and standards into a new norm, what Gallop calls a "normalizing moralism" or "a comforting representation." The problem with the platitude, the norm, the stereotype is not that they are false or trite in themselves but that they are false or trite in being detached from the contexts that gave rise to them. As Woolf shows in *Orlando,* what enables Alexander Pope's scathing remark on the character of women (a remark so famous that the narrator need not repeat it) to survive to shape future attitudes toward women is its being loosed from its generating context, which was this: Orlando inadvertently offended Mr. Pope by dropping a sugar cube "with a great plop" into his tea (214). A witty remark may be a petty retort. Unmoored from their contexts, literary standards, sexual traits, and social values appear to be incontestable; yet they are responses to particular historical and rhetorical situations. Taking Woolf's statement about androgyny out of its context in *Orlando,* repeating it as an unambiguous truth about human nature, trivializes it. What gives the concept its force are the contextual, textual, and sexual relationships in which it plays its part. "If you cannot give something up for something of like value," Gallop writes, "if you consider it nonsubstitutable, then you don't possess it any more than it possesses you" (76). We need to look at what Woolf *does* in a particular text and context, not at what her writing *represents* for all times or for all women.

Like Orlando herself, her critics must avoid the tyranny or folly of sex pride (160).[11] They must avoid setting up a feminist referential in place of a masculinist one. They must resist reestablishing a natural, even necessary, relation between self and narrative when they have exposed such a relation as arbitrary and provisional in conventional novels.

What *Orlando* presents, then, is not a metaphysical theory but a play of forms. Woolf's androgynous vision affirms Gallop's "permanent alternation," a persistent oscillation, as our binocular vision allows us to see both duck and rabbit in Wittgenstein's sample sketch (*Philosophical Investigations*, II, section xi). The double discourse of *Orlando* enables Woolf to set up exchanges between opposing positions, between different orders of discourse.[12] What appears to be an opposition between positions is tolerated as difference without belligerence, as different options on a spectrum of possibilities, not a *choice* of position but a *doubling* of vision. The double discourse enables Woolf to present a bistable vision, not a univocal theory. This double discourse does not deny a feminist reading. As Gallop says, "This problem of dealing with difference without constituting an opposition may just be what feminism is all about" (93). Woolf's gesture in *Orlando* is much like Gallop's in *The Daughter's Seduction:* she undercuts her own writing, or as Woolf puts it, mocks her own lyric vein (*Writer's Diary* 104); she changes her viewpoint; she alters her narrative voice. The ironic, mocking tone, the vacillating narrative voice, and the pastiche of literary allusions in *Orlando* check our efforts to read for a personal argument, check our tendency to take Woolf at her word, which is to take her discourse for granted. The double discourse, in Felman's terms its "play of undecidability," encourages us to suspend our analytical, judicial, end-seeking, purposive reading for the delight in speculation, equivocation, rhetoric, and play. Feminist readings of *Orlando* read only the law, or the counterlaw, of this novel, not its desire.[13] They stress the purposive and polemical over the playful and pleasurable. They would suppress the very multiplicity and flexibility by means of which Woolf defies authority, systems that shut out (*Writer's Diary* 183), and "the desire to make others believe as [she] believes" (149). *Orlando* is feminist not in what its language says but in what its discourse achieves. *Orlando* gives us not a theory of androgyny but a performance.

If androgyny were a triumph over the tyranny of sex (Maria DiBattista), a resolution to the contradictions between female and male (Rachel DuPlessis), or a transcendence of a gendered reality (Sandra Gilbert), then in writing *Orlando* Woolf would more than likely have defeated the need for literature, for sex cannot be separated from text, the grammatical from the gendered. Orlando's androgyny and diuturnity are not a testament to some essential and enduring human nature but an affirmation of adaptation and change and of the life-sustaining impulse to create fictions. The novel ends at the present moment, the moment of Woolf's writing ("Thursday, the eleventh of October, Nineteen Hundred and Twenty-eight"), with Orlando's sighting of the wild goose: "It is the goose!" Orlando cried. "The wild goose . . ." The wild goose and the ellipsis assure us that nothing is concluded, that the chase will continue. We can only respond, "Encore!"

Notes

1. Some feminist critics I'm referring to are Rachel Blau DuPlessis, *Writing beyond the Ending: Narrative Strategies of Twentieth-Century Women Writers;* Sandra M. Gilbert, "Costumes of the Mind: Transvestism as Metaphor in Modern Literature"; and Maria DiBattista, *Virginia Woolf's Major Novels: The Fables of Anon.* But the reading of *Orlando* and of androgyny that I take issue with throughout is a common one in Woolf and feminist criticism.

2. Jane Gallop, *The Daughter's Seduction: Feminism and Psychoanalysis*, 122, 126. All references to *Orlando* are to the Harcourt Brace Jovanovich paperback edition.

3. Shoshana Felman, "Rereading Femininity." I wrote this essay before reading Mary Jacobus's *Reading Woman*. In her introduction, Jacobus presents a reading of *Orlando* that is similar to my own, drawing as I do on Felman's essay.

4. See Jacqueline Rose's introduction to Lacan's *Feminine Sexuality*, 50.

5. Thomas Kuhn writes that "nature and words are learned together" in *The Structure of Scientific Revolutions*, 191. In Chapter Two of *Orlando*, the narrator remarks that the change in language and prose style in the seventeenth century is accompanied by a change in external conditions, such as in the natural landscape, in the character traits, and in the sewage system of London (113).

6. To say androgyny is a refusal to choose is not to deny the *possibility* of choice.

7. See Jacobus's first chapter, which contains a similar discussion of this novel in terms of language and clothing. See also Felman's "Rereading Femininity" in which she discusses sexual identity as "conditioned by the functioning of language" (29).

8. The narrator of *Orlando* often leads us to a big conclusion, and then omits it: "and so at last she reached her final conclusion, which was of the highest importance but which, as we have already much overpassed our limit of six lines, we must omit" (291). Other examples of this device can be found on pages 253 and 271.

9. Woolf, *A Writer's Diary*, 134. In this entry (November 7, 1928), Woolf comments on one effect of this play side: "I rather think the upshot will be books that relieve other books; a variety of styles and subjects: for after all, that is my temperament, I think, to be very little persuaded of the truth of anything . . ."

10. This is a characteristic tendency not only of feminist readings of *Orlando* but of feminist readings of the androgyne in women's literature in general. See, for example, DuPlessis's *Writing beyond the Ending*.

11. In "Women Novelists," Woolf writes: "any emphasis, either of pride or of shame, laid consciously upon the sex of a writer is not only irritating but superfluous. . . . a woman's writing is always feminine; it cannot help being feminine: the only difficulty lies in defining what we mean by feminine" (*Women and Writing* 70). Woolf's feminism, like Lacan's psychoanalysis, does not produce definitions but tries to account for how definitions are produced. See Rose's introduction to *Feminine Sexuality*, 57, and Jacobus's *Reading Woman*, 20–21.

12. The double discourse, like our binocular vision, gives us not just additional information but a different *kind* of information, a different way of organizing or processing what we experience. The shortsightedness of many feminist appropriations of *Orlando* comes from incorporating its double discourse into a monostable vision, into the one-to-one correspondence model of the reference theory of meaning. Rather than representing a new concept of self and

narrative, *Orlando* presents a different way of conceiving of the various relationships both within and between self and narrative. It does not represent a type; it enacts relations. (For a discussion of the binocular vision, see Gregory Bateson's *Mind and Nature.*)

13. It is the Law that gives *meaning* to sexual difference. *Orlando,* though, is not answering the question of the *meaning* of sexuality; it is exploring, as Felman puts it, the complex relations between sexuality and meaning. See Shoshana Felman, *Writing and Madness,* 156.

Works Cited

Abel, Elizabeth. *Writing and Sexual Difference.* Brighton, Sussex, England: Harvester, 1982.

Barthes, Roland. *The Pleasure of the Text.* Trans. Richard Miller. New York: Hill and Wang, 1975.

Bateson, Gregory. *Mind and Nature: A Necessary Unity.* New York: Bantam Books, 1979.

DiBattista, Maria. *Virginia Woolf's Major Novels: The Fables of Anon.* New Haven: Yale, 1980.

DuPlessis, Rachel Blau. *Writing beyond the Ending: Narrative Strategies of Twentieth-Century Women Writers.* Bloomington: Indiana Univ. Press, 1985.

Felman, Shoshana. "Rereading Femininity." *Yale French Studies,* 62 (1981), 29.

———. *Writing and Madness.* Ithaca, N.Y.: Cornell, 1985.

Gallop, Jane. *The Daughter's Seduction: Feminism and Psychoanalysis.* Ithaca, N.Y.: Cornell, 1982.

Gilbert, Sandra M. "Costumes of the Mind: Transvestism as Metaphor in Modern Literature." In Abel, *Writing and Sexual Difference.*

Jacobus, Mary. *Reading Woman: Essays in Feminist Criticism.* New York: Columbia Univ. Press, 1986.

Kuhn, Thomas. *The Structure of Scientific Revolutions.* 2d ed. Chicago: Univ. of Chicago Press, 1970.

Lacan, Jacques. *Feminine Sexuality.* Ed. Juliet Mitchell and Jacqueline Rose. Trans. Jacqueline Rose. New York: Norton, 1982.

Wittgenstein, Ludwig. *Philosophical Investigations.* Trans. G. E. M. Anscombe. New York: Macmillan, 1953.

Woolf, Virginia. *The Common Reader: First Series.* New York: Harcourt Brace Jovanovich, 1925.

———. *Orlando: A Biography.* New York: Harcourt Brace Jovanovich, 1928.

———. *The Pargiters: The Novel-Essay Portion of "The Years."* Ed. Mitchell Leaska. New York: Harcourt Brace Jovanovich, 1977.

———. *Women and Writing.* Ed. Michele Barrett. New York: Harcourt Brace Jovanovich, 1979.

———. *A Writer's Diary.* Ed. Leonard Woolf. New York: Harcourt Brace Jovanovich, 1953.

The Case of the Two Cultures:
Psychoanalytic Theories of
Science and Literature

RUTH SALVAGGIO

The relations between science and literature have always somehow managed to be charged with discontent, which is perhaps what makes them so suitable for psychoanalytic analysis. Although the infamous "two cultures," at least ever since C. P. Snow popularized them as such, have continued to attract theories about their relationship, to my knowledge no one has ever proposed any kind of psychoanalytic theory to account for the different positions they occupy in the intellectual world. What I offer is not a single psychoanalytic theory but an exploration of how the changing assumptions of psychoanalysis account for the remarkably different values assigned to each discourse in a culture which grants precedence to the scientific.

In doing this, I will be treating science and literature not only as two distinct discourses but as discourses which—like human individuals—have developed within cultural contexts and have therefore assumed specific gender characteristics. Psychoanalytic theories themselves, of course, have hardly escaped their own kinds of gender identification—at once addressing questions of sexuality and reflecting the perspectives associated with male and female behavior. Is it possible to use these sexually infused theories to understand not only human subjects but cultural modes of discourse as well? And if, as I will be suggesting, both literature and science are also discourses which have assumed their own gendered identities, then how might changes in psychoanalytic theory—especially those reflecting a shift from male-centered theory to various feminist and feminine critiques—

affect the ongoing reconstructions of discourses that have already been constructed according to gender identification?

The Gendering of Discourse

Let me begin by suggesting something about science and literature that reflects traditional beliefs: science is a masculine pursuit and literature a feminine one. Because such beliefs are deeply embedded in "cultural myths," they might easily be disputed by empirical researchers, and for a variety of reasons. Nonetheless, especially in recent years, a good deal of both empirical research and theoretical criticism has been consumed with the question of sexual difference in general, and the specific roles that gender plays in the formation of such cultural myths. For instance, Sherry Turkle, in her study of human response to the computer, has observed the different approaches of boys and girls to computer programming. She describes boys as "hard masters," as tending "to see the world as something to be brought under control." Girls, on the other hand, "are more likely to see the world as something they need to accommodate to, something beyond their direct control."[1] Carol Gilligan arrived at similar conclusions in studying male and female responses to moral conflict. When faced with moral decisions, males tend to respond by separating themselves from the situation, establishing their autonomy, and reaching clear-cut decisions that derive from and reinforce "systems of rules." Females, on the other hand, tend to see themselves connected to the situation, establish "relationships" rather than autonomy, and seek solutions in a "world that coheres through human connection."[2]

It should hardly seem surprising that both of these researchers rely on psychoanalytic explanations of behavior to account for their findings. Psychoanalysis, after all, has been preoccupied with the sexual origins of human behavior that might account for such gender-specific responses. But what is just as important to recognize here is that these different forms of behavior are at once affecting and affected by different modes of discourse. In Turkle's observations about computer programming, for instance, she finds that boys and girls not only "master" and "relate" differently to programs but create different computer languages. Those languages developed by males tend to reflect their desire for "the pleasures of mastering and manipulating a formal system," while those developed by females tend to be intimate, visual, and verbal (pp. 112–14).

Are these different approaches to language related to gender differences that mark the discourses of science and literature? Much of the feminist criticism emerging in both literary and scientific studies would suggest that this is the case. Just as language and behavior shape each other, so are discourse and identity mutually formed and informed by gender difference. "Self and identity," as Teresa de Lauretis explains, "are always grasped and understood within particular discursive configurations," and the process of becoming aware of identity is "a process by which one begins to know . . . that and how the subject is specifically and materially en-gendered in its social conditions and possibilities of existence."[3] Any subject, necessarily functioning within discourse, forms an identity as a subject according to the ways it speaks and behaves in these discursive modes. If the same is true not only for subjects that function within discursive systems, such as language and computer programming, but *for discourse itself,* then we need to explore the ways in which literature and science and psychoanalysis have come to form their own sexual identities—have come to be "engendered" in their "social conditions and possibilities of existence." What I want explore, in other words, are not so much the differences between men and women as their identities are "engendered" within "discursive configurations" but the ways in which particular discursive systems—which we know as science, as literature, and as psychoanalysis—have themselves assumed the characteristics of specific genders and have behaved according to their gendered identities.

Let us look more closely, for instance, at the feminist critiques of science, since they have been devoting attention to the very processes through which science assumes its gendered identity. In posing the question "How much of the nature of science is bound up with the idea of masculinity?" Evelyn Fox Keller argues that the modes of inquiry which have been culturally cast as masculine—objectivity, reason, intellect—have also shaped scientific discourse.[4] In psychoanalytic terms, as Turkle explains and Keller elaborates, the desire to distance oneself from phenomena and obtain mastery over them may reflect anxieties typically experienced by males who feel threatened by being too close, too indistinguishable, from the phenomena to be mastered.[5] Thus scientific attempts to create systems—such as Newton's "System of the World" or Darwin's classifications of biological life—appear as characteristically masculine. The very metaphors used by scientists, as Carolyn Merchant observes, again and again show us a male scientist seeking to discover, tame, and "master" the mysteries of a female natural world.[6] Mother Nature becomes the subject of analysis conducted by the fathers of science. In this system of discourse, science is already culturally encoded as masculine. Ruth Bleier summarizes the feminist critique of science by insisting that "science is in and of culture," and argues that the various critiques have demonstrated "the gendered and sexualized structure, the ideologies, and the symbolism that characterize the institution, the practices, the methodologies, and the theories of science."[7]

If objectivity, reason, and intellect have been culturally constructed as "masculine" attributes informing the construction of science, then "subjectivity, feeling, and nature"—responses which, according to Keller, our culture regards as "female"—might well be seen as feminine attributes not only purged from science but delegated to the world of the literary. Sandra Harding confirms this implication when she describes the "world hidden from the consciousness of science" as rich in literary associations—a "world of emotions, feelings, political values; of the individual and collective unconscious; of social and historical particularity explored by novels, drama, poetry, music, and art—within which we all live most of our waking and dreaming hours under constant threat of its increasing infusion by scientific rationality."[8] Yet even this world of subjectivity and feeling, even this literary and artistic world, is dominated by men who engage in a kind of discourse which has been long associated with the values and characteristics of women. If we are to understand the differences between engendered systems of discourse, and if we are to analyze them—as I want to— in terms of psychoanalytic theories, then we need to remember that while "masculine" pursuits, such as science, are traditionally associated with the achievements of men, "feminine" pursuits, such as literature, can and have been associated with both men and women but are often ultimately appropriated by men. Recognizing this historical pattern, the feminist critiques of science and of literature have each approached their subjects differently. While feminist critics of science are exposing the masculine construction of a scientific discourse dominated by a long tradition of male scientists, feminist literary critics are preoccupied with taking back a discourse which has been appropriated from women's specific cultural heritage and dominated by select male writers. We see this not only in the attempts to reclaim woman's image, which has traditionally served as a primary object of literary figuration, but in attempts to recover lost women writers who have not been assigned respectable positions in the culturally approved literary canon.[9] If science can be regarded as masculine in its construction because it reflects modes of inquiry which are traditionally associated with male behavior, then we must understand literature as feminine in a slightly different way: literature assumes a feminine identity because it reflects modes of response which, though historically expressed by men, are traditionally and culturally associated with female behavior.

With these distinctions in mind, we can understand the "identities" assumed by literature and science not so much as fixed or absolute categories of sexual difference but as modes of discourse which have themselves been engendered within cultural and ideological systems. The question arises, then, as to whether we can ever speak within any discursive system without being imprisoned by the constraints of certain gendered perspectives. Can we ever escape, in other words, the "discursive configurations" that have already shaped our identities as subjects? I believe that we cannot, that we are always engaged in the dynamics of coming to terms with our sexual identities and the effects of gender, among other things, in shaping discursive systems. And it is exactly for this reason that I rely on psychoanalysis—a discourse which itself speaks from and continually adjusts gendered perspectives—to adopt positions from which we can analyze the discourses of literature and science. De Lauretis, criticizing theories of discourse which explore sexual difference while articulating the fixed position of the male subject, argues that "even as they assert that sexual difference is culturally produced, the discourses of science, philosophy, and literary and critical theory concern themselves, finally, only with the production of Oedipus (or anti-Oedipus)" (pp. 12–13). I rely on psychoanalytic discourse for the very reason that it has, ironically, been able to produce something other than the story of Oedipus. In suggesting this, I do not want to vindicate psychoanalysis or claim that it is the one position from which we might speak about questions of sexual difference. On the contrary, I want to suggest that changing psychoanalytic assumptions can profitably be used to see, from varying positions, the ways in which discursive systems are engendered—and the effects of this gendering process on the identities assumed by writers and scientists, by women and men.

Psychoanalytic Theories and Gendered Perspectives

De Lauretis's claim that much discourse is only aimed at the production of Oedipus invites us to explore the gendered identities assumed by psychoanalytic discourse itself, since nowhere has the theoretical production of Oedipus been more obvious than in Freud's own theories. Can we use this Oedipal model—the story which relates human development in terms of the son's sexual quest—to explain the gendered construction of discursive systems? Let us consider the possibility of applying Oedipal theory to the development of literature and science as discourses, all the while keeping in mind the distinct gendered construction of Freudian theory as it explains human development in terms of the interaction of father, mother, and child. Until Oedipal trauma begins to manifest itself, the child's relations with father and mother, male and female, are largely devoid of conflict. But this state of pre-Oedipal satisfaction is interrupted when the child begins to experience sexual anxieties—in particular, feelings of desire for the mother and jealousy of the father. In the simplest account of this Freudian narrative, the child, typically figured as a son, overcomes his troublesome sexual desire by achieving distance and autonomy: he "objectifies" himself, assuming the independence that will allow him to move away from the mother and thus mature into a successful father.

Freud's account of human development may well constitute a science of its own, but it surely has its narrative dimensions as well, and we are reminded of its distinct narrative quality when we keep in mind that Freud himself used a "grand narrative" to name his theory—the story of Oedipus. Psychoanalysis, we might then say, uses narrative to legitimize itself, a notion elaborated by Jean-François Lyotard when he explains the way in which any science legitimates itself by "making an explicit appeal to some grand narrative."[10] I would like to consider not only the workings of such narratives in legitimizing a science such as psychoanalysis but also the ways in which all science defines itself in relation to other discourses. Since the case I am exploring concerns science and literature, let us consider a possible psychoanalytic understanding of their relationship. For this purpose, we need to recast the story of the so-called rise of modern science in terms of a family narrative. We can do this by considering a pivotal historical period in the inception and development of science, the seventeenth century—in particular, the history of science and literature in seventeenth-century England. During this time, modern science was born—fathered by the men we now associate with the emergence of scientific academies and societies and mothered by the mysteries of the natural world, traditionally associated with women and traditionally the subject of artistic discourse. The great scientist of this period was, of course, Isaac Newton, a man who calculated the mathematical design of the universe and who explained this "System of the World" as the product of his own father God.[11] If we can think of the history of modern science in terms of the pursuits of men who have, by and large, followed the Newtonian calling—men who have sought to explain and control the mysteries of the universe in the name of patriarchal design—then we might conclude that the sons of the father science have indeed overcome any Oedipal trauma, any desire to give in to mysterious and maternal nature rather than distance themselves from it.

It would be easy enough to relate the progress of this story by focusing on the masculine directions in which science developed after the seventeenth century. Brian Easlea, for instance, treats just this subject when he studies the split between the hermetic and mechanical scientific traditions during this age and shows how witchcraft and alchemy, and all their feminine associations, ultimately gave way to a masculine, mechanical science.[12] The heirs of science, in other words—the individuals and the discourse which we might regard as its sons—developed into men resembling their fathers, and perpetuated the Oedipal narrative of science. Carolyn Merchant offers a view of the history of science that would explain the perpetuation of this narrative. She describes "a cultural research program extending from the seventeenth century to the present day," which has regarded itself as engaged in the control of both "nature" and "natural resources," and concludes: "During the three centuries in which the mechanical world view became the philosophical ideology of Western culture, industrialization coupled with the exploitation of natural resources began to fundamentally alter the character and quality of human life. . . . Nature, women, blacks, and wage laborers were set on a path toward a new status as 'natural' or human resources for the modern world system" (pp. 287–88). Science controls nature in the same way that man controls woman—for woman has taken on one of the "discursive configurations" of those resources which function as the object of scientific inquiry.

It should come as no surprise, then, that nature and women, particularly throughout the last three centuries, have been more prominently featured in the discourse of literature. In England, for instance, after the brief reign of a group of neoclassical writers, poets and novelists were increasingly turning their attention to concerns that have been traditionally regarded as feminine. We begin to hear the voices of solitary and sentimental writers, and we see the flowering of the novel and especially its preoccupation with the plight of women characters. Moreover, we see a growing number of women novelists exploring their own subjective experiences that in turn shape the ways in which the novel develops.[13] If, as I have been suggesting, the seventeenth century marks a period when science assumed its masculine demeanor and literature became a kind of feminine discourse, then we might well account for the gendering of both science and literature by regarding each in terms of their respective fatherly and motherly roles. The mother discourse, like the body of the mother in Freudian theory, has been abandoned by sons who turn their attention to orderly, scientific matters. Oedipus must distance himself from the mother discourse and speak the symbolic discourse of the father.

Or should we say, switching the terms of our observation, that scientific discourse—instead of being legitimized by Oedipal theory—has itself legitimized this pseudoscientific theory? Has Freudian psychoanalysis explained the development of two different discursive systems, or have the discourses of science and literature themselves become subjects informing the construction of psychoanalytic narrative? Questions such as these invite us to enter into an even larger question concerning the construction of psychoanalytic discourse itself. What we need to consider now are not only changes in psychoanalytic theory since Freud but the ways in which these changes have been affected by the adoption of different gendered perspectives and the effects of these perspectives on theories of discourse. From these perspectives, we might explain the formation of discursive theories as deriving *from cultural constructions,* such as Oedipal narrative—and then engage in the process of effecting *reconstructions* of gendered identities and discourses that produce something other than Oedipus.

In considering other psychoanalytic theories which might account for the tensions between science and literature, I suggest that we turn our attention to several current feminist critiques of psychoanalysis. What is fundamental to all of these critiques is the realization that Freudian psychoanalysis is profoundly gendered in its construction. In emphasizing the role of father and son in its account of human development, Freudian theory necessarily speaks from the position of male subjectivity and ignores—or, more accurately, is baffled by—the experience of women. In shifting their attention to the role of woman, the feminist critiques of psychoanalysis explore narratives which question the "grand narratives" of "man" and generate different stories of human behavior. Several of these "other" narratives help explain the gendered discourses of and relations between science and literature—relations which are very much part of the sexual dynamics of culture and which therefore can be psychoanalyzed in other narrative terms.

Consider, for instance, what happens to conventional psychoanalytic theory when attention is directed away from the father and son and toward the mother. Nancy Chodorow's ideas about the "Reproduction of Mothering" are relevant here—along with those of Carol Gilligan, Adrienne Rich, Julia Kristeva, and others who have been exploring the role of the mother and her associations with relationship, closeness, emotion, and desire.[14] When such ideas come to inform and influence psychoanalytic theory, then psychoanalysis becomes engaged in the process of producing something other than Oedipus—something other than the son who must distance himself from the mother in his quest to become the father. In turn, such psychoanalytic perspectives offer us a very different means of understanding the relations between gendered discourses. Instead of seeing literary discourse in terms of the repressed mother, we might see it as engaged in articulating modes of response—charged with emotion, closeness, subjectivity—that have been largely excluded from the domain of science. If mothering, as Chodorow suggests, has not been assigned value in a culture which grants precedence to fathering, then we might say that literary texts—traditionally viewed as being secondary to and somehow less important than scientific facts—have only been playing the part of the woman in our culture. They have failed to be legitimized by "grand narratives" which only repeat the story of Oedipus.

Much recent work in critical and feminist theory would confirm this suspicion. Exploring the phenomenon she describes as "gynesis" or "woman-effect," Alice Jardine argues that postmodern discourse—which questions the master narratives of the past—is engaged in the "configuration" of woman.[15] "Woman," Jardine explains, occupies "a new rhetorical space," and represents changes in "conceptual positions" that are taking us "from time to space, the same to other, paranoia to hysteria, city to labyrinth, mastery to nonmastery, truth to fiction" (pp. 38–39). If this feminine configuration has, as Jardine suggests, "become the site of inquiry within a period of profound binary crisis," then we have grounds for reconsidering her effects in reshaping the gendered construction of literature and science. For the construction of these two discourses reflects, at the very least, a profound "binary crisis" in the cultural production of two very different discourses—discourses which reflect modes of response that have been associated with "woman" and "man." What will happen to our historical and theoretical construction of these discourses if we begin to understand their relationship not in terms of some Oedipal narrative but in terms of "feminine" concerns which have, until recently, been suppressed in cultural systems and have produced a "binary crisis"— two cultures—which represent human experience so differently?

Let me return briefly to our narratives about seventeenth-century science. As we have seen, it is possible to explain the "rise of modern science" in terms of an Oedipal narrative—if, of course, the story is related from the position of male experience. According to such a narrative, science forms its sexual identity by not only distancing itself from the maternal world of nature but also assuming the role of father as the force which will demystify the natural world. The result of this attempt to explain and control natural phenomena, as Merchant argues, is the mechanical "program" of science which we have inherited from Newton and Leibniz—a program which, according to Easlea, resulted in the repression of the feminine phenomena associated with alchemy, witchcraft, and the hermetic tradition. Let us now switch the terms of the psychoanalytic narrative which I have used to explain the "rise of science" and explore what happens when the story is related from the position of female experience.

Consider, for example, the question which Luce Irigaray poses about science, specifically "about its *historical lag in elaborating a 'theory' of fluids.*"[16] In arguing that science has maintained a *"complicity of long standing between rationality and a mechanics of solids alone,"* Irigaray claims that science participates in a discursive system in which fluids have been and must be suppressed. But what is most significant about Irigaray's argument is that she associates fluidity with women. "It is already getting around," she writes, "that women diffuse themselves according to modalities scarcely compatible with the framework of the ruling symbolics. Which doesn't happen without causing some turbulence, we might even say some whirlwinds, that ought to be reconfined within solid walls of principle, to keep them from spreading to infinity." Unless science minimizes the characteristics of fluidity and woman, then the "transgression and confusion of boundaries" which they represent may disturb the "proper order" desired by science (p. 106).

Irigaray's purpose in her own discourse, as she explains it, is to "(re)discover a possible space for the feminine imaginary" (p. 164). But in order to do this, she must break with narrative structures—including that of traditional psychoanalysis—which are bent on the control of phenomena conventionally described in both fluid and feminine terms. (One need only recall here Freud's attempts to come to terms with women hysterics.) Such a narrative transformation would not only alter the masculine construction of science but necessitate the revaluation of the feminine and fluid material long associated with literary discourse. The transformation would produce neither Oedipus nor the opposite of Oedipus—but open discourse to the effects of woman, feminine experience, and offer a radically different account of discourse itself as a symbolic mode which can accommodate turbulence and flow. What is ultimately at stake here is a reconfiguration, in psychoanalytic terms, of the relationship between the masculine and the feminine. This reconfiguration would not invert the positions occupied by science and literature, masculine and feminine, solid and fluid, but instead allow us to reposition ourselves so that we can respond to phenomena—respond to the world and human experience—in ways other than those that privilege one discourse over another, one sex over another.

"Since historically the properties of fluids have been abandoned to the feminine, *how is the instinctual dualism articulated with the difference between the sexes? How has it been possible even to 'imagine' that this economy had the same explanatory value for both sexes?"* (p. 116). Irigaray's question urges us to "imagine" discursive economies that have not abandoned the feminine, that allow us to adopt more than one or two perspectives—the scientific or the literary, the hard or the soft—to represent and construct cultural experience. We can begin to discover these other discourses in psychoanalytic narratives which have themselves been consumed with the articulation of sexual difference—and which have, for almost a century now, been changing and shifting their perspectives about the cultural effects of sexual difference. In a sense, it seems appropriate that this should be the fate of psychoanalysis, itself a hybrid, the product of scientific methods and narrative models. But the hybrid nature of psychoanalysis is also its bisexual nature. If psychoanalysis can split its own gendered construction without diagnosing itself as schizophrenic, then it holds forth the possibility of imagining discourses other than those which have bifurcated and hierarchized our culture. It does not give us a way to escape gendered discourse but to reposition ourselves and continually participate in the reconstruction of discourse and identity—particularly those discourses that we now know as literature and science and those identities that we now label feminine and masculine.

Notes

1. Sherry Turkle, *The Second Self: Computers and the Human Spirit* (New York: Simon & Schuster, 1984), pp. 105–6.
2. Carol Gilligan, *In a Different Voice: Psychological Theory and Women's Development* (Cambridge, Mass: Harvard Univ. Press, 1982), p. 29.
3. Teresa de Lauretis, "Feminist Studies/Critical Studies: Issues, Terms, and Contexts," in *Feminist Studies/Critical Studies,* ed. de Lauretis (Bloomington: Indiana Univ. Press, 1986), pp. 8–9.
4. Evelyn Fox Keller, *Reflections on Gender and Science* (New Haven: Yale Univ. Press, 1985), p. 7.
5. See Turkle, pp. 109–10, and Keller's discussion of "The Inner World of Subjects and Objects," pp. 67–126.
6. Carolyn Merchant, *The Death of Nature: Women, Ecology, and the Scientific Revolution* (San Francisco: Harper & Row, 1980).
7. Ruth Bleier, "Lab Coat: Robe of Innocence or Klansman's Sheet?" in *Feminist Studies/Critical Studies,* p. 62. Also see Bleier's *Science and Gender: A Critique of Biology and Its Theories on Women* (New York: Pergamon Press, 1984).
8. Sandra Harding, *The Science Question in Feminism* (Ithaca: Cornell Univ. Press, 1986), p. 245.
9. Elaine Showalter summarizes these two historical tendencies in explaining that feminist literary criticism has "gradually shifted its center from revisionary readings to a sustained investigation of literature by women." See "Feminist Criticism in the Wilderness" in *The New Feminist Criticism: Essays on Women, Literature and Theory,* ed. Showalter (New York: Pantheon Books, 1985), p. 248.

10. Jean-François Lyotard, *The Postmodern Condition,* trans. Geoff Bennington and Brian Massumi (Minneapolis: Univ. of Minnesota Press, 1984), p. xxiii.
11. On the connections between Newton's science and his devotion to God the Father, see Frank Manuel, *A Portrait of Isaac Newton* (Cambridge, Mass.: Harvard Univ. Press, 1968), especially pp. 117–32.
12. Brian Easlea, *Witch Hunting, Magic and the New Philosophy* (Brighton: Harvester Press, 1980). Also see Easlea's *Fathering the Unthinkable: Masculinity, Scientists and the Nuclear Arms Race* (London: Pluto Press, 1983).
13. For a discussion of only one example of this transformation, see Margaret Doody, "Deserts, Ruins and Troubled Waters: Female Dreams in Fiction and the Development of the Gothic Novel," *Genre* 10 (Winter 1977), 529–72.
14. Nancy Chodorow, *The Reproduction of Mothering: Psychoanalysis and the Sociology of Gender* (Berkeley: Univ. of California Press, 1978); Carol Gilligan, *In a Different Voice;* Adrienne Rich, *Of Woman Born: Motherhood as Experience and Institution* (New York: W. W. Norton, 1976); and Julia Kristeva, "Stabat Mater," in *The Kristeva Reader,* ed. Toril Moi (New York: Columbia Univ. Press, 1986), pp. 160–86.
15. Alice Jardine, *Gynesis: Configurations of Woman and Modernity* (Ithaca: Cornell Univ. Press, 1985), see esp. pp. 25–28.
16. Luce Irigaray, *This Sex Which Is Not One,* trans. Catherine Porter (Ithaca: Cornell Univ. Press, 1985), pp. 106–7.

SECTION II

Representation and Distortion

Displaced Feminine Representation
in Woody Allen's Cinema

RICHARD FELDSTEIN

In a world where Oliver North is viewed as a hero and Robert Bork promoted as an unbiased, even apolitical, nominee to the Supreme Court, it seems fitting that members of the liberal intelligentsia would celebrate Woody Allen as a man who loves and understands women. We need only listen to the teleguidance of Siskel and Ebert or consult a local newsstand to find this popular myth perpetuated. For years such sources have sung hosannas in praise of *Annie Hall* and, more recently, have instituted a chorus of acclaim for *Hannah and Her Sisters,* a film they say is sensitive to the needs and desires of women. To believe such reviews, however, we must develop a convenient amnesia like John Poindexter's, allowing us to discount Allen's early films in which women became specular icons in a circuit of desire which repeatedly shifted its focus to the subject's scaffolding and the modern-day schlemiel that Allen invariably portrayed— a nebbish intellectually developed and verbally adept but sexually ineffectual if not absurd. Consequently, then as now, Allen's female protagonists have been staged as scopophilic objects-to-be-looked-at while the schlemiel/protagonist has remained the visual, aural, and narrative center of attention.

It follows, then, that commentary has centered on Allen the pop cultural satirist, whose rhetorical extensibility finds its limit when the filmmaker represents his female characters in a system of signification whose phallic prejudices Allen depicts ironically yet persistently mirrors. Like Allen, most of his critics have ignored his repeated representation of women as supplementary commodities in a patriarchal system of exchange, refusing to acknowledge what privilege the writer/director/protagonist retained for himself and what significance he bestowed on his female protagonists, be

69

they Lasser, Keaton, or Farrow, depending on the period of his career we examine. Instead, critics have fixated on "the 'I' dramatized as inept, inadequate, foolish, exploited, or self-deceiving in a situation that elicits the audience's sympathy or tears" (Goldman 12). Like other Jewish comedians of our time (Philip Roth and Lenny Bruce, to name two), Allen altered the schlemiel's image, making him humorous rather than sad, a bespectacled bumbler who habitually measures himself against Svengali-like rivals that successfully seduce pinup-perfect women. In Allen's cinema, women not only sustain the gaze from scopophilic ego ideals and the schlemiel who alternately debunks and imitates them, but from the institutional apparatuses which film the spectacle and from that segment of the audience which identifies with the privileged, masculine position of spectatorship. Considering that Woody Allen merely imitates mainstream classical cinema when perpetuating this masculine bias produced through such a confluence of identifications, it becomes understandable why Mary Ann Doane charges that historically "the simple gesture of directing a camera toward a woman" is "equivalent to a terrorist act" (23).

In Allen's early films, his female characters are inscribed within this phallocentric loop of interchange between inept ego and ego ideal. Many of Allen's jokes trace this circuit, taking either a sadistic swipe at the romanticized male lead or a masochistic poke at self-deprecation, but regardless of which option Allen chooses, his jokes are often at the expense of women. For example, in *What's New, Pussycat?*, *What's Up, Tigerlily?*, and *Casino Royale*, Allen parodies the James Bond formula that Hollywood successfully exploited by presenting male protagonists who encounter a series of violent events that, in an inversion of coitus interruptus, are spelled by occasional sexual intrigues with women. In *What's Up, Tigerlily?* Allen himself plays a Hollywood director who wields his casting couch like a sexual weapon positioned between an actress's professional aspirations and the part she might play. In fact, *Tigerlily* ends with a filmic footnote featuring China Lee, a Playboy model who performs a striptease for director Allen, who nibbles on an apple while exclaiming, "I promised I'd put her in the film—somewhere." Even if we grant Allen's intention to satirize Hollywood's tendency to exploit those who cast their fate on the director's couch, the sheer repetition of phallocentric examples reveals a misogyny that repeatedly depicts his female protagonists as those who complement the Bond hero by masquerading themselves as the mimicked objects of male desire. Luce Irigaray critiques this phallocentric strategy in *This Sex Which Is Not One,* when relating how women exist (much as they do in *Playboy* magazine) as specularized commodities in a system of patriarchal exchange: "The production of women, signs, and commodities is always referred back to men . . . and they [women] always pass from one man to another, from one group of men to another" (171). Here Irigaray uncovers a so-called heterosexual system she unmasks as a "hom(m)o-sexual" monopoly in which the law that orders society valorizes the desires of men as they exchange women. Whether Irigaray's claim is valid as a blanket condemnation continues to be subject to debate, but, as a succession of examples attest to, in Allen's comic cinema unfunny caricatures often display a phallocentrism that is reflected in box-office sales.

Continuing the search through films whose social legitimation has been ensured by a liberal bestowal of Oscars, we encounter unapologetic misogynous depictions that become more and more revealing. In *Tigerlily* an underworld flunky boasts that the gangsters have just received another shipment of women, "loin, flank, sirloin: why this is the best shipment of meat we had this year. Now, boss, aren't you glad you gave up being a vegetarian?" As in the sequence featuring China Lee, where Allen eats an apple while a woman strips, there is again introduced a term-by-term reconversion exemplifying a gastronomical equation between food and sexuality. Interestingly, it is such oral needs coupled with sexual aggression that drives the various gangland factions in an overriding compulsion to find their fetishized object of desire, the great egg-salad recipe: "one so good you could plotz." In *Bananas,* however, situations depicting phallic rivalry, rather than oral aggression, predominate as Allen jousts with female protagonists whose threat of castration becomes so pronounced that the schlemiel feels impelled to counter it. In *Bananas* Allen trades bromos for boxing gloves when Fielding and Nancy perform sadomasochistic sexual variations in a media event covered by Howard Cosell, who announces the intimate details of their wedding-night rendezvous before Nancy divulges in a post-honeymoon interview that Fielding is "not the worst I've had. Not the best, but not the worst."

From this compilation of sexist examples we find that Allen initially conceived mock-Bond characters as rivals to be ridiculed and satirical female protagonists as specularized objects subject to oral and phallic economies of desire. To escape from an all-encompassing orality equated with the (m)Other, Allen created female protagonists with Diane Keaton in mind, who, in the early stages of their collaboration, played women who promised love and sexual gratification without the threat of oral-cannibalistic incorporation. Yet risks attended this strategy because incarnations of the (m)Other kept reappearing, a disturbance Allen tried in vain to quell until, by *Manhattan,* Keaton herself became yet another desirable but threatening woman who confronted the male protagonist.

In *Play It Again, Sam,* however, there is no radical or irreducible difference detectable in Keaton's character, but Allen does transform his role, recasting the prototypical schlemiel by de-emphasizing his sexual inadequacy while highlighting his verbal dexterity. As a consequence, the schlemiel becomes capable of sharing a less conflictual relationship with women. Thus, although Allan Felix initially bemoans that there are "ten million women in the country and I can't wind up with one," later he does ironically maintain an ongoing relationship with Linda, his best friend's wife. Suffering from conjugal neglect, Keaton's character finds Felix attractive and sexually stimulating, but Felix only seduces Linda because he can enlist the aid of Humphrey Bogart, an ego ideal whose tough-guy counsel helps him to assert a nonchalant air of machismo when entering into prophylactic relations. In other words, Felix takes Bogart's advice, and, in colluding with this Bond-like character, demonstrates that at some level the schlemiel and the ego ideal are doubles, split to counter a fear of castration associated in this film with Felix's ex-wife Nancy. Developed in counterpoint to the conjured Bogey fantasm is an animated memory of Nancy, which, overlaid with associations to the women Lasser portrayed in earlier films, taunts the childlike nebbish, disturbing his fragile self-image and newly won confidence. But at the end of *Play It Again, Sam,* it is Bogart, not Nancy, who holds center stage while reenacting a scene from *Casablanca* in which he praises the nerd-turned-hero for having developed a "little style" and not "needing me anymore."

The Keaton Era

At the beginning of the Keaton era, the shift in the schlemiel's depiction is paralleled by Allen's according himself a power—a privileged path of access that repeatedly intercuts the narrative trajectory. In *Everything You Always Wanted to Know About Sex* (*But Were Afraid to Ask), Sleeper,* and *Love and Death,* Allen's schlemiel wields this fantastic power by doubling the historical consciousness depicted in the film with parodic asides from a protagonist schooled in Catskills humor and an existential appreciation for the absurd. In this way a fantastic hybrid is constituted, as Allen's protagonist uses his explicative illogic to read against the temporal grain while defying the linear impetus of plot that moves toward the closure of its denouement. The exegetic reconfigurations produced by this type of cross-reading prove uncanny on some occasions: a court jester from the Renaissance tells subversive, arcane jokes to an uncomprehending king; a sperm cell anxiously comments on the futility of understanding the mission of impregnation; and in *Love and Death* Boris confers with Death's obliging shade, which tells him to partake of life's illusion until they next meet. Until *Love and Death,* however, Allen's schlemiel exists in a centered, not heterogeneous, space while all other characters are subject to the dictates of the script's spatiotemporal dimensions.

With *Love and Death* Allen gives his female protagonist the fantastic license usually reserved for males only. In the film Keaton's kooky character converses with the schlemiel in literary and philosophical dialogues that comment reflexively on the unfolding narrative. At given moments in the script both characters disengage themselves from the narrative impetus and exchange ideas in verbal patterns so complex as to belie their being the spontaneous repartee of natural conversation. Take for instance the following passage:

Sonja: What prevents you from murdering somebody?
Boris: Well, murder is immoral.
Sonja: Immorality is subjective.
Boris: Yes, but subjectivity is objective.
Sonja: Not in any rational system of perception.
Boris: Perception is irrational and implies Immanence.
Sonja: The judgment of any system or a priori relationship of phenomena exists in any rational or metaphysical or at least epistemological contradiction to an abstracted empirical concept such as being or to be or to occur in the thing itself or of the thing, itself . . . Boris, we must believe in God.

This conversation occurs because Boris questions God's existence. Even in a Godless universe, Boris claims, people should not murder each other because murder is morally reprehensible. He takes this position, however, while posing an absurdism that colors perceptions born of an intersubjective matrix he typifies as irrational. Sonja, on the other hand, counters that "immorality is subjective," only to argue that perception is rationally structured, and that this structuration, though it leads to contradictions, must be taken as proof of God's existence. That they should have this conversation wherein God becomes equated with "an abstracted empirical concept such as being" indicates an alterity that calls attention to itself as existing outside the purview of narrative design, which, like a decoy, lures readerly desire within the entanglement of plot.

Boris and Sonja also defy spatiotemporal boundaries when confronting Death, lifting up the veil of impenetrability, and, if only for short-lived moments, defying assignable limits to converse with a caricature of lack. That they perform such fantastic exploits could lead Allenian apologists to contend that this bestowal of power on Keaton demonstrates that parity had been achieved between Allen's male and female protagonists. This "equivalency," they would argue, continues in *Annie Hall*, where all characters appear to be more equally situated.

Woody Allen's most celebrated film, *Annie Hall* was named for the female protagonist, a part for which Diane Keaton received an Oscar. In order to establish Annie's position, Allen encouraged the subject/spectator to identify with her, but only within the confines of narrative desire. In other words, the "maker of stories and captor of images" himself more frequently identified with his female protagonists who now shared center stage with his schlemiel (Mulvey 16). But within this paradigm of identificatory merger, how does the subject/spectator situate her- or himself in relation to the filmic image of the other? To answer this question, we can revisualize the subject's identification with celluloid characters so that it does not represent one pole in a binary set, the alternative being the scopophilic fantasy in which women become objects of visual pleasure, separate yet appropriable to sight-stimulated fantasies. Rather, both structures—scopophilic and identificatory—become alternating and/or simultaneous modes of representation. The subject/spectator of Allen's films is confronted with this combinatory logic revealing scopic inscriptions of desire persiting alongside of ego identifications with film characters that are untouchable yet incorporable through appropriative fantasy. And *Annie Hall* proves no exception to this interplay.

Trace its code of narrative arrangement and you will find that *Annie Hall* is not about its namesake, because the primary sequence of events depicts Alvy's life, not Annie's. Although Annie is a historical subject who progresses through perceptible transformations, each passage is supervised by Alvy as part of his tutorial. Like Eliza Doolittle, Annie is prepped—introduced to theoretical texts, told to take adult education courses, to enter into analysis. Annie is persuaded to listen to Alvy on other matters that pertain to her future; on one occasion she actually passes up a possible opportunity to sign a record contract because Alvy feels insecure about her working with Tony Lacey. Unfortunately, once Annie does recognize Alvy's possessiveness as suffocating, she leaves him for Lacey, who also treats her as a partial term of reference because, the narrative suggests, she sacrifices her career for Lacey's, a jet-set life-style, money, and a house where Charlie Chaplin once lived.

This narrativized account, concerned with Annie's life only in so far as it relates to the exposition of Alvy's history and her evocation of desire within that account, is itself framed, like a play within a play, by Alvy's introduction at the beginning of the film and the concluding sequence in which he extricates himself from the narrative of duration by turning to the audience in a manner reminiscent of George Burns on "The Burns and Allen Show." Burns, you might remember, often interrupted the ongoing narrative to perform a vaudevillian monologue which sometimes referred to Gracie's confusion with language, her propensity to take literally what others said. Like Burns, the Alvy/Allen protagonist also establishes a collusive pact with an audience of confidants encouraged to view events through the screen of his mediating perspective and the positionality of desire it implies. Thus, when Annie returns home from her first analytic session and she and Alvy quibble about whether Annie uttered a slip of the tongue ("my wife" for "my life"), Alvy revives the monologue format to argue his case: "She said, 'will it change my wife.' You heard that because you were there so I'm not crazy." It seems that Alvy invokes a medical-juridical discourse to judge sanity on the evidence of one parapraxis, but on closer examination this assumption proves only partially true because he does not summon psychoanalytic thunder to indict Annie for a slip in speech or a lapse in mental operations, since he is not really interested in analyzing the "antagonism between the subject's conscious intentions and what [s]he has repressed" (Laplanche 300). Rather, Alvy Singer raises the specter of psychoanalytic normality and the adaptive ego it implies because he also wants to dissuade Annie Hall from raising that specter herself now that she has been to an analyst. This form of authoritarian foreclosure fits a pattern that is finally predictable in Woody Allen's cinema: spectatorial engagement respecularized through the intrusive and compromising logic of the schlemiel's position and Allen's overidentification with it.

Another strategy hidden by this overinvolvement is Allen's use of the gaze as a structuring principle in *Annie Hall,* where one form of phallocentrism is replaced with another that, while it includes Keaton within the intentionality of narrative design, would entrap the viewer in a cinematic look controlled by the apparatus. Although Allen and Keaton share a relative inequality as protagonists, Allen takes further advantage of his position(s) as writer/director/character to manipulate our perspective by using the camera to organize color, image, and sound in reference to his gaze, a cinematographic centering that presents an intersection of voice and image tracts to create an illusion of continuity "restored from discontinuous elements" (Baudry 29). As film theorist Jean-Louis Baudry suggests, "the [filmic] world offers up an object endowed with meaning, an intentional object, implied by and implying the action of the 'subject' which sights it" (31). This sighting, not to be confused with seeing, is what Lacan calls *le regard* or the gaze, the sense we have about us that we "are beings who are looked at, in the spectacle of the world" (*Four* 75). The gaze is an imagined vision of ourselves seen from the field of the Other. When we watch a filmmaker's work, then, we are not only lured by narrative desire but, as imagined objects from another perspective, we are enticed by a subtle summons to lay down our gaze before a distinctive imaging or signature.

By using the camera eye to color perceptions in a biased light, Allen sustained the gaze to create a fictitious filmic totality, a frame of reference that has subjected Keaton and other characters to the constitutive effect of the apparatus. In a recent interview in *The New York Times Magazine* Allen blatantly stated, "If I had to make films without complete control from start to finish, I definitely would not do it" (James 18). Despite his claims to the contrary, then, Woody Allen first and foremost inscribes himself as the primary object of an autobiographical filmic discourse that grudgingly allows women their agency as subjects in the narrative production. At his best, he still displaces feminine representation with autobiographical analysis that becomes the source of enunciation and object of scrutiny in the metacinematic commentaries of *Stardust Memories* and *Zelig*, mainstream films that failed at the box office because they focus reflexively on the cinematographic process of representation.

Allen's Avant-Garde Phase

In her famous article "Visual Pleasure and Narrative Cinema," Laura Mulvey advances the argument that radical filmmakers can reveal the illusions perpetrated by classical narrative cinema, whose "formal preoccupations reflect the psychical obsessions of the society which produced it" (8). Exposing such obsessions and revealing the eroticism encoded for the filmic look forms an integral link in her analysis of the film text's iconicity, its attachment of meaning to images. For Mulvey, feminist analysis should replace the pleasure produced from the camera's identification with the male protagonist who "draws the spectators deeply into his position, making them share his uneasy gaze" (15). In *Alice Doesn't* Teresa de Lauretis compliments Mulvey for "marking and summing up an intensely productive phase of feminist work with film," but de Lauretis carefully delineates their positions while demonstrating that Mulvey reaches a theoretical impasse by resting her argument on a binary logic with its series of oppositions, "type A and non-A: 'mainstream' (Hollywood and derivatives) and 'non-mainstream' (political-aesthetic avant-garde)" (59). In Mulvey's analysis these terms are skewed to idealize the radical avant-garde cinema whose work is to politicize desire and free "the look of the camera into its materiality in time and space and the look of the audience into dialectics, passionate detachment" (Mulvey 18).

De Lauretis's critique of binarisms can be applied to Woody Allen's avant-garde phase because of its cautionary warning not to idealize any mode of representation since it can be appropriated for an antifeminist politico-aesthetic agenda that showcases itself as egalitarian, democratic, or the like. With this in mind, films like *Stardust Memories* and *Zelig* become more problematical because, from first shot to last, they self-consciously remind us of their filmic referentiality and our place in the chain of signification. Yet, though these narratives are multilineal structures that call attention to the manipulation of visual pleasure, Allen's films displace their sociohistorical dimension with a narcissistic fixation on Allen's autobiographical propensities, the *I* that reappears in successive films, revisualizing itself, a solidification of presence. This need to celebrate himself as *auteur, auteur* during the avant-garde phase reveals disparate, uneven ratios of development.

For example, *Stardust Memories* imbues Allen's filmic correlative with his own traits—directorial accreditation, fame, and money. Sandy Bates, however, is an embittered public figure that detests admirers who shower him with affection. Not a scriptbound character, Bates is aware that he exists as part of an author/character conflation in a metacinematic study superimposed onto the narrative. Allen had used this technique before, most notably at the end of *Annie Hall*, when the narrative of duration was framed as a play within a play rehearsed as a means of rewriting a less painful ending for a failed relationship. But *Annie Hall* partially adheres to a realism that *Stardust Memories* parodies, a film beginning with Sandy Bates's realization that he is on the wrong train, not a suite filled with convivial company, drink, and *la joie de vivre,* but another site littered with ambulating cadavers on their way to a twentieth-century burial ground, a version of Eliot's modernist wasteland. A self-conscious spinoff of Fellini's *8½,* the central narrative of *Stardust Memories* concludes, as did *Annie Hall,* by calling attention to the film within a film and director Allen's part in having structured both.

But if Allen parodies himself in such projects, does it follow that he accepted the (k)not of castration which required a counterstrategy, the creation of numerous schlemiels whose function was to localize lack in a coherent caricature of ineptitude? In all likelihood Allenian apologists would credit the filmmaker for working through, and later for parodying this working-through of, desire, which, since it is for something-other-than-self, always leaves a remainder, a *manque-à-être,* a want-to-be. As

Ellie Ragland-Sullivan argues, desire is predicated on lack even as it testifies to an intrasubjective split, "an anxiety or metonymy" (82). Keeping in mind that desire is subject to a series of displacements, we find that even Allen's avant-garde films deny this fundamental lack, work rather to contain the sliding of displacement by taking the same initiatory path that leads repeatedly to the boundary of *self*-limitation. Allen never abandons this yellow brick road and his knotty entanglement within the temporal dimension; from mirror-stage objectifications to secondary Oedipal self-dramatizations, it is this psychic interplay that engenders Allen's schlemiels. But at what cost?

What cost is there in becoming one's ego ideal, in exceeding the illusion, in recognizing it as such? This is a pertinent question in *Stardust Memories* and *Zelig*. In the former, the schlemiel-turned-director tells a captive audience that he did not have to study filmmaking at New York University; "they studied me." Responding to an accusation of narcissism, Bates quips that "if I did identify with a Greek mythological character, it would not be Narcissus . . . it would be Zeus." Such a hotshot director is a mock-schlemiel, a veritable patriarch-in-schlemiel's-clothing that acknowledges the blurred, tenuous boundary between Allen and protagonists who had become famous directors, writers, and media personalities. None of them, however, more closely resembles Woody Allen than Sandy Bates, who defends his right to make serious films, to leave behind the vaudevillian techniques that entertained moviegoers in his early period. Completing the circuitry of selfhood developed in *Play It Again, Sam,* Sandy Bates becomes a Bogey-like ego ideal when projecting before him "the substitute for the lost narcissism of his childhood in which he was his own ideal" (Laplanche 144).

This attempt at narcissistic recuperation invariably displaces feminine representation, which is the case in *Zelig* where the schlemiel mimes ego ideals whose presence provokes him to undergo transformations through which he becomes the embodiment of the objectified other. When in the presence of Frenchmen, Zelig becomes a Frenchman; when in Chinatown, he takes on Oriental characteristics; when with Orthodox Jews, he grows a beard and becomes a rabbi. But, in a crucial scene where Zelig enters into the psychoanalysis with Eudora Fletcher that eventually frees him of his compulsion to mime others, Zelig underidentifies with the female psychoanalyst by becoming an analyst, not a woman. It becomes apparent, then, that at some fundamental level these two terms are not equivalent, that "female" must retain its adjectival position, disallowed the nominal status of the "psychoanalyst." In fact, in Allen's films the ego ideal is never a woman. Instead, films like *Zelig* study the ego's *méconnaissance* while parodying Allen's previous psychodramatic self-reenactments. But, even as *Zelig* substitutes the structuralist's statement on the system of signification within the medium of expression, Allen creates female protagonists who must be "perfect" enough to conjure the illusion that they too have become their ego ideals. In *Stardust Memories* Dorrie suspects as much when, confined to a mental hospital, she lucidly states that "you were searching for the perfect woman, and settled for me."

The female protagonists in this film are a troubled lot, especially Dorrie, who is beautiful, sometimes charming, and the object of a stardust memory that momentarily "takes the film into a no-man's-land outside its own time and space" (Mulvey 12). In this evanescent reminiscence, Dorrie resembles Linda in *Play it Again, Sam,* a woman demarcated from the (m)Other that threatened to incorporate the schlemiel within the realm of nondifferentiation. But elsewhere in the film Dorrie refuses to allow Sandy to forget what he would repress: "I'm beautiful, but I'm trouble," a refrain echoed later by Daisy, a statement with a special resonance for the nostalgic schlemiel. Later, in a subsequent sketch, Allen and Tony Roberts dress up as brain surgeons to operate on two women, to combine them surgically in an attempt to find the perfect specimen. One woman is "an animal, nasty, mean, trouble" while the other has a "great personality" but is sexually unstimulating. The point of the operation is to put "wonderful" Doris in Rita's body and therefore entertain a butchershop ménage à trois. Charlotte Rampling, who also plays Dorrie, is one of the women that undergoes brain surgery. It seems that her beauty is so arresting, her power to evoke the look so pronounced that she must be punished twice (as Dorrie and as Rita), victimized in direct proportion to her ability to transfix desire and provide the illusion, if only momentarily, that the split, noncoherent subject is whole, safe from difference. This illusion is further perpetuated by the film's final scene, when Sandy pledges to forget Dorrie and Daisy in favor of Isobel, a woman whom the director finds nonthreatening, like the narrative conclusion that sentimentally replicates the first scene aboard Allen's train of sorrows.

A similar image repertoire of degradation awaits Mia Farrow in her films, for she portrays a gum-chomping gun moll in *Broadway Danny Rose* and a romanticist in *The Purple Rose of Cairo* who falls in love with a celluloid protagonist whom she idealizes. But in *Interiors,* Allen's first "serious" film, there is no comic division of interest nor bicolumnar contrast in plots where women are strategically suppressed to the margins while the schlemiel remains the principal catalyzing agent of humor. Instead, unfunny *Interiors* analyzes the anxiety attached to Allen's representation of women who are no longer the image of his eye and the unacknowledged support of his system. This confirms that years before Allen found such flimsy support in fleeting stardust memories, he had decided that another tactic was necessary to prevent further slippage.

Feminine Representation in *Interiors* and *Hannah and Her Sisters*

In "Woman as Symptom," Jacqueline Rose discusses Lacan's concept of the "pas tout" or "not all" in terms of cinematic representation: not-allness is a vanishing point indicating irreconcilable difference, a moment of unintegrative Otherness that undermines the possibility of systematic unity for the cinematic structure. As Rose's title suggests, this argument lends itself not only to a deconstruction of systemic logic but to a feminist critique of iconicity, images of women superimposed compensatorily for the rupture-in-difference that must be refused or bound "back into the logic and perfection of the film system itself" (219). In accordance with this strategy, woman becomes equated with sexual difference, a differentiation that the system attempts to elide even as it establishes her as a limit or boundary that guarantees against the illimitable boundarilessness of an unsupported system. In other words, woman becomes the support of systemicity itself in relation to which "she comes to represent two things—what the man is not, that is, difference, and what he has to give up, that is excess" (Rose 219).

Such terms as vanishing point and unappropriable difference are useful when applied to Woody Allen's *Interiors*, a film that is not formulaic in the usual sense because Allen does not recycle the same old schlemiel, slapstick, and sexual innuendo. *Interiors* takes itself seriously, but its dramatic intentionality brings with it a depiction of the (m)Other, which, like the return of the repressed, appears at the precise moment when comedy is abandoned. Gone are the nostalgic melodies that accompany the introductory and concluding credits of Allen's films and, like them, the schlemiel/protagonist is noticeably absent. One might suspect as a result of the latter omission that Allen's female protagonists would fill the vacuum left by the male lead's departure, but *Interiors* defies expectation, reversing field as figure and ground alternate and the existential anguish (usually candied over by the comedian's witticisms) becomes predominant, fore-grounded in a series of familial conflicts that erupt on-screen. In fact, it is questionable whether, at some level, Allen's female protagonists are not thinly veiled replicas of Allen. Any hope that Eve, Renata, Joey, or Flyn would be agents of their own interests is illusory, since they utter Allen's words under his direction while sharing common attributes with the writer/

director/actor as well. It is also no coincidence that Flyn is an actress, that Renata, Frederick, and Michael all write for a living. If we could find a director through which Allen objectifies himself, this colloquy of one would be complete.

This director/character conflation is found, like Poe's purloined letter, in the most obvious of hiding places, in the characterization of Eve as the (m)Other whose directorial gestures become a narrative focal point and source of commentary by characters in *Interiors*. Eve is portrayed as an interior designer incapable of expressing love directly. Instead she fetishizes desire in a series of art objects and their spatial arrangement to convey the shape and limitation of her love. Emotionally removed from her daughters and husband and often dissociated from her own feelings, Eve watches helplessly as her desire fossilizes into objects of exchange. After Eve's suicide, her husband Arthur remembers his wife as "distant . . . always poised and distant," a woman with dignity who created an environment resembling "an ice palace." Her daughters, however, know her as a geometrician of fantasy who objectified herself in the objets d'art which she bought, then arranged in accordance with her grand design. Daughterly desire for their mother's desire impelled each to identify with and transform herself through these objects of exchange in hopes of provoking a response from Eve, albeit mediated by the geometric gaze of the director whose distance characterized her relation to family members.

What is unique about Allen's unfunny film is the displacement of his bespectacled schlemiel by a Janus-faced mother-director who becomes central to narrative engagement. Eve's nonmaternal relation to her daughters and her excessive concern about their social status positions her as a phallic figure who enjoys pitting Joey against Renata—always undermining the former's efforts to comfort her, always praising the latter in front of the family. This competitiveness, juxtaposed with Eve's obsession with spatial representation, makes her so phallocentric that it leads one to wonder whose eyes focus behind her sunglasses—Eve's or director Allen's—whose numerous window shots offer a correlative image to his spectacles, which in turn metonymically invoke the gaze that situates characters and audience alike within the fixed optics of his vision. Allen thus insinuates himself into the narrative, and, although the schlemiel is not a factor in *Interiors*, the film offers another example of Allen's self-referential need to carry himself like a remainder across his canon, a means of self-presencing established to compensate for a perceived loss, one so great he could not depict the (m)Other without allegorizing his position as the choreographer of cinematographic inscription, a psychodramatic stance he habitually projected onto characters who acted as screens for this ritualistic reenactment. Allen enacts this ritual in *Interiors,* where he masquerades as a vanishing point of unrecognizable difference when he scripts himself as the mother-in-drag whom he substitutes for the (m)Other that is finally not so different after all. Because of this ploy, a measure of control is retained, the yawning gulf denied, and difference remains under erasure.

The Eve/Allen conflation serves as a model for the mother-daughter bonding which creates further difficulty in delineating boundaries, recognizing where one woman begins and the other leaves off. Renata suggests as much when she accuses Joey of changing places with their mother: "for a while there you were her, weren't you?" Renata herself needs Frederick to remind her that "you are not your mother" when she also closely identifies with Eve, the late-night pacer who undergoes shock treatment before eventually committing suicide. This permeability of mother-daughter boundaries finds a filmic correlative in the opening and closing shots of the sisters, who, lodged in their beach house within carefully decorated interiors, look out their windows at a natural site impervious to Eve's designs, which paradoxically remains a guilt-ridden reminder of a mourned seascape. Furthermore, these windows, a corollary for Allen's spectacles, open onto an external vista even as they reflect the sisters' mirrored images, an iconic division indicative of the identity confusion linked to this type of cross-representation.

As if this framing tactic were not sufficiently heavy-handed, Allen also arranges his narrative so that its denouement presents a delirious, rapid-fire progression of drug euphoria, rape, and suicide. Part of the narrative function is to structure the (m)Other's death, but Eve's drowning is purposely juxtaposed with Flyn's use of cocaine and another traumatic moment of rupture, Frederick's attempted rape of Flyn, who is his wife's sister. A writer who wants "to knock someone over" with his prose, Frederick grows more and more aggressive until he admits his joy in attacking perceived literary enemies "under the guise of high standards." It is not long after Frederick declares "my anger scares me; I don't like what I'm becoming" that he verbally, then physically, assaults Flyn, telling her that "it's been such a long time since I made love to a woman I didn't feel inferior to." This verbal salvo is followed by physical aggression that Flyn wards off before penetration occurs—a violation that elicits no follow-up response from Flyn or other family members, who, caught in an Allenian politics of representation, are repositioned for the duration of the film in relation to Eve's act of self-willed annihilation. The pacing here is significant: one event so quickly follows another that they disallow a response to the rape scene while depicting a pattern wherein the pleasure

Allen associates with Flyn's to-be-looked-at-ness cannot mask the anxiety-ridden, compromised knowledge that on some level the daughter is conflated with the manipulatable, negotiable (m)Other Allen would disavow as the support of his cinematic project.

Hannah and Her Sisters parallels *Interiors* in using a recursive logic that transfers Eve's role as a perfectionist onto Hannah, the sister/mother whose contained self-assuredness family members both admire and resent. Husband Eliot thinks of Hannah as a maternal figure that "came into my empty life and changed it . . . and I paid her back by banging her sister in a hotel room." Lee expresses ambivalence toward her sister by going to bed with Eliot, then measuring her performance against Hannah's: "I was so worried I wouldn't compare with Hannah." Sister Holly reinforces this pattern by repeatedly borrowing money from Hannah but resenting the advice that comes with it: "you really know how to cut me down," to belittle ideas which eventually help Holly to rescript her future. But the most dramatic example of ambivalence toward the sister/mother figure comes from the bespectacled hypochondriac Mickey, who was once Hannah's husband but later marries Holly. The narrative purposely intimates that Sachs's impotency was psychological in nature, influenced by his relationship with Hannah. Diagnosed as impotent while married to this maternal figure, Sachs disproves that diagnosis by the end of the film when he learns that Holly will give birth to their child.

Hannah and Her Sisters, then, recycles the *authori*tarian maternal figure from *Interiors* in the guise of the sister. Another in a line of Allenian comedies, *Hannah* situates family members in a series of sexual triangles that fray and tear at interpersonal relations, but, because of the film's comedic effect, never sever the cord of love entirely. Although deceived by her husband and sister, Hannah happily accepts Eliot's newfound admiration once Lee meets Doug, the literature professor she eventually marries. The same can be said for Evan and Norma, the parental figures who threaten to redress perceived wrongs but never venture beyond a certain point of petty faultfinding. Their inability to cross over the tragic boundary invoked in *Interiors* is the difference between the two films. For while Evan accuses his wife of getting "drunker and drunker and finally she became Joan Collins," he does not leave Norma, nor does she desert him.

Subjects like the pain of separation and the recognition of one's mortality are also mediated differently in comedic films like *Hannah and Her Sisters*. For instance, the question of mortality is obsessively reconsidered by Mickey Sachs who, after succumbing to the fear that he has a brain tumor, changes his life-style with the realization that "you're gonna die,

I'm gonna die, the audience is gonna die, the network's gonna—the sponsor. Everything." With this pleasantry in mind, the hypochondriac drops out for a year, considers converting to Catholicism, ponders becoming a Hare Krishna devotee, then enacts a mock existential suicide by shooting his image in the mirror. "In a Godless universe, I didn't want to go on living," he declares; "I want certainty or nothing," he rails until saved in the proverbial nick of time when his gun misfires, splintering a mirror and his reflected image of representation. It is at moments like these, when Sachs is saved or Eliot's marriage is retrieved from impending failure, that the comedic plot alters the codification of events.

Woody Allen, however, does write into Sachs's plot a conversion motif triggered by, of all things, the Marx Brothers' movie *Duck Soup,* which succeeds where Christ and Krishna failed in rousing Mickey out of a year-long stupor, a depression that lifts once he realizes that life has its moments, some of them humorous, some bittersweet. The paradisiacal promise of comedy for Allen holds out hope that maybe there is an all-pervasive power greater than ourselves: "I know maybe is a very slim reed to hang your whole life on, but that's the best we have." It is not surprising, then, that Woody Allen's central concern in recent years has not been with politics or psychoanalysis but with religion and our place in a structured universe. Allen was quoted in *The Miami News* as saying that "everything is based on that enormous fear and anxiety that human beings deal with, that sense of total bewilderment and total anxiety about mortality . . . that to me is the only significant struggle . . . until you come to terms with that, everything else is putting Band-Aids on something" (Berger 3C). We know that in *Hannah and Her Sisters* the concept of God fails the protagonist; it is replaced, of necessity, by the affect evoked by humor, a pattern that harkens back to one established in *Stardust Memories* where Og, "a superintelligent being" from Mars, tells Sandy Bates that he is "not Superman, you're a comedian. You want to do mankind a real service? Tell funnier jokes." In both films Allen mediates conceptualized lack with humor to present another type of difference, a metonymic displacement not seemingly riddled with anxiety. For, as Mario Levin has stated, comedy is "produced as a discharge of energy resulting from the difference between two forms of a representation: between the alien and the known, the habitual and the modified, or between what is expected and what actually happens" (78). A hierarchal pattern thus presents itself, writ large across Allen's canon, exemplified by a series of displacements including the daughter's slippage into and confusion with the (m)Other, the subsequent failure of woman as the basis of fantasy and support of Allen's phallocentric system of representation, and the inability of God (at some level confused with the *jouissance* of woman which is radically Other) to pose an alternative support system and thus prevent such slippage. All of these developments call for a counter-response that introduces the comic into the field of signification.

We must beware of reading Allen's humor apolitically precisely because he believes it to be a definitive answer, a mythologized end point and source of certitude. It is not surprising, then, that superintelligent Og speaks with Allen's voice in a narcissistic circuit of self-replication. Lacan reminds us in "A Love Letter" that when "one is made into two, there is no going back on it. It can never revert to making one again" (156). This considered, such Ogian intonations of wisdom become a form of self-prophesying propaganda, especially when attended by the not-so-innocent gaze situating the specular subject in a comedic relation. Allen's is not a case of mid-life crisis where psychoanalysis and Oedipus are displaced by religion and Mort Sahl. Rather, like Allen's celluloid directors, writers, actors, and media personalities, his comedians present a self-replicating persona depicting the masculine subject of enunciation. Perhaps his most powerful incarnation, the comedian offers Allen hope in a world torn by incestuous longing and Oedipal deadlocks, an ideological world in which Allen's female protagonists are customarily displaced by an author-centered roundabout. With this in mind, *Hannah and Her Sisters* becomes a more insidious film than *Interiors* because of Mickey Sachs's plot where humor is resistant to political analysis.

Works Cited

Allen, Woody, dir. *Annie Hall.* United Artists, 1977.

———, dir. *Bananas.* United Artists, 1971.

———, dir. *Broadway Danny Rose.* Orion, 1984.

———, dir. *Everything You Always Wanted to Know About Sex* (*But Were Afraid to Ask).* United Artists, 1972.

———, dir. *Hannah and Her Sisters.* Orion, 1986.

———, dir. *Interiors.* United Artists, 1978.

———, dir. *Love and Death.* United Artists, 1975.

———, dir. *Manhattan.* United Artists, 1979.

———. Screenplay. *Play It Again, Sam.* Paramount, 1972.

———, dir. *The Purple Rose of Cairo.* Orion, 1985.

———, dir. *Sleeper.* United Artists, 1973.

———, dir. *Stardust Memories.* United Artists, 1980.

———, rerelease dir. *What's Up Tigerlily?* American International, 1966.

———, dir. *Zelig.* Orion, 1983.

Baudry, Jean-Louis. "Ideological Effects of the Basic Cinematographic Apparatus." *Cinematographic Apparatus: Selected Writings*. Ed. Theresa Hak Kyung Cha. New York: Tanam, 1980. 25–61.

Berger, Joseph. "Films Find Saints as Compelling as Sinners." *The Miami News*. 8 Jan. 1986: 3C.

de Lauretis, Teresa. *Alice Doesn't: Feminism, Semiotics, Cinema*. Bloomington: Indiana Univ. Press, 1984.

Doane, Mary Ann. "Woman's Stake: Filming the Female Body." *October* 17 (1981): 23–36.

Goldman, Albert. "Boy-man, Schlemiel: The Jewish Element in American Humour." *Explorations: An Annual on Jewish Themes*. Ed. Murray Medlin. Chicago: Quadrangle Books, 1968. 3–17.

Irigaray, Luce. *This Sex Which Is Not One*. Trans. Catherine Porter. Ithaca: Cornell Univ. Press, 1985.

James, Caryn. "Auteur! Auteur! The Creative Mind of Woody Allen." *The New York Times Magazine*. 19 Jan. 1986. 18–30.

Lacan, Jacques. "A Love Letter." *Feminine Sexuality*. Trans. Jacqueline Rose. Ed. Juliet Mitchell and Jacqueline Rose. New York: Norton, 1982.

————. *The Four Fundamental Concepts of Psycho-Analysis*. Trans. Alan Sheridan. New York: Norton, 1978.

Laplanche, J., and J.-B. Pontalis. *The Language of Psycho-Analysis*. Trans. Donald Nicholson-Smith. New York: Norton, 1973.

Levin, Mario. "The Comic Difference." *Che Vuoi?* 1, no. 1 (1984): 69–80.

Mulvey, Laura. "Visual Pleasure and Narrative Cinema." *Screen* 16, no. 3 (1975): 6–18.

Ragland-Sullivan, Ellie. *Jacques Lacan and the Philosophy of Psychoanalysis*. Urbana: Univ. of Illinois Press, 1986.

Rose, Jacqueline. *Sexuality in the Field of Vision*. London: Verso, 1986. 215–23.

"Laughing in a Liberating Defiance": *Egalia's Daughters* and Feminist Tendentious Humor

MARLEEN S. BARR

> Too bad for them if they fall apart upon discovering that women aren't men, or that the mother doesn't have one. But isn't this fear convenient for them? Wouldn't the worst be, isn't the worst, in truth, that women aren't castrated, that they have only to stop listening to the Sirens (for the Sirens were men) for history to change its meaning? You only have to look at the Medusa straight on to see her. And she's not deadly. She's beautiful and she's laughing.
>
> HÉLÈNE CIXOUS
> "The Laugh of the Medusa"

Egalia's Daughters, Gerd Brantenberg's satire of the sexes, posits a society where women are empowered because they don't have one. Women in Egalia change history by refusing to listen to men and by valuing castration. Brantenberg allows us to gaze directly at a feminist utopia where reversing ideology, not sex roles, is most important. Although the women of Egalia are more beautiful than deadly, they epitomize men's worst fear. And the novel's female readers are laughing.[1]

Reactions to the novel are divided by gender. Men are not amused, while women are "laughing in a liberating defiance."[2] Why do men close the book while women read and laugh? What does their laughter mean? I will put Norman N. Holland's *Laughing: A Psychology of Humor* to the good feminist use of answering these questions. And I will discuss *Egalia's Daughters* according to ideas generated by Catherine Clément, Freud, and Kristeva.

But first, my own brief response to the novel: Its humor reminds me of a morning when I was chatting on a patio with three close female friends. Our conversation was interrupted by the sight of my male cat approaching with a live rabbit in his mouth. I screamed and grabbed a beach towel to subdue him while the rabbit escaped. My friends observed these doings and laughed. The realization that I had saved the bleeding, innocent creature from certain death stopped me from laughing. This situation was at once funny and not funny, comic and tragic, humorous and serious.

My response leads me to view the novel's humor in terms of Kristeva's comment about Menippean discourse: "Menippean discourse is both comic and tragic, or rather, it is *serious* in the same sense as is the carnivalesque; through the status of its words, it is politically and socially disturbing. It frees speech from historical constraints, and this entails a thorough boldness in philosophical and imaginative inventiveness" (52). The novel's comic moments are at the same time tragic and serious. Here, for example, is the experience Petronius, the protagonist, faces when he purchases his first peho (an article of clothing analogous to a bra for the penis): "The boys said it was awkward and uncomfortable, cramming your penis into that stupid box. And it was so impractical when you had to pee. . . . Ought he to have a size five with a B-tube or a size six with an A-tube, they would debate, sizing him up with their heads cocked to one side, pretending that having a penis was the most natural thing in the world" (12–13). Readers chuckle while remembering the serious mental and physical consequences caused by their own discomfort with impractical feminine garments. The novel's tragic scenes also juxtapose seriousness with tragedy and comedy. Readers might both laugh and cry when Petronius becomes the victim of gang rape: "He felt her wet crotch against his thigh. . . . The grip on his penis tightened. She was breathing hard against his ear, bouncing violently up and down, forcing his thigh against her crotch, pumping and moaning. . . . This wasn't happening to him, but to someone else" (65). These comic and tragic components are politically and socially disturbing. The above passages, for example, speak to the personal and public restrictions directed toward inhibiting the movement of women's bodies. They heighten awareness of woman as victim and accuse patriarchy of being her victimizer.

At the same time, the novel frees speech from historical constraints. Armed with a female-centered and female-authored history, Egalia's women define human biology in a manner which empowers them to control their language and their world: "The menstrual cycle in the wom [woman] was precisely what bound the huwom [human] race to life, to nature's own great cycle and to the phases of the moon. By virtue of this endlessly recurring rhythm in her body, she was bound in a very different way, to nature, and this contact with her natural surroundings gave her an inner power and strength, which allowed her to dominate nature and the environment. . . . Wim [women] therefore had great control over everything—over their own bodies, over the cultivation of the soil, over the world" (168). This biological explanation of women's dominance derives justification from more than a simple sex-role reversal. Instead, it is best justified by a reversal of ideology—socialization rules indicating that sexism is an artificial construction. Hence, although the novel might at first appear to stop short by presenting a limited and obvious role reversal, upon closer analysis it becomes clear that the work is a bold example of feminist philosophical and imaginative inventiveness.

Feminist theorists currently assert that patriarchy is merely one of many possible representations of human reality. The following passage provides one example of how the novel uses feminist imaginative and philosophical inventiveness to self-consciously—or metafictionally—articulate the same argument:

They [menwim] had accepted the inferior position wim had allotted them. They must have believed wim when they said it was part of the natural order. Why did they believe them? . . . They could just as well have said that it was part of the natural order for wim to mind children and for menwim to go out and make decisions. Nothing was really in harmony with any so-called "natural order." Everything was the contrivance of huwom beings. A systematic contrivance with a laugh in view: to hold huwom beings of one sort down, so huwom beings of another sort can exploit them and thrive as parasites. (173)

This juxtaposition of role reversal and ideological reversal announces that patriarchal law is merely a systematic contrivance.

Serious laughter is evoked by these reversals, which cannot be correctly defined as either patriarchal law or a simplistic parody of patriarchal law. Instead, the reversal becomes something other, a new law which is other from prevailing patriarchal law. The reader's laughter in response to this new law is analogous to Kristeva's thoughts about the laughter of the carnival: "The laughter of the carnival is not simply parodic; it is no more comic than tragic; it is both at once, one might say that it is *serious*. This is the only way that it can avoid becoming either the scene of law or the scene of its parody, in order to become the scene of its *other*. Modern writing offers several striking examples of this omnified scene that is both *law* and *others*—where *laughter* is silenced because it is not parody but *murder and revolution*" (50). Because the reader's laughter is not merely a response to a simple parody but rather a bold call for nothing short of a revolution against patriarchal law—murdering a social father—it soon becomes silenced.

This response is metafictionally commented upon within the novel when Petronius writes a masculinist utopian novel which reflects our world. His novel within Brantenberg's novel forms an ideological reversal within an ideological reversal. The Egalian response to Petronius's novel reflects men's response to Brantenberg's novel: "Some people disliked the book and stopped reading halfway through. There was nothing particularly funny about portraying 'men' as muscle-bound supermen, always carrying on and shouting and ordering people about, while 'women' went round smiling and behaving like servile dolls in pretty dresses. It was grotesque. No culture which managed to distort the natural characteristics of the two sexes to such a degree could be regarded as a real culture" (266). The subversive laughter of the Other is dismissed and silenced instead of acknowledged and understood.

Brantenberg correctly and self-consciously predicts men's response to her novel. Here, for example, is what a male expert on utopian fiction (who will remain happily anonymous) said to me about *Egalia's Daughters:* "I found it predictable and because I found it predictable I found it boring. Well, I mean, I went and read the last chapter to see if I was right and I was. My recollection of it is that one of the patterns within SF or utopian fiction it fits is gender reversal. It is predictable once you figure out that it is written by a feminist." This theorist of utopian literature assumes the voice of Petronius's Egalian reviewer as he dismisses the text, closes the book, silences the laughter. He is blind to the text's juxtaposition of comic and tragic and oblivious to its subversive ideological reversal. Yet, despite the attitude this man's particular response represents, female readers continue to laugh. Their laughter is important and serious. I wish to explain, rather than dismiss or silence, this female laughter. And I want to understand why gender schism divides the laughers.

Psychoanalytic theory can facilitate an understanding of these issues. Freud leads me to conclude that Brantenberg's novel is a long, feminist, tendentious joke, the type of joke which, according to Freud, is "able to release pleasure even from sources that have undergone repression. If . . . the overcoming of external obstacles can . . . be traced back to the overcoming of internal inhibitions and repressions, we may say that tendentious jokes exhibit the main characteristic of joke-work—that of liberating pleasure by getting rid of inhibitions" ("Jokes" 134). Women are taught to abide by patriarchal rules, to be feminine—and laughing at patriarchy breaks the rules and is unfeminine. When she enjoys Brantenberg's humor, the reader overcomes inhibitions and repressions against being unfeminine, laughs, and experiences the liberating pleasure of getting rid of patriarchal inhibitions. Overcoming such inhibitions, however, has not been easy for women. They habitually repress their own jokes and smile demurely when they are debased by men's misogynistic jokes. Hence, when women laugh with Egalia's daughters, they enact a feminist achievement. Freud explains why this is true:

> Experience with tendentious jokes shows that ... the suppressed purpose can, with the assistance of the pleasure from the joke, gain sufficient strength to overcome the inhibition, which would otherwise be stronger than it. The insult takes place, because the joke is thus made possible. But the enjoyment obtained ... is so much greater than the pleasure from the joke that we must suppose that the hitherto suppressed purpose has succeeded in making its way through.... It is in such circumstances that the tendentious joke is received with the heartiest laughter.... They [tendentious jokes] put themselves at the service of purposes in order that, by means of using the pleasure from jokes as a fore-pleasure, they may produce new pleasure by lifting suppressions and repressions. ("Jokes" 136–37)

When the reader laughs, she successfully gains sufficient strength to overcome inhibitions against finding fault with her place in the patriarchal construction of reality. The pleasure she derives from laughing with the novel's commentary about arbitrary partriarchal constructions is greater than the pleasure she derives from laughing with its sex-role reversals. Her reaction explains why women's and men's responses to the novel differ. Men stop short at the humor of the sex-role reversals without taking the time to consider the more pleasurable (but obviously not more pleasurable to men) joke of unmasking patriarchal constructions. Men, unlike women, refuse to smile demurely at the opposite sex's gender-related humor. They refuse to be amused by the observation that an unnatural arbitrary system makes their dominant position possible. Women, on the other hand, can now muster the strength to insult patriarchy. Their reaction to the novel's sex-role reversals is a fore-pleasure preceding the new pleasure of seeing the text as a means to lift sex roles' suppressions and repressions.

The novel's insult directed at patriarchy can take place because women finally have the strength to make feminist jokes possible. Although feminists were once accused of having no sense of humor, feminist humor has now successfully made its way through the patriarchal repression directed against it. In fact, feminist humor is strong enough to serve as a power fantasy for women. Look, for example, at this Egalian joke: " 'In the old days all the wim used to carry a PS—it stands for prick-scissors, if you really want to know. And if any big menwim bothered them they pulled them out. Snip!' She [Petronius's sister] laughed" (103). The novel functions as a metatextual PS, a tendentious joking postscript to patriarchy, a phallocentrism suppressor. The laughing reader snips patriarchy with her eyes while realizing that man's system cuts short the full potential of her mind and body.

She constructively enacts Freud's notion that "humour has in it a *liberating* element." He continues: "[W]hat is fine about it [humor] is the triumph of narcissism, the ego's victorious assertion of its own invulnerability. It refuses to be hurt by the arrows of reality or to be compelled to suffer." While engulfed within the novel's matriarchal world, the reader is "impervious to wounds dealt by the outside world" ("Humour" 265). She roars with rebellious laughter at specifically feminist jokes instead of demurely smiling at men's misogynistic jokes. Her ego triumphs as she insists upon deriving pleasure from humor which speaks the truth to her instead of constructing lies about her. She avoids patriarchy's compulsion to make her suffer by using humor as a means to evade adverse circumstances. She, in other words, appropriates Freud's ideas: "Humour is not resigned; it is rebellious. It signifies the triumph not only of the ego, but also of the pleasure principle, which is strong enough to assert itself here in the face of adverse real circumstances. . . . By its [humor's] repudiation of the possibility of suffering, it takes its place in the great series of methods devised by the mind of man for evading the compulsion to suffer" ("Humour" 265). Rather than resigning herself to patriarchy, the reader uses humor to rebel against it.

This positive attitudinal shift is further explained by Holland's observation that "[c]haracteristically for Freud, laughter embodies a frontal assault on adult reality" (53). The reader's laughter is one such assault on her adult reality, a reality which demands that she play the role of diminutive and less-than-human being—and then laughs at her subhuman behavior. Women are convinced by patriarchy to meet the frontal assaults on their adult reality by literally handicapping themselves with further frontal assaults: padded bosoms, made-up faces, and deodorized genitals. They act in complicity with the male jokes directed at these assaults. *Egalia's Daughters*, on the other hand, changes woman's laughter. Her impulse to laugh with those who laugh at her—a complicitous, self-directed frontal assault—is turned away from herself and becomes a tendentious gratification of the forbidden impulse to laugh at men. "In tendentious joking, not only do we get the pleasure of the word play or jesting, but we also gratify forbidden impulses. . . . That is, only if they are disguised as word play do we allow ourselves to gratify these tendencies without anxiety'' (Holland 48). Or, although we can laugh at prick-scissors, we would be made anxious by carrying poultry shears as a means of self-defense.

Laughing at men no longer makes us anxious, however. The novel gratifies the forbidden impulse to turn men's misogynistic jokes back upon themselves. "Seawim," for example, enjoy the following reversal of men's humor:

> "He was just a sex maniac. . . . I couldn't get anything done when I had to go and rub it every half hour. . . . So one day I threw a bucket of cold water between his legs. Plop, it went, and it just dangled there. I don't think I've ever laughed as much. Ha, ha, ha!"
>
> They all shrieked with laughter. Petronius glanced at Gro [his female lover]. She was laughing, too. Even Gro. (79)

Like Petronius watching Gro laugh, women watch men laugh at normal aspects of female sexuality and anatomy. Men often fail to realize that it is wrong to use laughter to insult women. On the level of simple reversal, Brantenberg's novel is an innocent joke which makes men realize that their humor is extremely damaging to women. On the level of ideological reversal, Brantenberg's novel becomes a tendentious joke, a social corrective—a weapon. "We distinguish . . . between laughing *at* and laughing *with* someone, because laughter, by withholding pity, can serve as a weapon. We use it as a social corrective. We attack individuals, types, institutions, even deities by laughing at them (Holland 17). The entire novel laughs at patriarchy and shows no pity for men. It is a tendentious, feminist, social corrective which attacks the institution of patriarchy by laughing at it, not with it. And male readers are reluctant to laugh with us.

Women have been dissuaded from wielding the weapon of laughter, restrained from public speaking and public laughing. Johnny Carson is more welcome on late night television than Joan Rivers. Rivers and the laughing Egalians are monstrous, frightening women, women breaking out of patriarchal constraints, crossing dangerous lines. As Catherine Clément explains, "She laughs, and it's frightening—like Medusa's laugh—petrifying and shattering constraint. . . . All laughter is allied with the monstrous. . . . Laughter breaks up, breaks out, splashes over. . . . It is the moment at which woman crosses a dangerous line, the cultural demarcation beyond which she will find herself excluded" (Cixous and Clément 32–33).

The reader crosses an especially dangerous line while laughing at male anatomy. Our culture, after all, exploits the female body and shields the male body from exploitation. *Egalia's Daughters* brazenly crosses Clément's line by positing new male psychological constructions of body images. When Egalian men try not to be ashamed of their bodies, try not to feel inadequate because their anatomy differs from the female norm, the novel breaks out and splashes over, acting as a postscript to patriarchy. Male Egalians resolve to no longer feel "ashamed of the fact that they had a cock. They would therefore show it openly and unashamedly" (162–63). The reader's reaction to the men's shame includes both laughter and pain.

This passage is especially funny and serious: "The menwim recognized so many common experiences among the things they were telling one another. The shame of having a manwom's body. The shame of having a penis and a shamebag. . . . The shame of lacking breasts and hips and proper thighs and buttocks. The shame of not menstruating. . . . The shame of nocturnal emissions. The shame of lacking the ability to bear children. Shame, shame, shame" (248). The realization that women's shame is a patriarchal construction emerges from this dual reaction. The same realization about psychical differences between the sexes also emerges: "Various psychologists had undertaken studies, all of which tended to show that the child became frustrated and maladjusted if it did not stay with its father for the first five years of its life. . . . As long as one sex held power over the other, they would never be able to find out what differences there really were between the sexes—psychically—if there were any at all" (209).

Brantenberg uses humor to deconstruct the "anatomy is destiny" argument. She shows that woman can break out of the definition of herself as castrated man, that her so-called anatomical lack is positive, that having one can be a social and biological hindrance. She crosses a dangerous line, breaks up the integrity of the masculine body image, creates a new feminist psychoanalytic order to follow the disordered Imaginary. As Clément explains, "To break up, to touch the masculine integrity of the body image, is to return to a stage that is scarcely constituted in human development; it is to return to the disordered Imaginary of before the mirror stage, of before the rigid and defensive constitution of subjective armor. It is dangerous. . . . An entire fantastic world, made of bits and pieces, opens up beyond the limit, as soon as the line is crossed" (Cixous and Clément 33). Egalia is dangerous. It is the place of the new feminist Ego, the place of the new feminist symbolic system, the feminist fantastic world which opens up beyond the limits of patriarchal constructions. This fantastic world can become real when women use laughter to cross the dangerous line of woman's inscribed, proper, socially acceptable place.

The novel also confronts the constructed notion of woman's proper place during the sex act. As we saw during the rape scene, in Egalia the standard sexual position is for the women to grasp the man's penis while she rubs her genital area against his thigh. A man does not expect to have many opportunities to insert his penis into a vagina: " 'It takes a lot of courage to say you want to do it like that. And a wom has to be incredibly tolerant and considerate before she'll let you do it that way . . . ,' " explains Petronius (186). The most crucial aspect of the humor evoked by this sexual role reversal occurs when Petronius learns that he shares his specific sexual desire with others: "He knew he would enjoy doing it in the way Baldrian [his friend] had described, but he'd thought he was alone in having such desires" (186). As the reader watches Petronius realize that he is not alone, she laughs and reaches the same awareness about herself. Her laughter, a marker for her pain, merges with the laughter of other readers and universalizes her particular pain. It generates an "I am not alone" encounter-group reaction, a reading experience fruitfully articulated by Bella Abzug: "It makes you laugh, but it's not funny" (Holland 107). Readers form a group of laughers reacting to a juxtaposition of feminist humor and female pain. This group of laughing female readers can be discussed in terms of Holland's *Laughing*. His ideas can be called upon in a discussion of a specifically feminist humor and an exploration of the question of why women laugh.

Holland believes that "laughter is a social signal to other members of the group that they can relax with safety" (43). Brantenberg certainly creates a literary space for women's humor, a signal to her readers that they can relax and safely laugh at the vicissitudes of being a woman living under patriarchy. Holland continues to speak to Brantenberg's signaling: "laughter serves to show to other humans a willingness to cooperate and a desire to continue with whatever activity is in progress. . . . Laughter is a disguise within which one can communicate secret, forbidden ideas, because it makes people aware of mutual identifications and social relations" (84). When the reader laughs with *Egalia's Daughters,* she expresses her willingness to cooperate with the aims of feminists. As she identifies with other feminists, her laughter becomes a disguise allowing her to communicate her secret, forbidden desires for liberation. The point is that feminist laughers manifest a specific sense of humor. As Holland imagines a "macroperson" to illustrate the characteristics of a specific group of laughers—an American sense of humor, for example—the same composite can be drawn for feminist humor, a humor which has been called nonexistent. *Egalia's Daughters* is considered to be funny by women, not men, because it appeals to a specific macroperson, a female feminist laugher.

This particularly feminist group humor can be best understood by describing it according to what Holland calls the "Aha!" experience of psychoanalytic interpretation: "the feeling that suddenly all the data are so unified that it is as though mute stones have spoken. . . . We reason the same way in more commonplace situations, such as figuring out the function of an unknown device. Once I know that this conglomeration of handle, clamp, socket, and plunger is a cherry pitter, I understand that the clamp holds the device to a table. . . . In short, once I have grasped the central theme of pitting cherries, I can use it to relate a host of otherwise baffling details. If the machine is truly functional, one theme will relate all its details" (133–34). Brantenberg's humor unifies and unmasks the data of patriarchy's subordination of women. It figures out how the unknown device called patriarchy works, that patriarchy uses the conglomeration of shame and sexual inhibition as a sexist clamp to hold women in a secondary position. The novel's feminist humor, then, emanates from the "Aha!" experience of seeing how patriarchy functions. Brantenberg stresses that patriarchy is a machine for subordinating women. She isolates patriarchy's identity theme and creates a novel which is a well-functioning feminist humor machine.

Holland discusses one particular feminist laugher, "Ellen," and her reaction to Kliban's cartoons. Even though he does not call particular attention to the fact that Ellen is a woman, I want to direct her response to Kliban toward an understanding of the humor of *Egalia's Daughters* in general and feminist humor in particular. Her response helps me to answer my version of the question "What does the reason I laugh have to do with the reason 'we' laugh?" (Holland 20). In my version of Holland's question, "I" is the individual reader of *Egalia's Daughters* and "we" is the macroperson of feminist laughers. Holland explains how Ellen's humor functions: "I had asked Ellen why she found it amusing when Kliban took some unpleasant, ugly piece of reality and put it into a cartoon. She answered that Kliban was demonstrating that someone else sees the world in the same 'very critical' way she does. . . . and the fact that Kliban puts very ugly things in his cartoons simply proves that 'somebody else sees what I see' " (158). Similarly, the reader finds *Egalia's Daughters* amusing because it demonstrates that someone else sees patriarchy in the same "very critical" way she does. When Brantenberg puts ugly, sexist things in her novel, she proves to the reader that "somebody else sees what I see." The reader responds to a tendentious joke and so does Ellen: "In effect, Ellen did just what she imagined Kliban doing. He created a real world. She created a real world. He said that world is ugly. So did she. . . . Kliban's picture of the world confirmed Ellen's, yes, but more important, it proved you could be safe in holding this view of people, provided you were intelligent and witty enough" (161). When the reader responds to Egalia, she confirms her view of her world. She is told she can safely express this view in an intelligent and witty way. The reader reacts to the novel as an innocent joke, as Holland says Ellen reacted to the cartoons: "Why did Ellen laugh at the King Kong cartoon? . . . Because it presents something harmful (King Kong) harmlessly. Because it is playful. Because it shows people eating the slain god. . . . Because it let her feel superior. . . . Ellen laughed because she found she could confirm her identity through Kliban's cartoons" (170, 172). Similarly, *Egalia's Daughters* playfully and humorously renders the patriarchy harmless. It slays phallocentrism and proclaims that god is female. Its textual world gives the reader the superiority patriarchally constructed reality denies her. Above all, the reader laughs because she can use the text to confirm her feminist identity.

When the laugh of the individual feminist reader combines with that of a macroperson representing an entire undefined and untapped category of feminist humor, her response becomes a psychological and social event, a powerful defense—a powerful weapon: "A laughing audience gives rise to a particularly powerful defense, for the laughter of others . . . reassures the human animal. The sound of others' laughing says there *is* a frame" (Holland 183). Holland continues: "Only when some person laughs has the joke become a psychological event. And only when many people laugh does it become a social one. . . . As Freud pointed out, the joke . . . serves the benign but paradoxical social function of asserting our shared inhibitions by the very act of loosening them. By laughing together, Ellen and I let each other know that we held certain values in common" (187–88). The laughter of other feminists reassures the individual feminist. Feminist laughter says there is a frame, a demarcation, to patriarchy's power to control, dominate, and inhibit women. (No wonder, then, that patriarchy has acted to silence women's laughter.) The reader is strengthened when the psychological event of her individual laughter combines with the social event of the feminist macroperson's group laughter. Laughter loosens women's inhibitions and signals that they share values in common.

Egalia's Daughters is important because instead of simply functioning as a predictable sex-role reversal utopia it acts as a catalyst to encourage the untapped and unpredictable power of women's shared laughter. It shows that instead of having patriarchy construct women's identity, laughter can help women to avoid complacently accepting demeaning identity constructions. Laughter is one small step to help women arrive at identities which are free of patriarchal definitions of "female." Holland seems to speak to this point:

Identity, then, offers but one small step in a dialectical understanding of many laughings. . . .

Why do we laugh? Because we are, as the children's song says,
Free to be
You and me.
Precisely. (198–99)

Many feminist laughers can help the individual feminist to understand her particular identity better. Why do feminists laugh? Precisely because we are not free to be you and me. Rather, we are like the rabbit who has just escaped from the startled cat's mouth. Wounded, we seek refuge so that we can heal.

Laughter is a liberating force which can facilitate this healing. Northrop Frye informs us that comedy's "significance . . . is ultimately social significance, the establishing of a desirable society" (169–70). The feminist laughter evoked by Brantenberg's text can be channeled to build a more desirable feminist society. We are laughing together. We realize that the cliché about the impossibility of a feminist sense of humor is a lie. If we do not use the power of our shared laughter to change the world, the joke is on us.

Notes

1. Throughout the text, I will use "readers" to indicate "the novel's female readers."
2. The phrase "laughing in a liberating defiance" appears on page 248 of *Egalia's Daughters*.

Works Cited

Cixous, Hélène, and Catherine Clément. *The Newly Born Woman*. Minneapolis: University of Minnesota Press, 1986.

Freud, Sigmund. "Humour" (1928). In *Character and Culture*. New York: Collier Books, 1963. 263–69.

———. "Jokes and Their Relation to the Unconscious" (1905). In *Standard Edition of the Complete Psychological Works of Sigmund Freud*, trans. James Strachey et al., ed. James Strachey. 24 vols. London: Hogarth Press, 1953–74. Vol. 8.

Frye, Northrop. *Anatomy of Criticism: Four Essays*. Princeton: Princeton University Press, 1957.

Holland, Norman N. *Laughing: A Psychology of Humor.* Ithaca: Cornell University Press, 1982.

Kristeva, Julia. "Word, Dialogue and Novel." In *The Kristeva Reader.* Ed. Toril Moi. New York: Columbia University Press, 1986. 34–61.

The Match in the Crocus:

Representations of Lesbian Sexuality

JUDITH ROOF

The "illumination, a match burning in a crocus, an inner meaning almost expressed" (47) is the succession of terms by which the omniscient narrator in Virginia Woolf's *Mrs. Dalloway* describes Clarissa Dalloway's perception of her feelings for women. This series of definitions which ranges from a sudden light to the masked and burning phallus to a failure of expression approximates the evolution and complexity of strategies for representing lesbian sexuality in Western literature. The "illumination," like a flash of enlightenment, intuition, and arousal, conflates vision and perception, introducing a visual component which carries over into the image of the burning match. This visibility is paramount; it introduces and enables the last two definitions but is also reversed and extinguished by them, ending in the invisibility of the "almost expressed." These three attempts to describe Clarissa's feelings are neither equivalents nor successive refinements; imparting incongruous perceptions, they are radically different in their representability and in their relation to the visible. Homeless in a terrain of normative heterosexism, representations of lesbian sexuality migrate from visible, expressible flashes of a masquerade of heterosexuality to an observation of the failure of language in the face of the unaccountable combination of lesbianism. In any case, what is evident in the narrator's description is the difficulty of locating the place of lesbian sexuality in relation to the requisite visibility of a phallocentric system of representation.

Because of its superficial absence of penis, lesbian sexuality provokes a crisis in a system of representation which is reliant upon a symmetry, if not sameness, between the sexes, a crisis that reveals the mechanisms which suppress difference in the depiction of heterosexuality. The fantasy of complementariness inherent in the sexual symmetry Luce Irigaray unveils in the work of Freud is an illusion premised upon the presence/lack dichotomy of a phallic economy (Rose 33; Irigaray, "Blind Spot"). In a system in which "everything turns on the penis-phallus and the potential disturbance of its identity by the woman" (Heath 107), the lesbian threatens to reveal the frightening aspect of a doubled lack—a negative Medusa—rather than the comforting and regularly represented template of the mimetic negative/positive, presence/absence of the biological penis and its warm envelope. The impetus, as Irigaray observes, may be "the desire for the same, for the self-identical, the self (as) same, and again of the similar, the alter ego, and, to put it in a nutshell, the desire for the auto . . . the homo . . . the male, dominates the representational economy" (26).

Visibility, as a crucial feature of this "sameness" economy, appears in the representation of lesbian sexuality as an additional, necessary term. While sexuality itself is a product of the impact of culture, language, and representations of sexuality on the unconscious (Rose 43), the representations themselves adhere to a preference for the visible something, not only in a desire for same, but in a desire for that which narcissistic fantasies can fix, in other words, the phallus. The phallus, as Lacan states, "is something the symbolic use of which is possible because it can be seen, because it is erect" (quoted in Mykyta 50). Though the phallus and the visible are not identical since the phallus is reduced to a *seeming* value (Rose 42), in the representation of sexuality itself the phallus/penis defines poles of difference in terms of visibility. In the portrayal of sexuality, this symbolic phallus becomes reassociated with its anatomical model, which is then symbolically projected onto the woman who either becomes the phallus—object of desire—or displays a phallus—fetish. Though still larger than life, this phallus operates as a privileged signifier of desire in an imaginary zone of sexuality comprised of the satisfying and visible potential unity of matching parts. Less visible female genitals, victims of this homogenetic impulse, are represented as the invisible opposite of the phallus, as a phallic attribute, or as a place for the phallus to fit in an inverted version of itself. Completing this symmetry, Lacan says: "of what cannot be seen, of what is hidden, there is no possible symbolic use" (quoted in Mykyta 50). Rendering sexuality in terms of the visible engages the scopophilic pleasure of the male gaze. Seeable, sexuality becomes a source of voyeuristic pleasure particularly associated with Freud's observation of the connection between the eye and the phallus ("The Uncanny" 231).

The lesbian, instead of imparting the implicit phallic desire of the "normal" woman, conveys a different, concerted absence which frustrates both symmetry and visibility. The possible presence of a double lack in the representation of a sexuality between two women—a double ϕ, since "the female body in itself indicates ϕ" (Mitchell 33), would tend toward the invisible, toward an affirmation of lack which could not reflect back a reassuring symmetry of presence/absence, thus creating a disturbance of phallic identity. If woman "is represented as . . . what cannot be represented" (Mykyta 51), lesbians cannot be represented at all except in terms of this unrepresentability. Their representation would seem to cancel out the phallus rather than permit the phallocentric erection of the woman as phallus, a construction which would cover over the castrated state of the woman with the desired phallic projection or fetish (Mykyta 54). Under these circumstances the unmitigated lack necessitated by the representation of lesbian sexuality might evoke a castration anxiety that would remain uncured. However, the gyroscope of symmetry by which sexuality is perceived and represented would tend to correct the tipping imbalance of this lesbian double lack. By trimming this excessive absence to a comfortable balance, the rules of a phallocentric representation (and there may be no truly "other" kind) would hide, translate, and re-create lesbian sexuality in terms of a superimposition of visibility. A component of visibility, the illusion of complementariness cures the discomfort of lack caused by the overabundant absence of woman and regulates the perception and understanding of a behavior particularly troublesome to any notion of phallic preeminence.

Because sexuality is inseparable from representation, since it in a sense arises from it (Rose 43), the capacity of a phallocentric representation limits rather than renders lesbian sexuality and delineates it in ways predictably reassuring to a phallic identity. The correctives to be found in phallocentric representations of lesbian sexuality consist of versions of Woolf's three diagnoses. The solution suggested by both "the illumination" and "the match burning in a crocus" is a superimposition of the visible phallus upon the unseeable woman, a masquerade ("sexuality belongs for Lacan in the realm of masquerade" [Rose 43]) which hides lack and translates a lesbian scenario back into heterosexuality.

In this context Woolf's "match" image is a double masquerade, a layering. The phallic match, concealed once by the flame of its burning, its "illumination," is cloaked again by the petals of the crocus, a flower with a phallic shape. The superimposed "phallic" tends to layer, bandage, and bind the woman in narcissistic clothes, covering this gap in the system, displaced as her "sickness," with masculine behavior or phallic imagery which re-creates the malady it hides. In this masquerade, phallic solution, the lesbian is always a sore because she's never a woman and not a man. The representation of lesbian sexuality as an assumption of the phallus functions as a telling symptom of the phallocentric operation of representation which must skew and force potential asymmetries into a malleable mold by which its anxieties are controlled and even turned to its aggrandizement.

The other solution suggested by Woolf's "inner meaning almost expressed" is consonant with the paradoxical representation of both women and lesbian sexuality as unrepresentable. Enfolded as a present yet hidden and invisible third term in the phallic register of representation, this solution, modeled after female genitalia seen other than as lack, re-creates the conditions of its own representational impossibility: it can be there, but it cannot be seen in its own terms since such terms do not exist.

The phallic matrix into which lesbian sexuality is fit is nowhere more symptomatically evident than in Sigmund Freud's inadvertent relegation of it to extratextual footnotes in "Fragment of an Analysis of a Case of Hysteria" (the "Dora" case) and his attempts to explain it in "The Psychogenesis of a Case of Homosexuality in a Woman." The prominence of a male model and perception is evident in Freud's terminology and in his quasi-solutions; in his terms the lesbian is the woman all too attached to penile powers rather than one who spurns them. Not evolving peacefully within the measured rhythms of the family romance, the potential lesbian in Freud's terms suffers from an excessive love of the father which shifts to an excessive resentment when she is rejected by him. The father's rejection of her causes her to turn away "from men altogether" ("Psychogenesis" 144). In both cases the adolescent female's intense love for her father, her attendant penis envy, and some special predisposition, "factors . . . probably of an internal nature" ("Psychogenesis" 155), create her homosexuality. To Freud, lesbian sexuality is like water dammed in its desired flow toward the father and rerouted, displaced, onto an object of the same sex, an inherent masquerade with its foundations deeply routed in heterosexual desire (*Dora* 78).

In his analyses of lesbian sexuality, Freud fails to find its etiology. In the Dora case, his tracing of the series of repressed and displaced desires which manifested themselves as hysterical symptoms ends in footnotes where he recognizes the importance of Dora's homosexual desire for Frau K (*Dora* 126). Mainly hidden outside of the text, yet rooted within as the foundation for all of the other displacements (*Dora* 142), Dora's lesbian propensities are a hidden internal factor masked by the text and by a curiously blind phallocentric analysis caused in part by Freud's failure to recognize his own countertransference—his own desire situated in Dora (Gearhart 115). In "Psychogenesis" Freud leaves the ultimate determinant of lesbian sexuality to an undefined "internal" factor which he assumes to be present but cannot define. He describes the girl's overt behavior as an assumption of masculine traits, a masquerade of having the penis which covers up that unknown internal disposition. In both cases the representations by which Freud makes known his analyses reflect his inability to come to the point, to make lesbian sexuality visible unless it is conveyed by the attribution of a false penis, a kind of fetishization of the lesbian who has tried to wrest from male control the phallus projected upon her. Even if the lesbian's phallus is a fake, its presence continues the reassuring reciprocity of heterosexuality. Freud passes over the site of lack and comes to rest on the masquerade of hysteria or of masculinity, anticipating Woolf's solutions. The masquerade of masculine behavior is very much the match in the crocus; the "internal factor" which he cannot penetrate is "an inner meaning almost expressed."

The Phallic Solution

In literature, as in Freud's analyses, the superimposition of the phallus is a means employed primarily by male writers to represent lesbian sexuality. The use of masquerade concurrently with denominations of sickness and/ or perversity suggests the ambivalent position of the lesbian in literature. While allegations of illness hint at a castration anxiety displaced from the male provoked by lesbian sexuality, the inclusion of lesbians in literature is a corrective to the threat of castration evoked by women in general. The representation of lesbians, often both a voyeuristic occasion and a warning to women who are out of their proper place, is for the benefit of the phallocracy, reinforcing phallic presence and attesting to its privilege. In this way, a great threat is turned to a great reassurance; a crisis becomes a cure.

The superimposition of a phallic masquerade sexualizes the suspect, manless world of the convent in Denis Diderot's *The Nun*. In the convent, the phallicization of sexual women is necessary to depict sexuality: the binary oppositions of heterosexuality include not only male/female but the virgin/whore, saint/sinner, internal/external dichotomies which overload the meaning of sexuality in a community of religious women and make lesbian sexuality a perversion of both nature and sanctity. In *The Nun* Sister Sainte-Suzanne, forced to enter the convent and take vows because of her illegitimacy, is mistreated in this unnatural "homosex" community of women. Going from a sadistic Mother Superior to a lascivious one, Sister Suzanne is depicted as the innocent victim and truly feminine woman in the midst of costumed, masculinized, diseased Mother

Superiors whose power and control exist in direct relation to their assumption of male prerogative. Stripped of her habit, the symbol of her
chastity, Sister Suzanne's corporal punishment is a spectacle for the sadistic
Mother Superior and her followers in scenes staged not for the nuns but
for the male reader's eye. Suzanne is punished because she is reluctant to
take her vow, to join fully in the community of women, to comply with
the will of the fathers who wish to take her lack of paternity out of
circulation. Already outside of the patriarchal order because of her ille-
gitimate birth, Suzanne continues to resist patriarchal disposal of her.
Sadism is the extreme means necessary to take care of this excessive problem, yet its execution is shifted into the hands of the Mother Superior.

Saved from further punishment by the intervention of priests, Suzanne
is courted by the next Mother Superior, whose sexual advances are described by Sister Suzanne as a "malady" she claims not to understand.
The disguised nature of the sexual behavior—no one will tell Sister Suzanne
what is going on—as well as the nuns' disguise of celibacy create a climactic
phallic masquerade in Sister Suzanne's first clearly sexual encounter with
the Mother Superior:

> By now she [the Mother Superior] had raised her collar and put one
> of my hands on her bosom. She fell silent, and so did I. She seemed
> to be experiencing the most exquisite pleasure. She invited me to kiss
> her forehead, cheeks, eyes and mouth, and I obeyed. I don't think
> there was any harm in that, but her pleasure increased, and as I was
> only too glad to add to her happiness in my innocent way, I kissed
> her again on forehead, cheeks, eyes and lips. The hand she had rested
> on my knee wandered all over my clothing from my feet to my girdle,
> pressing here and there, and she gasped as she urged me in a strange,
> low voice to redouble my caresses, which I did. Eventually, a moment
> came, whether of pleasure or of pain I cannot say, when she went
> as pale as death, closed her eyes, and her whole body tautened vi-
> olently, her lips were first pressed together and moistened with a sort
> of foam, then they parted and she seemed to expire with a deep sigh.
> (122–23)

The sexual scene in this passage is a spectacle of fragments; growing within
this collection of eroticized parts, the Mother Superior becomes a phallus,
stiffening and emitting a froth. Her assumption of masculine privilege, a
problem worse than Sister Saint-Suzanne's illegitimacy, must also be punished by men (the priests). In a kind of phallic justice, the Mother Superior
is demoted from her position of power. The lesson is clear: sexuality

among women is phallic and connected to privilege and power. Women who usurp the phallus must be punished by castration.

In Théophile Gautier's *Mademoiselle de Maupin,* as in *The Nun,* ignorance cloaks and enables episodes of lesbian sexuality; however, in *Mademoiselle de Maupin* ignorance of gender rather than of the sexual nature of the activity creates the ironic quasi-consummation of the triangle of D'Albert, Rosette, and Théodore. Mademoiselle de Maupin, cross-dressed as the man Théodore, captures the interest of the two bored lovers, D'Albert and Rosette, who both believe themselves to be in love with her. On one level a novel about the authenticity of love, particularly from D'Albert's point of view, *Mademoiselle de Maupin* plays on assumptions about the appearance of gender as a way of testing love. Rosette, who is first smitten by Théodore, cannot understand "his" failure to return more than friendship. Théodore, in language which echoes Freud's theory of lesbian development, reflects: "as I have not loved any man, the excess of my affection has in a way overflowed into my friendship with young girls and young women" (276). However, to Théodore, the disguise of masculinity lacks the real thing—she wishes for the wherewithal to properly return the ardor displayed by Rosette and even begins to enjoy Rosette's caresses, almost, as she states, forgetting the "similarity of sex" (283). Sexuality between the two women can be depicted as reciprocal only as long as Théodore, believing the masquerade to be true, forgets that she isn't a man. The phallus is there by default as long as she doesn't remember that she doesn't have a penis. However, her fear that the disguise will be penetrated prevents her from going too far with Rosette. The maleness of the masquerade triggers and allows sexuality; the fact of the disguise arrests it.

The constant masking and unmasking of Théodore's masculine guise represents lesbian sexuality as tangled in a paradox of presence and lack. When Mademoiselle de Maupin is Théodore she may enjoy a sexual encounter with Rosette—a lesbian sexuality—which disappears when she remembers she's a woman: she can only be a lesbian when she's a man. Théodore's confessions of forgetfulness function as reminders to the readers that what is being depicted is sexuality between two women, though the phallus is there quite literally in the constant evocation of its absence. Seen as a necessary signifier of both sexual enjoyment and the narration of it, the phallus acts as a kind of symbolic master-of-ceremonies, introducing the erotic encounter for voyeuristic perusal by the reader, then cutting it off when the phallus is announced as absent. On the edge of impropriety, Théodore is finally not the arbiter of her own sexual enjoyment. Not only does she constantly invoke the missing phallus but the encounters are interrupted each time by Rosette's brother, the real censor of their activity, who defends heterosexual virtue and its representation.

While the name of the absent phallus evokes its presence, depicting lesbian sexuality threatens to disrupt the phallic identity of the male. The insidious threat of the representation of lesbian sexuality in nineteenth- and twentieth-century literature is its disruption of the symmetry of displaced identity, of the male projection of self-unity onto the woman. Predictably, the representation of lesbian sexuality by male authors during this period is more concerned with the male anxiety created by its disturbing presence. Rather than representing sexual encounters between women, male authors represent lesbian sexuality as a male reaction to it. Like Freud's analysis of the Dora case, the aggressively hostile responses of male protagonists refer offstage, to the footnotes, to that identity-jolting scene represented metonymically by its visual and auditory symptom evinced by the male who is located center stage. Covered by the phallic crocus, the phallus whose desired unity veils all, the lesbian becomes that hidden, covered gap which is depleted at all cost, displaced, and represented as a male symptom in a disruption of narcissistic desire.

Such displacement is evident in Henri de Marsay, the protagonist of Balzac's *The Girl with the Golden Eyes.* Young Henri falls in love with his ideal woman, the golden-eyed Paquita in whom he sees, as Shoshana Felman points out, "his own phallus" (25). Paquita, whom Henri erroneously believes to be the mistress of an aged marquis, is a well protected, almost inaccessible possession. With the help of Paquita and her friends, Henri himself finally "possesses" Paquita, only to have that possession defect at the height of passion. When Paquita calls out a female name instead of Henri's, she evokes another scene of passion which divests Henri of both ownership and identity. Fragmented, Henri reacts violently and determines to murder Paquita only to find that his rival has beaten him to it. The rival, the marquise instead of the marquis, turns out to be Henri's half sister, daughter of the same prolific, philandering father. Faced, as Felman observes, with himself, Henri is split, forced to see the feminine which has destroyed the illusion of his unity and mastery.

In *Lady Chatterley's Lover,* the gamekeeper Mellors is also enraged at a lesbian sexuality which he sees as women's unauthorized assumption of phallic privilege. The lesbians' independence and disregard for phallic power and efficacy threaten his own shaky identity grounded entirely in the powers of the penis. His description of the lesbian reveals his own fear:

—Then there's the hard sort, that are the devil to bring off at all, and bring themselves off, like my wife. They want to be the active party.—

Then there's the sort that's just dead inside: but dead: and they know it. Then there's the sort that puts you out before you really "come," and go on writhing their loins till they bring themselves off against your thighs. But they're mostly the Lesbian sort. It's astonishing how Lesbian women really are, consciously or unconsciously. Seems to me they're nearly all Lesbian.

"And do you mind?" asked Connie.

"I could kill them. When I'm with a woman who's really Lesbian, I fairly howl in my soul, wanting to kill her." (262–63)

In masquerading as the male, in usurping what Mellors believes to be his sexual role, the lesbian reduplicates Mellors, displaces him, and multiplies the phallus, fragmenting his oneness and his primacy. Instead of finding a reassurance of his identity in the otherness of the female, Mellors must fight with her; and his hatred, like that of Henri de Marsay, is a symptom of the instability of phallic currency. Later in the novel Mellors says, "When I get with a Lesbian woman, whether she knows she's one or not, I see red. No, no! But I wanted to have nothing to do with women any more. I wanted to keep to myself: keep my privacy and my decency" (263). Mellors's desire for retreat, couched in terms of morality and "decency," is the transparent expression of another desire; instead of keeping his "privacy," he wants to keep his primacy. Evidence of the lesbian scene decenters the phallus and the man. Like Henry de Marsay, Mellors is faced with his own impotence and uncertainty about his own ability to possess.

That this decentering makes the man "different" is also the subject of Ernest Hemingway's short story "Sea Change." A slice-of-life at the moment of the dissolution of a relationship, "The Sea Change" depicts a heterosexual couple's final discussion of the woman's choice of a female lover. Like Mellors and Henri, the man threatens to kill his ex-girlfriend's new paramour. Calling the women's activities "vice" and "perversion," the man wants both to keep and reject the woman. Trying to save something of the relationship, she asks the man not to categorize lesbian behavior in such a way. Echoing the image of inexpressibility, she says, "You don't have to put any name to it" (400) and asks him to accept difference and multiplicity. However, the woman's choice visibly changes the man: "He was not the same-looking man as he had been before he told her to go" (401). The phallus and phallic relationships have been decentered; his identity as the projection of that phallus is also shattered. Even his mirror image has changed: "I said I was a different man, James," he says to the bartender. "Looking into the mirror he saw that this was quite true" (401).

Directly representative of the phenomenon of a displaced identity resulting from lesbian activity at another scene, "The Sea Change" documents lesbian sexuality as a response, as a break in identity and loss in the male, the return image of what man projects into his mirror. Instead of the projection of phallic wholeness onto the woman, the lack of phallus evident in lesbian sexuality reflects back division and uncertainty.

The "Other" Solution

Since the phallus is *the* term of the representation of sexuality, in service of symmetry it appears superimposed as the visible term which both permits and denies sexuality between women. Whether the phallus plays a role in lesbian sexuality as it occurs between women is less important in a consideration of the representation of sexuality than the role of the phallus as signifier and the dangers created by its potential absence. In a circumstance which excludes the penis, the phallus is predictably manifest and necessary to retain the symmetry which soothes the anxiety of castration. The representation of the lesbian is an open site for the play of sexual difference in its relationship to the perception and representation of sexuality. Conscious of a kind of phallic preeminence, women writers are faced with the difficulty of representing perceptions unaccounted for in a phallic economy in terms of that economy. Though invisibility is not synonymous with unrepresentability, the problem of representing other in terms outside of the homogeneous phallus/absence of phallus opposition remains. The reinsertion of the phallus in representation recolonizes lesbian sexuality even if the phallus is the only term available for such a sexuality in a phallocentric system. Strategies for representing something other than a mere absence of phallus tend to return to the phallic; Woolf's "match burning in a crocus" is a prime example of this pattern. However, Woolf's match image combined with the following "inner meaning almost expressed" functions as a possible means for subverting the phallic. A crocus is finally not a phallus—its petals peel back to reveal something other, a flame rather than a stick, radiance rather than solid unity, a transformation which renders the phallus itself invisible as either presence or absence.

The problem of representing lesbian sexuality in terms other than phallic is addressed by Luce Irigaray in her essay "This Sex Which Is Not One." Irigaray suggests an alternative representation which rests on the autoerotic arrangement of "two lips which embrace continually." Substituting female genitalia for those of the male, Irigaray attempts to elevate the female genital model to a somewhat mystic, symbolic level, to create an alternative, but evasive, seeability that can become symbolic, not because female genitals are erect but because they encompass more than themselves, because they are excess. To Irigaray the female "is neither one nor two," and though her "sexual organs are simply absent from the scene: they are masked and her 'slit' is sewn up," her sexuality is ubiquitous. We can't see sexuality because it is no single point but is everywhere at once. Irigaray's solution embodies the unrepresentability of the female, overtly placing her outside the realm of the visible and replacing the visible with a general class of the sensory, multiple signifiers of the body that translate via sensory imagery into language. Irigaray's view suggests two strategies for the representation of lesbian sexuality: sexuality as hidden or masked, but revealed in the removal of the layers of that mask, and female sexuality as everywhere at once—as two and one and radiant.

The second half of Woolf's series of metaphors anticipates Irigaray and perhaps more deftly treats the problem of representing lesbian sexuality. In its context in the novel, the match burning in the crocus, while appearing to superimpose phallic layers, also works to strip those layers, to reveal the inexpressibility of an inner radiance which is ubiquitous and invisible, but which is initially couched in phallic terms. Subverting and metamorphizing phallic layers, the visual metaphor of the burning match situates lesbian sexuality in the flame, a visible but amorphous entity, hardly solid, which obscures and consumes its agent, the phallic match. The illusion of the phallus seated in the match and the crocus dissolves into paradoxically visible representations of the combustion of a match whose physical transformation gives us fleeting glimpses of the energy such transformations release.

In *Mrs. Dalloway* Woolf represents lesbian sexuality mimetically as both the hidden, potent other figured by female genitalia and as generalized radiance. The two strategies are conflated in an early passage in *Mrs. Dalloway:*

> yet she could not resist sometimes yielding to the charm of a woman, not a girl, of a woman confessing, as to her they often did, some scrape, some folly. And whether it was pity, or their beauty, or that she was older, or some accident—like a faint scent, or a violin next door (so strange is the power of sounds at certain moments), she did undoubtedly then feel what men felt. Only for a moment; but it was enough. It was a sudden revelation, a tinge like blush which one tried to check and then, as it spread, one yielded to its expansion, and rushed to the farthest verge and there quivered and felt the world

come closer, swollen with some astonishing significance, some pres-
sure of rapture, which split its thin skin and gushed and poured with
an extraordinary alleviation over the cracks and sores! Then for that
moment, she had seen an illumination; a match burning in a crocus;
an inner meaning almost expressed. (p. 47)

Though the image of swelling recalls phallic dimensions, the portrayal has
shifted to one of a generalized rather than a focused response. Vaguely
suggestive of female genitalia, the image is not a likeness of absence or
lack, nor is its plenitude given phallic proportions. Evasive, the unnameable
"it" can be captured only by the approximations of simile and metaphor
and by its effect, the feeling of it.

The glimmer of radiance which appears in the narrator's first attempt
to approximate Clarissa's feeling becomes clearer in the narration of the
episode of Clarissa and Sally Seton: "Then came the most exquisite moment of her whole life passing a stone urn with flowers in it. Sally stopped;
picked a flower; kissed her on the lips. The whole world might have turned
upside down! The others disappeared; there she was alone with Sally. And
she felt that she had been given a present, wrapped up, and told just to
keep it, not to look at it—a diamond, something infinitely precious, wrapped
up, which, as they walked (up and down, up and down), she uncovered,
the radiance burnt through, the revelation, the religious feeling!" (p. 52).
The image of the wrapped diamond is like that of the match burning in
the crocus; while the images appear to strip away obscuring layers in an
effort to see the source of the pleasure felt, the end of the stripping is a
feeling, a revelation which evades sight but provides insight. The visibility
of the images are transitory attempts to capture the feelings which slip
by; however, the visible equivalents, the marks of the attempt, remain as
parts of the rendition. No longer masquerade, lesbian sexuality is transparent, invisible, and ubiquitous, figured as light rather than shape, as
extrahuman though natural, rather than an effect of costume or behavior.
The flowers are metaphors of hidden sexuality; hiding within radiating
petals is something indescribable, something other than the phallus. Sally's
plucking of the flower and her kissing of Clarissa are recognitions of this
sexuality; plucking the flower is a symbolic acquisition and transmission
of sexuality which enables Sally to kiss Clarissa. The flowers are transformed into the hidden diamond, the burning match, the radiance of the
specific hidden point which overwhelms its wrapping and becomes generalized, infuses everywhere at once, offering new significance to Woolf's
initial "illumination."

In these two passages, Clarissa's sexual feelings are contrasted to those
of men, suggesting that lesbian sexuality results from the assumption of

a male role, or again, masquerade. This comparison is superseded by the latter half of the passage in which Clarissa's sexual feeling infuses the entire world, which like an omnipresent female organ swells and splits to gush forth in a kind of all-encompassing *jouissance*. That the image of the match in the crocus is followed by the observation that it was "an inner meaning almost expressed" demonstrates the problem of expression. Clarissa can find only approximations and analogies "what men felt," "a match in a crocus." Like female genitalia and at the same time like Freud's footnote in the case of Dora, the match in the crocus hides the source of light, reveals its radiance, and simultaneously expresses its own inexpressibility. The written passage is a visible trace of a sexuality never defined but somehow communicated in its absence as an effect of the efforts to verablize. The passages are the shell from which it has been released, but in which it is still blocked off, screened, contained, encapsulated by petals, footnotes, wrapping, and words.

Similar imagery of flowers and flames occurs in Violette Leduc's *La Bâtarde* in the descriptions of Violette and Isabelle's nightly trysts in the boarding school. Not only do the meetings take place at night in secret, they occur inside the curtained bedchambers largely in silence. The portrayals again reflect the process of stripping away the boundaries and containers while remaining inside of them: "Her tongue began to press against my teeth, impatient to make me warm all over. I shut myself up, I barricaded myself inside my mouth. She waited: that was how she taught me to open into a flower. She was the hidden muse inside my body. Her tongue, her little flame, softened my muscles, my flesh" (73). While the tongue might be suspiciously phallic, only waiting and not using the tongue enabled the sexuality. In this passage, Isabelle herself is the "hidden muse," Freud's "internal factor" both inside and outside of Violette (herself a barricaded flower). Isabelle's tongue, which first unsuccessfully pressed, becomes a flame, an other-than-phallus which softens her, which makes her "warm all over," radiant. Violette's opening recaptures the image of the flower, hidden, now opened by flame, radiating warmth. Later, Violette describes Isabelle's kiss: "A tiny bluish egg fell from her lips onto the spot she had left as her mouth returned to it" (75). Like Clarissa's diamond, revealed yet wrapped, the hidden spot is hidden again by lips.

Again expressed mainly in terms of nature, lesbian sexuality is a series of approximations and transformations contained within, yet exceeding, their verbal base. As Violette declares: "A flower opened in every pore of my skin" (75). "Isabelle's fingers opened, closed again like the bud of a daisy and brought my breasts through pink mists out of their limbo. I was awakening to spring with a babble of lilacs under my skin" (76). Like

Clarissa's swelling world, Violette's sexuality is a life-force, a portion larger than herself yet within herself: "The springtime that had been crying its impatience with the voice of tiny birds under my skin was now curving and swelling into flower" (84). This organic base, the human body, is the opposite of masquerade; a stripping, a peeling back, a revelation, it seeks the source of light, the diamond, the pearl, the match, not to lay it open to the gaze but to assure that it is hidden so that its radiance might spread, since only in secret may it burn and avoid a phallicizing visualization. This process of peeling back is described by Leduc: "the hand stripped the velvet off my arm, halted near the vein in the crook of the elbow, fornicated there amongst the traceries, moved downward to the wrist, right to the tips of the nails, sheathed my arm once more in a long suede glove" (84). The match burns, consumes itself because of its sequestration; the removal of layers is simultaneously their replacement. Without its wrapping, without the petals of the crocus, the miracle match burns out, fades, or is transformed into the priapus. Revealed, it is no longer neither one nor two as Irigaray describes it, but monolithic, at once phallus and absence of phallus.

The representation of lesbian sexuality as being simultaneously stripped and hidden is characteristic of a textual process which functions as both an accumulation of words and revelation of images. Monique Wittig's *Lesbian Body* embodies this figuration; a compendium of organic components accompanies the joinder of the women, appearing to reveal their sexuality, but simultaneously burying them in words and fragments. The book itself, the leaves closed on words, is Irigaray's neither one nor two. Like the lovers sinking together in the sand, the pages, the mounded words and language, obscure the illumination as they describe it:

The engulfment continues steadily, the touch of the sand is soft against m/y legs. You begin to sigh. When I am sucked down to m/y thighs I start to cry out, in a few moments I shall be unable to touch you, m/y hands on your shoulders your neck will be unable to touch you, m/y hands on your shoulders your neck will be unable to reach your vulva, anguish grips m/e, the tiniest grain of sand between your belly and m/ine can separate us once for all. But your fierce joyful eyes shining hold m/e against you, you press m/y back with your large hands, I begin to throb in m/y eyelids, I throb in m/y brain, I throb in m/y thorax, I throb in m/y belly, I throb in m/y clitoris while you speak faster and faster clasping m/e I clasping you clasping each other with marvelous strength, the sand is round our waists, at a given moment your skin splits from throat to pubis, m/ine in turn from below upwards, I spill m/yself into you, . . . (48)

This image of each woman was vulva meeting, joining, but hidden by the sand, is another frustration of both the spectacular and the phallic. Again reprising the image of splitting skin, Wittig's passage portrays an excess founded in but escaping the body. The narrator centers the eyes themselves as the agents of illumination, conflating the eye and the phallus and escaping that equation as the eyes extend, become like arms holding the women together.

The representation of lesbian sexuality as either masquerade or the hidden but radiant other-than-phallus illustrates the distinction in the way lesbian sexuality is perceived by the phallic system and by systems which attempt to comprehend lesbian sexuality in other-than-phallic terms. The masquerade is above all spectacle; as masquerade, lesbian sexuality is presented in the guise of and for the eyes of the male reader. Its reassuring function in part explains its appearance; what monstrous self-confirmation might be gained by the conquest of the usurping woman. The simultaneous revelation and hiding of lesbian sexuality in texts where lesbianism is not an exemplar insists that one not see, not gaze upon the source of the *jouissance,* or perhaps that it cannot be made to be seen though language seeks its equivalents. The lesbian as spectacle is never the lesbian, not because she should be hidden or is by nature secretive (though perhaps is by necessity), but because the act of expression renders her a function of the symmetry by which all complementary parts fit into the whole, reenfolded in the system of binary oppositions by which we represent and understand sexual difference and sexuality.

This is not to say that the hidden other-than-phallus is anything other than a description of a mode of representing lesbian sexuality that can coexist, in fact is produced and predicted by a phallic system. The implied secrecy and bondage of the match in the crocus are facts of peaceful coexistence rather than sources of eroticism. The representation of lesbian sexuality cannot help but at least partly function as the phallic, but in reproducing the symbolic facsimile of female genitalia, in separating lesbian sexuality from the text by means of a veil or barrier, and by simultaneously permeating the text with radiance which flows from the hidden source of *jouissance,* the match in the crocus succeeds in breaking peacefully away from the phallic, while resting radiantly in the rupture it creates.

The representation of lesbian sexuality, the gap or break in a system which turns on itself, forces the revelation of the mechanism of representation which works to repeat itself as same. The clash of differing perceptions, male and lesbian, in the arena of representation, reveals the masquerade, the reappropriation and reabsorption of both woman and sexuality into a homogeneous community which invests identity in the other and capitalizes on the reassurance offered by the reflection of unity it sees there. The mechanism is nowhere more clearly revealed; like the unconscious, the lesbian is the gap, the slip by which the unconscious may be deduced. The representation of the lesbian is characteristic of the representation of the female and of sexuality in general. Disruptions themselves, women employ guerrilla tactics to disrupt the system again. The women authors who attempt to represent lesbian sexuality are not representing pure perception and idyllic self-expression, but are instead reacting to representation itself, to an awareness of the suppressive and homogenizing mechanisms by which they are phallicized. Their efforts to express something outside must still be filtered through the ponderous machinery of symmetry. Thus, though the working of phallocentric representation is revealed, the position of representations by women is also exposed as derivative, dependent upon the system they attempt to subvert. Other, like the unconscious, like woman, is finally only expressed in the breaks and paradoxes resulting from play on the phallus and yet perhaps that is the only way it can escape.

Works Cited

Balzac, Honoré de. *The Girl with the Golden Eyes.* In *Droll Stories.* Trans. J. Rudd. London: Subscription, 1899, 257–341.

Diderot, Denis. *The Nun.* Trans. Leonard Tancock. London: Folio Society, 1972.

Felman, Shoshana. "Rereading Femininity." *Yale French Studies* 62 (1981): 19–44.

Freud, Sigmund. *Dora: An Analysis of a Case of Hysteria.* Ed. Philip Rieff. New York: Crowell-Collier, 1965.

———. "The Uncanny." *Standard Edition* XVII, 217–56.

———. "The Psychogenesis of a Case of Homosexuality in a Woman." Trans. Barbara Low and R. Gabler. *Sexuality and the Psychology of Love.* Ed. Philip Rieff. New York: Collier, 1963, 133–59.

Gautier, Théophile. *Mademoiselle de Maupin.* Trans. Joanna Richardson. Harmondsworth, Middlesex: Penguin, 1981.

Gearhart, Suzanne. "The Scene of Psychoanalysis: The Unanswered Questions of Dora." *In Dora's Case: Freud—Hysteria—Feminism.* Ed. Charles Bernheimer and Claire Kahane. New York: Columbia Univ. Press, 1985, 105–27.

Heath, Stephen. *The Sexual Fix.* New York: Schocken Books, 1982.

Hemingway, Ernest. "The Sea Change." *The Short Stories.* New York: Scribners, 1966, 397–401.

Irigaray, Luce. "The Blind Spot of an Old Dream of Symmetry." In *Speculum of the Other Woman.* Trans. Gillian C. Gill. Ithaca: Cornell Univ. Press, 1985, 13–129.

————. "This Sex Which Is Not One." In *This Sex Which Is Not One*. Trans. Catherine Porter. Ithaca: Cornell Univ. Press, 1985, 23–33.

Lawrence, D. H. *Lady Chatterley's Lover*. 1928; rpt. New York: Grove Press, 1959.

Leduc, Violette. *La Bâtarde*. Trans. Derek Coltman. New York: Farrar, Straus and Giroux, 1976.

Mitchell, Juliet. "Introduction I." In *Feminine Sexuality: Jacques Lacan and the Ecole Freudienne*. By Jacques Lacan. Trans. Jacqueline Rose. Ed. Juliet Mitchell and Jacqueline Rose. New York: Norton, 1985, 1–26.

Mykyta, Larysa. "Lacan, Literature and the Look: Woman in the Eye of Psychoanalysis." *Sub/Stance* 19 (1983): 49–57.

Rose, Jacqueline. "Introduction II." In *Feminine Sexuality: Jacques Lacan and the Ecole Freudienne*. By Jacques Lacan. Trans. Jacqueline Rose. Ed. Juliet Mitchell and Jacqueline Rose. New York: Norton, 1985, 27–57.

Wittig, Monique. *The Lesbian Body*. Trans. David LeVay. New York: Avon, 1975.

Woolf, Virginia. *Mrs. Dalloway*. New York: Harcourt, Brace, Jovanovich, 1925.

Scribe, Inscription, Inscribed:
Sexuality in the Poetry of
Robert Bly and Adrienne Rich

VICTORIA FRENKEL HARRIS

Robert Bly has said that he danced his first college dance with Adrienne Rich. What dance they learned in college, Bly at Harvard, Rich at Radcliffe, probably had more to do with a waltz of language, formed and informed by their ivy fathers, leading phallocrats of modernism. Since the symbolic, however, does not arrive ready-made at high school graduation, perhaps a glance at some retrospections each shares about their formative years would edify.

In Lacanian terms, the symbolic register refers to language, the signifying phallus, the father's law. Clearly, success is determined in our culture by how well one accedes to the symbolic. Lacan suggests that a female determines in the symbolic that she is constituted by a lack, lacking the phallic signifier, symbolized by the father. Some cognitive development, thus, for a girl in patriarchy, includes an awareness of insignificance in the signifying system.

In *Nice Jewish Girls: A Lesbian Anthology*, Rich's essay about her beginnings is significantly entitled "Split at the Root." The forms and sources of her perceived division are manifold, but the article notably begins with a telling forbidden by her father: "I have to break his silence, his taboos; in order to claim him I have in a sense to expose him" (Beck 67). Rich describes her father as an intellectual, "a young teacher and researcher in the department of pathology at the Johns Hopkins Medical School." What he fathered in Rich was alterity, creating a divided woman who learned to speak brilliantly her father's language, which, in fact, she rehearsed for his approval. Recalling a time she practiced her lines for a school production of *The Merchant of Venice,* she writes: "As always, I read my part aloud for my father the night before, and he tells me to convey, with my voice, more scorn and contempt with the word 'Jew' " (Beck 70). Rich, divorced from a part of her identity, a Jew only in the abstract (her father not denying but ignoring his heritage), prepared her language for her father. "He prowled and pounced over my school papers, insisting I use 'grown-up' sources; he criticized my poems for faulty technique and gave me books on rhyme and metre and form. His investment in my intellect and talent was egotistical, tyrannical, opinionated and terribly wearing. . . . He taught me . . . to feel that I *was* a person of the book, even though a woman; to take ideas seriously" (Beck 76). It appears that Arnold Rich embodies the symbolic for which the daughter must strive, her earliest engagement with language coming prescribed, prohibitive—validity coterminous with masculinist values.

In *Of Woman Born* Rich in fact proclaims that she "identified more with men than with women; the men [she] knew seemed less held back by self-doubt and ambivalence, more choices seemed open to them" (193). With agility, Rich gained access to the dominant symbolic, not questioning the logos or her invisibility within its terms. Indeed, she is split at the roots, not only of her Jewishness but of her intellectual and emotional life. Of her tutor-father, Rich says she "never in [her] whole life [knew] what he was really feeling. . . . It was a difficult force-field for a favored daughter to disengage from" (*Of Woman Born* 77). But Rich broke some of the grounding, ironically, by marrying a Jew, one whose family very much announced its Jewishness. In a kind of variation of Plath's "Daddy," Rich marries a Jew, instigating the father's retreat, her family not attending the wedding, not to be seen by the daughter for several years, while she learns an ethnicity denied her by her Jewish father. Rich realizes that what the father "demanded [was] absolute loyalty, absolute submission to his will. In my separation from him, in my realization at what a price that once-intoxicating approval had been bought, I was learning in concrete ways a great deal about patriarchy, in particular how the 'special' woman, the favored daughter, is controlled and rewarded" (79).[1]

Bly's retrospective, entitled "Being a Lutheran Boy-God in Minnesota," just as candidly reveals his awareness of being special. "I grew up as a typical 'boy-god.' As I understand the idea, boys toward whom the mother directs a good deal of energy, either warm or cold, tend to become boy-gods. . . . I was the favorite son. This embodied itself in a sense that I was 'special' " (209). That specialness conditioned him to recoil from emotional life, commitments, and, Bly says, from "the body—that is, woman—[as] evil" (210). In Bly's signifying system the recoil from emotion always complies with a patriarchal recoil from that which is female. He learned to be cheerful, cherished, physical, competitive (as evidenced by a piece of his young boy's journal in which he enters scores he earns at school that are always higher than his brother's scores). While the essay tells of the mother's goodness and lists several characteristics Bly finds praiseworthy, she exists as Woolf's "angel in the house," "a good mother, without envy or malice, affectionate, excitable, living with simplicity and energy—one of the servants of life" (209), and, I suspect, one of the servants of men. His memoir concludes, however, by paying homage to his father, whose righteousness made a real difference in the life of a hired man mistreated by local law and significantly impressed his son. This portrait signifies the deepest respect for the father as logos.

Bly and Rich, then, share a sense of privilege, but its terms augur difference. Both enter the ivy halls filled with a sense of self. Rich feels privileged to engage in a linguistic world embodied by the father, the mother apparently only in the background. Bly's sense of esteem derives from a nurturing mother, one who fits comfortably within sexist stereotypes. My point, then, to which I will return in detail, is that the specificity in each of these poets' stories derives from traits in the father.

With feminism's radical questioning of that which is inscribed into our patriarchal culture, ways to avoid the perpetuation of patriarchal inscriptions need to be found. Indeed, even the word *feminist* contains an undeniable reference to patriarchy. I prefer *feminist* to *feminine,* however, because of its unmistakable ideological basis. *Feminine* is at times treated as predisposition, as if language were neutral rather than a signifying system inscribing ideology. While one response to subjugation is muteness, as Tillie Olsen's *Silences* eloquently describes, a felt urgency for redefinition rescues us from the recourse to silence within a dominant masculine discourse. Indeed, the situation Virginia Woolf describes in "A Room Of One's Own" persists today, as some feminists feel the need to justify writing for an academic audience that is founded undeniably upon patriarchy. As Luce Irigaray explains, "Female sexuality has always been conceptualized on the basis of masculine parameters. . . . About woman and her pleasure, this view of sexual relation has nothing to say. Her lot is that of 'lack,' 'atrophy' (of the sexual organ), . . . the penis being the only sexual organ of recognized value. Thus she attempts by every means available to appropriate that organ for herself: through her somewhat servile love of the father-husband capable of giving her one, . . . through access to the cultural values still reserved by right to males alone and therefore always masculine, and so on" (*This Sex* 23–24). Such distortion of the woman—physically, psychologically, and emotionally—through omission and by the dominant class is precisely what Adrienne Rich addresses in "Diving into the Wreck," where she concludes that she must "explore the wreck": "a book of myths / in which / our names do not appear." A woman telling her story in its particularity seldom appears in the texts we routinely read.

Likewise, Robert Bly distinguishes himself from routinization, particularly in such early volumes as *Silence in the Snowy Fields* and *The Light around the Body*. A male addressing the imperialism of male power, Bly turned to such sources as Erich Neumann's *The Great Mother* and the psychoanalytic theories of Carl Jung, where he found material he thought could undermine an authority that practiced war and imperialism, exemplified by our slaughter of civilizations at least as good as our own. Bly found in the Jungian quadrant a four-part structure of the psyche in which intellect and emotions, the senses and intuition, are portrayed as binary opposites. The traits valorized within our culture, senses and intellect, are attributed to the male. Only by balancing these characteristics with the devalued "feminine" traits can a person achieve individuation. For Bly, this organization paralleled in many ways much that he found in the Taoism and Buddhism he was reading at the time, in particular the yin/yang sigmoid as emblematic of harmonious psychic development. Bly departed from the modernist poetry he inherited by breaking its rational enclosure, debunking some of modernism's most cherished concepts, such as the notion of the aesthetic artifact as a self-contained unity. By valorizing intuition, a female element according to the Jungian quadrant, Bly attempted to invest his poems with the elemental female and in some way to disrupt academic discourse as well. The sincerity of his desire to recuperate the fallen status of woman is unquestionable. His cultural reading about matriarchies is tireless, as is his effort to organize his annual Conference on the Great Mother, where about a hundred people convene at a designated place to study, read, write, and gain deeper understanding of the archetypal woman.

The neglect of the unconscious, then, is of particular concern to Robert Bly. His association of the unconscious with the feminine is not without analogies among feminist thinkers and poets. Rich herself has said: "Well, I still believe that the energy of poetry comes from the unconscious and always will. So a poetry which could affirm woman or the female, which could affirm a bisexual vision, or which could affirm a whole other way of being male and female as part of its consciousness, as part of its tradition, such a poetry of the future would still, it seems to me, be churning up new unconscious material, which we would be fascinated and influenced by. If it's not doing that, then it's not poetry as far as I'm concerned"

(Gelpi 113). Similarly, in her essay "The Powers of Difference," Josette Feral argues that the female unconscious "is 'the noise' in the system, the defect. It is a surplus which patriarchal society has always wanted to get rid of by denying it any specificity" (Eisenstein 90).

Specificity, however, is a complex territory, which may be variously approached. While some French feminists accede to a specifically feminine mode of inscribing (usually in terms of the body, as in Irigaray or Hélène Cixous), the separatist paradigm seems to break down at the very moment of language, the symbolic register in Lacanian terminology. Though language is, obviously, not seriously considered more easily acquired by either males or females, its content just as obviously reveals sexism in all its manifestations. The perspectives couched in linguistic formulas that are acquired and self-perpetuating must be exposed by feminists, and through a variety of ways. In distinct ways, Cixous, Clément, Irigaray, and Kristeva urge an understanding of the politics of language. Writing the body apparently inculcates female rhythms, or female sexuality, or female propensities within the text, and most beautifully in many cases such as Irigaray's *This Sex Which Is Not One* or Monique Wittig's *Les Guérilleres*. Or, as Jane Gallop and Carolyn Burke point out in "Psychoanalysis and Feminism in France," the script may portray what Julia Kristeva calls the primordial semiotic, whose text "L'Héréthique de l'amour" ("Love's Heretical Ethics") intends in its analytical interruptions, "by a lyrical intertext composed of outbursts, cries, and flashes of an opening on the page," to link "the female subject and the semiotic, based upon the knowledge of a resemblance to the mother's body," a language of mothers and daughters that Kristeva terms "subliminal, subversive preverbal" (Eisenstein 113). These writings, like the writings of both Bly and Rich, intend to inscribe women into history, to restore to texts that which was heretofore the not-subject.

While it would be difficult to be unresponsive to these texts, I question any possibility of presenting Kristeva's semiotic, preverbal content. The status of the text remains linguistic—in other words, symbolic. *Ecriture féminine* more likely discards a rationality that, opting for linearity, appears to inscribe the male. In its refusal to be linear, Kristeva's move parallels Bly's intention to subvert rationalism, inadvertently implicating both in the patriarchy, for reasons to which I shall attend in depth presently. A more authentically revolutionary potential lies not in replacement but in inclusion, such as legitimizing intuition in public writing. While not preverbal, such writing depicts something about intuition, defying the latent sexism in all our discourse, which ascribes intuition to females but in an economy that devalues it. This might be seen metaphorically as writing the body—but whether that body is male or female would depend upon whether or not one is dealing with matriarchies or patriarchies, and whether or not the dominant gender values or devalues intuition. Linear development is gender neutral. Could not a linearity be posited that is also intended to inscribe the female? Might not gestation, for example, be envisioned as a progression toward a climactic birth? Perhaps the more pluralistic, surfaced body is the acculturated female body, the body of a woman who learns early not to go in one direction, whose lesser status makes her available for the varied burdens. Variousness, I feel, just might be a euphemism for the necessity to contend, conform, and conceal. Is not the female mind capable of developing a single thought? Irigaray makes an irresistible comment in *This Sex Which Is Not One* about the ideological imperative of sexuality, the coercion of the subjugated class extended even to physiology. The central sexuality of the male may compel female approximation, but perhaps one may alleviate this oppression by exposing it, countering its linguistic repression. As Christiane Makward suggests in "To Be or Not to Be . . . a Feminist Speaker," a possibility for females writing goes beyond the binary of either silence or a "phallocratic sham," since "characterizations of feminine creativity have emerged: ideas about nondetermination, open structures, nonlinearity, movement" (Eisenstein 100–101). I would like, however, to reiterate my sense that those characteristics are neither biologically male nor female. Because they are marginalized, they are attributed to the female. By reserving for men the traits recognized as more formidable, patriarchy maintains oppressive domination.

Denying the Freudian biological imperative, I maintain rather that the ideological basis of subordination is pertinent here to counter essentialist positions. How do certain elements in society become empowered while other things seem powerless? How do certain attributes become cathected, while others are ignored? When do these elements and traits comply with what is considered masculine or feminine? The masculinization of culture with its concomitant feminization of everything that does not empower is pervasive. Of course, in patriarchy that extends to the woman, whose specificity is depicted in terms of her difference from the dominant male.

A society that profits from its leaders will valorize those empowering traits. What is unprofitable, of course, is what the empowered attribute to the subjugated class, here woman. She, in turn, so privatizes difference from her assigned qualities that cultural becomes confused with natural. (Many American critics confront this confusion in addressing a variety of topics, such as the establishment of the literary canon. Annette Kolodny's observations are especially relevant. Adrienne Rich's assessment of motherhood as defined in patriarchy is chilling.) So, I choose to analyze the inscriptions of these two contemporary poets, who have in many ways enlarged our discourse. Both have written poetry that addresses the enormous consequences for a people whose culture is routinely sexist. While disagreeing with essentialist positions, I recognize how easily historically maintained characteristics may be mistaken for innate tendencies. I prefer to position my argument on how Bly and Rich describe patriarchy, how they are partially inscribed by patriarchy, how their positions in patriarchy affect their poetry, and how their poetry remains distinguishable because of the gender differences that are learned from earliest childhood.

Bly's first book of poetry, *Silence in the Snowy Fields* (1962), explodes the modernist authority thoroughly rooted in America at the time of its publication. So different was this poetry from conventional modes that early critics, such as William Heyen, confessed their inability even to read it at first. A new critical vocabulary commensurate to the response Bly's poetry demanded had to be fashioned. Slowly, words like "subjectivist" or "leaping poetry" or "deep imagery" or "neo-Romantic" emerged to deal with his poetry of spare surfaces, more like a Chinese painting than an American poem.

Bly's indefatigable effort to discover the causes of sexism in society and to analyze alternatives precipitates his internationalism. He has developed a vocabulary, outside the institutionalized language, that is simultaneously local and cross-cultural. Images of place give Bly his physical specificity, while his vast reading, traveling, and understanding of different cultures and languages take him out of the mainstream of American poetry. Departing from an academicism he found sexist, rationalistic, and tired, Bly privileges intuition and emotion, the two elements of the Jungian quadrant purported to be the female elements, as opposed to senses and intellect, those supposedly masculine traits. His effort shifts the criteria of significance, introducing what he finds to be the neglected female and unconscious. Bly turns away from a society privileging the mind, finding that his Lutheran background obliterated the body: "purity lay in the eternal, in what was 'up.' I already knew that" ("Boy-God" 210). By the time he finished high school he felt a "terrible longing to come down!" (212). What Bly comes to be known for as a poet has roots in these early days, when he focused on questions of right and wrong and on just what it is that society sanctions.

Rich's early books, *A Change of World* (1951) and *The Diamond Cutters* (1955), deal with change but, unlike Bly's volume, easily excel in modernist conventions. Lauded by exemplary modernists such as W. H. Auden, Rich's early poems attained to the dominant discourse, a discourse into which she had been so well indoctrinated that she only later realized she was "split at the root," merely mimicking what she perceived as powerful in patriarchy. One might assess Rich's modernism as a clear avoidance of anything specifically female, very different from the poetry for which she is now renowned. She was a brilliant student of what in her society was deemed important, clever in the use of language that would not consign her to the traditional separation of most females from public life. The price of excellence, however, is abstraction—not only the abstraction that Bly bemoans in academic poetry but one much more damaging to Rich who, in collusion with the defeminization of culture, abstracted herself. She failed to reckon with her own identity, living an alterity that co-opted her own sexuality. Her energy toward success involved denying some sense of selfhood, a denial severe enough to cause various manifestations of hysteria in other women, which Rich poignantly discusses in *Of Woman Born*.

Of course, Rich eventually does break radically from her inheritance. But, in order to show the actual tears in modernist closure, I should like first to examine Bly's formal break from modernism in order to reveal the vestiges of modernism which remain in his poetry. Then I wish to discuss Rich's more radical break from modernism, including her own early achievements.

As indicated earlier, Bly's *Silence* was difficult for the literary establishment to read, primarily because of its leaps of intuition. Appropriating "feminine" emotion and intuition, Bly attempts his departure from the objectivism informing modernism, which approaches a poem as separable from both its author and recipient. However, a biological determinant undergirds Jung's scheme, distinguishing a species fragmented in its majority/minority features. Thus Bly, attempting to inculcate those features he finds maligned in our patriarchal culture, excels in a poetry privileging intuition, all the while inscribing the male. The intuitive, that is, is appropriated thematically, but the gesture encompassing the entire volume is not the heterogeneity welcomed by Cixous, say, or Irigaray. The speaker remains originary, the source of vision. In other words, despite the intuition stated, the vision refracts upon a cathected "I" as repository, an "I" that is singular and defined and has arrived at a higher station than those other men in patriarchy who are not awakening the female elements in their psyches. Xavière Gauthier speaks to this point, stating that "certain qualities are attributed to women, and are seen as particularly 'feminine' (intuition, sensitivity, etc.); but it is men who render these judgments" (Marks 162). Bly's system lacks the radical deconstruction of gender identity as conceived in patriarchy which is necessary if the society that produced it is to be changed.

Bly must be seen as courageous for designating significance and value to that which patriarchy subordinates. Despite his sincere attempt to rectify a situation of male domination, however, perceptual modes that may be identified with male privilege persist in his early work. One poem ostensibly sensitive to the division existing between the male and the female in the *Silence* volume is "A Man Writes to a Part of Himself," which depicts a public and a private self, the private one, visualized as female and of an earlier historical moment, apparently deprived by the traveling public self. The poem concludes with the speaker asking "And how did this separation come about?" This poem clearly asserts Jung's economy of a psyche with both masculine and feminine sides, but the speaker is a man, dominant and empowered to nourish or starve the feminine element. The scaffolding, then, is patriarchal, and the author remains at its authoritative center, a figure unexposed in this poem. If, as Adrienne Rich or Audre Lorde, Hélène Cixous or Julia Kristeva suggest, a connection exists between language and transformation, the disconnection in *Silence* with any *real* woman might lead to what Domna Stanton terms in "Language and Revolution" a "regressive mystification of the 'feminine' and may yield nothing more than a new 'lingo' " (Eisenstein 80–81).

Since the speaker is never exposed in this book but stands instead as a creator behind the poems, he parallels the father, not seen but the originator, the logos behind the product. This stance retains the position of male power, omitting any vulnerabilities, and even the distinctions, of the person. Indeed, the poems renowned as most intuitive are those concluding the middle "Awakening" section of this volume, where a higher plateau is reached by a speaker earnestly trying to depart from Western patriarchal values. In "Watering the Horse," the speaker envisions thoughts of "giving up all ambition!" These thoughts, termed "strange," lead him to an epiphanic conclusion: "Suddenly I see with such clear eyes / The white flake of snow / That has just fallen in the horse's mane!" Despite his rejoicing at having attained a more-than-sensory perception, the position achieved is one that the speaker had already endorsed. He remains, that is, filled with ambition, the ambition to attain a completed psyche by relinquishing masculine ambition and gaining feminine intuition. We know very little of the speaker's subjectivity in any of these poems. What is revealed is a thorough thematics imported from Jung, ideationally behind the poetry, ideationally endorsed by the poet. While different visually from modernism, this poetry retains the constructive features of an originary voice, forging a poetry behind the scenes and inscribing patriarchal binary thought.

Thus Bly's well-intentioned brand of feminism conceals remnants of the patriarchy he denounces (an inevitable by-product, perhaps, of the Jungian schemata).[2] Nonetheless, Bly's achievement in *Silence* is momentous. He attempts to undermine a code that clearly perpetuates male domination. In a sexist society, those attributes most highly prized are assigned to the male. By eschewing one of these, the academic language echoing patriarchal institutions, Bly reverses the conventional terms of privilege, endorsing those attributes that are designated as female, celebrating a consciousness privileged with intuition.

But even if intuition is attributed to the female in Jungian terms that Bly endorses, no woman emerges from this book. While females are mentioned in nine of the poems, not one is actualized. At this stage of his career, that is, Bly the poet is interested in the archetypal feminine rather than an actual female. Even "At the Funeral of Great Aunt Mary," which describes an occasion certain to evoke particulars about a specific woman, focuses almost entirely on the speaker's unorthodox beliefs. Women in *Silence* exist only in an extremely symbolic language of horizontals, waters, and darkness,[3] those essences of the female myth that, as Barthes has demonstrated, often mask ideological positions. Feminizing the natural world in no way restructures phallocentrism. Rich has said that "Whatever is unnamed, undepicted in images, whatever is omitted from biography, censored in collections of letters, whatever is misnamed as something else ... buried in the memory by the collapse of meaning under an inadequate or lying language—this will become, not merely unspoken, but *unspeakable*" (*Lies* 199). Emblematic woman, adjunct and metaphoric, is coercive glorification, here augmenting male consciousness while ignoring specificity; the female here, dehumanized and depersonalized other, is significant as and exists only in service to the narrator's beatitude; the female omitted is she who has been historically oppressed.

When, in *Loving a Woman in Two Worlds* (1985), an actual woman appears, she often retains the position typifying patriarchal portraits of women; specifically, the object for the subject, man. This reductiveness is especially evident in the volume's sex poems. In these often explicitly erotic poems, which deal with an actual rather than a symbolic female, Bly seems unable to avoid the dichotomous tendencies of the Jungian schemata that served him so well during the earlier stages of his psychic and poetic development. Rather than effacing itself before the other, the ego in these poems tends to declare its independence, reducing the woman to the level of an object, thereby reversing Bly's persistent movement away from his culture's proclivity to think in terms of subject-object dichotomies.

Though *Loving a Woman* is Bly's most overtly sexual volume, no female sexuality is articulated. Woman is portrayed, rather, in the way Irigaray says that women must resist: as "a more or less obliging prop for the enactment of man's fantasies. . . . That she may find pleasure there in that role, by proxy, is possible. . . . But such pleasure is above all a masochistic prostitution of her body to a desire that is not her own,, and it leaves her in a familiar state of dependency upon man" (*This Sex* 25). Moreover, in our culture (and probably, I maintain, for cultural reasons), male sexuality is scopophilic, which Irigaray contends is "particularly foreign to female eroticism" (25–26). In the erotic poems of this volume, the woman is of specular interest to the speaker and is never particularized as a subject.

Thus, while *Loving a Woman* delivers an actualized female much of the time, the woman presented in the erotic poems is trivialized, existing as an object of the masculine gaze, a female of essences whose gap accommodates a fetishized penis. Lacan has said that woman does not exist if she does not speak herself. The woman in *Loving* never speaks herself. Although at times radiantly glowing, she is only an object. As subjects, the sexes are stylistically distinct from each other; the style of woman, according to Irigaray, "tends to put the torch to fetish-words, . . . well-constructed forms" (*This Sex* 12). Bly's woman, on the other hand, remains the other, whose sexual plurality is reduced to the gap, a house for his fetishized penis.

Consider, for example, "Come with Me," where the speaker takes the woman "away from the buildings and the high places." The poem concludes, "I love to go with you, and enter the valley where no one is king." In an ostensive movement away from patriarchy, abandoning the realm of kings, Bly perpetuates that realm by metonymically reducing the female to a valley, a house for his own form. This centralization repeats patriarchy physically, symbolically, and formally. Similarly, in "At Midocean," Bly begins his poem with the female other, object of his gaze and touch and never subject in her own specificity.

> All day I loved you in a fever, holding on to the tail of the horse.
> I overflowed whenever I reach out to touch you.
> My hand moved over your body, covered with its dress,
> burning, rough, an animal's foot or hand moving over leaves.
> The rainstorm retires, clouds open, sunlight
> sliding over ocean water a thousand miles from land.

The subject of the poem is the male—dominant, central, and source. The love in this poem is clearly masculine, fixing the woman in a gaze and moving in a linguistic/sexual gesture of ejaculation from the source "I" to the "overflow." The poem concludes in a universalism typified in patriarchy, but the access to natural landscape is gained through an association of the phallic overflow with the rainstorm and ocean water, a seminal concentration symbolically expanding, the female identity inscribed only by its patriarchal affiliation.

This gesture of subversion and dispersion repeats itself throughout *Loving a Woman*. Indeed, in "Ferns" the female body, fragmented and other, is in service to the male speaker's intuitive expansion: "It was among ferns I learned about eternity. / Below your belly there is a curly place. / Through you I learned." The speaker learns through the female other, who never materializes as a subject, differentiated only by an accommodating sexuality. Similarly, in "The Hummingbird Valley" the valley of the title becomes a point of entrance for the male, who inquires, "Isn't it a house? It has been a house to me." The kinesthesia in this volume is ejaculatory, from the nuclear, essential subject outward. Perhaps this constitutes the male version of inscribing the body. More likely, however, it reiterates patriarchy where the man, who is central, develops his ego. While there is more than a metaphoric woman present in this work, the love of the male exists phallocentrically. The plunging, entering imagery of Bly's first volume, where the subject enters a symbolically female milieu, is retained on these erotic poems, but now a real woman has replaced the archetypal feminine and remains an object serving the masculine subject.

In "The Laugh of the Medusa," Cixous laments that "man has been handed that grotesque and scarcely enviable destiny (just imagine) of being reduced to a single idol with clay balls" (884). Bly's most explicit poems of this kind of sexuality are "Conversation," "The Horse of Desire," and "The Whole Moisty Night," the latter portraying the act of coitus as a "Viking ship," which "sails into the full harbor." Again, the woman in the poem is identified in relationship to the subject: "The body meets its wife far out at sea." In a show of rather adolescent pride, the speaker, unable to break through the chrysalis of ego, metonymically reduces his sexuality to the penis, whose "lamp remains lit the whole moisty night." The light in the darkness, the lamp in the unexplored dark continent, here is evidence of a grid imposed upon human experience that feminists, that equalists, must strive to throw off. Those strategies of repression that valorize the masculine in binary logic reduce a woman to man's other, a negative of his positive, rather than identifying her difference. Indeed, in this poem the woman bears an inequitable designation: the "wife" of the "man."

Irigaray maintains that the system of thought that identifies sexual difference only in Freudian terms of the male phallus must be "radically convulsed" in order to realize a woman as a speaking subject (*Speculum* 176). To Kristeva, the identification of this speaking subject as a unity is a phallic conception which she seeks to undermine (*La Revolution* 160 and "Subject in Signifying Practice"). For the woman's body, in Irigaray's formulation, stays "in flux, without ever coagulating. Solidifying ... Multiple ... This body without fixed borders. This mobility without end" (*This Sex* 214). Because it represses her multiplicity, the dominant phallocentric discourse is a subversion of the female. If, as Cixous further contends, "phallic culture has created language and has silenced the expression of the female body and the female libido" ("Laugh" 884), Bly continues to subvert the female in his phallocentric declaration of love, whose words do not inscribe the female body in language but appropriate it, and then only its accommodating fragment.

Bly reifies sexuality, fetishizes the penis (in "The Horse of Desire" and "Conversation"), and concomitantly maligns the female causing his erection, who remains absent from its celebration. Such lacunae, Dianne Crowder suggests, "are absences which signify the absence of a discourse—women in male discourse" (128) and signify an idealized order. Bly concludes "The Horse of Desire" by metonymically evoking an idealized phallic order, first by proclaiming his love, then by apparently locating that love in his penis and testicles:

> The bear between my legs
> has one eye only,
> which he offers
> to God to see with.
> The two beings below with no eyes at all love you
> with the slow persistent
> intensity of the blind.

In "Conversation," Bly similarly addresses the fact that there is a woman whom he has loved, but he again reduces her to an object of his gaze. Indeed, he says she "walked by and [was] gone. That was all." In several of the poems in this volume, the woman is lauded for several virtues—firmness, spirituality, lack of triviality (virtues which he might just as easily attribute to his mother)—but, as a sexual partner, she appears as no more than an object of masculine desire, the focus shifting to the speaker's subsequent erection: "My sex, or rosy man, / reached on its own and touched the book." This phallogocentric discourse complies with the centrist male's physical and verbal response.

So, while in *Loving a Woman* a more-than-metaphoric woman appears, her depiction as having virtue, spirit, and strength identifies the timeworn metawoman, sexually serving to release the containment of the male. Such a discourse addresses human sexuality by marginalizing female sexuality. It is both distorted and ideologically consistent with a patriarchy that inscribes a superior male whose biologic economy becomes metonymic of central organization, logocentrism, monotheism, and rationalism. The image content of Bly's work is part of his ideational content or meaning. Bly remains the special one who receives from the female, retaining dominance to the extent that the woman is relegated to the status of other, fragmented and colonized, a relationship identifiable in his "Boy-God" memoir in the dispersal of the mother into universal attributes of goodness. The locus of authority, of the logos, is the father. The female in Bly's erotic poems remains diffuse, metaphoric, unarticulated, and inarticulate, while the subject with material status is clearly the male at the center of these logocentric verses.

When in *Loving a Woman* Bly turns away from the poems that deal explicitly with physical sex, particularly in poems such as "Secrets" or the beautiful " 'Out of the Rolling Ocean, the Crowd . . . ,' " he achieves that sense of unity typical of his best poetry, that sense of unity the erotic poems frequently affirm but seldom incorporate. But the dialogical situation of the erotic poems tends to resist Bly's lyrical, which is to say his monological, impulse. At that moment, his habitual gesture of incorporation appears self-enhancing, an effective extension of and metaphor for his developing psyche but not well suited to express meaningful interactions with other human beings. An actual woman has replaced the archetypal feminine of the earlier poems, and she seems threatened by Bly's essentializing imagination.

It is not my intention to label Bly a sexist. To the contrary, I have argued elsewhere that he has done more than any male poet in this century to interrogate and expose the patriarchal domination of Western culture (see my article " 'Walking Where the Plows Have Been Turning' "). That the lineaments of this domination may be traced in the erotic poems of *Loving a Woman* does not suggest weakness or hypocrisy on Bly's part; it reveals, rather, the pernicious authority of a discredited but still powerful patriarchy the sediments of which are virtually impossible to filter out. Indeed, the spirit of my critique is informed by Bly's similar critiques of a male-dominated society, critiques from which I and our culture have profited.

What surprises Gauthier is that "men and women seem to speak approximately the same language; in other words, women find 'their' place within the linear, grammatical, linguistic system that orders the symbolic, the superego, the law. It is a system based entirely upon one fundamental signifier: the phallus. And we can marvel . . . at the fact that women are alienated enough to be able to speak 'the language of Man' " (Marks 162). But the phallic signifier, according to Lacan, is not the penis but language (Ragland-Sullivan 267–308). Just as a female as male auxiliary is an affront to any woman, so would be any divestment of capacity based upon biology. The intuition granted a female in Jung's quadrant is appreciated within a patriarchy that valorizes the other end of the dyad, the purported male counterpart, intelligence. Lacan's symbolic register, attributed to both sexes, seems more apt. One could not, for instance, deprive Rich of her intellectual capacity. She identifies herself brilliantly as an articulate lesbian poet, reserving for herself a position as a subject with desire, without reducing another to a mere object of that desire. I believe Rich is attempting to recuperate the imaginary within which the child may still sense her ability and redress the deficiency, the split, that occurred when she entered the symbolic through the powerful father, wielder of the logos. But her language retains rigorous control in both her feminist prose and poetry.

In "Diving into the Wreck," Rich descends to salvage that which remains from patriarchal destruction. She descends practically crippled with "grave," "awkward," and "absurd" layers of protection. But the text is as yet uninscribed: the speaker is "here alone," and later confides, "I have to learn alone." She comes to "explore the wreck," but recognizes the danger lurking in symbolic inscriptions: "The words are purposes. / The words are maps. / I came to see the damage that was done." The words seem somehow complicit with the damage. Wrenching herself from the symbolic into the imaginary, the speaker says: "the thing I came for: the wreck and not the story of the wreck / the thing itself and not the myth." The symbolic has inscribed historically a patriarchy; this depiction of the identity located in the imaginary remains within the linguistic symbolic. It does, however, introduce patrilineage as such, and a great task for a feminist is to find "a book of myths / in which / our names do not appear." In other words, locating texts from which one is typically excluded redresses the damage by declaring that gaps exist, that the ellipses are to be texted.

The poetry subsequent to *Diving into the Wreck* (1973) is as exacting in its articulations and as convincing as any of Rich's writing. While Freud constructs sexual difference around the phallic economy, I believe Nancy Chodorow more appropriately locates female identity relationally. The female, unlike the boy, does not find her difference from the first identity, the mother figure, and therefore is not initially invested with the binary response: me/not me. Her identification is more informed by process, and becomes problematic only when she realizes that she identifies "with a negatively valued gender category, and an ambivalently experienced maternal figure, . . . accessible, but devalued. Conflicts here arise from questions of relative power and social and cultural value" (Eisenstein 14). This obviously pertains to Rich's memory of her identification with the male order and her performing for and subscribing to the father's approval. This also explains, to some extent, Bly's earlier encoding, which thematically addresses injustice but retains its inherited position of centrality. While language acquisition must be seen as relational and culturally coded, Rich maintains an ability to change, her sense of urgency perhaps greater than Bly's.

Catherine Clément warns about the struggle in such transformations:

> assuming the real subjective position that corresponds to this [revolutionary] discourse is another matter. One would have to cut through all the heavy layers of ideology that have borne down since the beginnings of the family and private property: that can be done only in the imagination. And that is precisely what feminist action is all about: to change the imaginary in order then to be able to act on the real, to change the very forms of language which by its structure and history has been subject to a law that is partriarchal, therefore masculine. Reflection on feminist action, therefore, calls into question and into play the transformational powers of language, its capacity to motivate change in both ideology and economy. (Marks 130–31)

A genuine female subject emerges in Rich's prose and poetry from the time of *Diving into the Wreck*. In the sequence of love poems at the heart of *The Dream of a Common Language*, for example, Rich offers a materialized female subject whose love is faceted and whose sonnets become supple enough to engender a love poetry without an objectified other, an object of the gaze, a resource for the speaking subject. The relaxation of boundaries applies to inner-outer, subject-object, and poetic form as well. Here is a language of mutuality rather than subordination, but typically depicting the struggle Clément addresses. In sonnet 19 Rich says, "If I could let you know— / two women together is a work / nothing in civilization has made simple."

This struggle comes in part from what Rich calls "revision," a philosophical imperative if we are to overcome obliterating devastations inherent in patriarchy. In Rich's feminist enunciations, for instance, she explicitly rejects some Freudian commentary that articulates a female in terms of binaries. In *Of Woman Born*, for instance, she disagrees with Freud's essay "On Negation," which posits a fundamental split between inner and outer. She retorts: "As the inhabitant of a female body, . . . the boundaries of the ego seem to me much less crudely definable than the words 'inner' and 'outer' suggest. I do not perceive myself as a walled city into which certain emissaries are received and from which others are excluded" (*Of Woman Born* 63). Rich denies a fundamental split in a female in terms of inner and outer as much as she denies the metaphorized woman of no material existence in the fabrications of a male subject who objectifies and fragments a female in terms of his desire. And yet her world is the symbolic, the world of the father and of her literary heritage. Rich claims that the "major influence in [her] life in many ways was poetry, was literature." She was "always looking to poetry and to literature to find out what was possible, what could be, how it was possible to feel, what kinds of things one could or could not do" (Bulkin 1, 64). These inscriptions, however, omit her experience, leaving Rich typically opting for change. It is "by now clear" to her "that a feminist renaissance is underway," although we do not "know precisely what forms will best accommodate the changes we want, or that the forms themselves will not change and develop." Rich opts for a *nascence*, "partaking of some inheritances . . . but working imaginatively far beyond them" (*Lies* 126, 131, 155).

And, indeed, her opening sonnet in the "Twenty-one Love Poems" claims that "No one has imagined us." "The 'Twenty-one Love Poems,' " Rich says, "in a sense delineate the end and the beginning of a certain part of my life" (Bulkin 2, 61). The change involves capturing the mirroring prior to the symbolic. Perhaps one might see even a hall of mirrors, each poem in the sequence apparently releasing its individual containment and refracting upon one another. Rich says she thinks of these poems as a single poem, "having a rhythm that kind of bound them together and a certain amount of reference back and forth" (Bulkin 2, 59). These poems, furthermore, do not build to a climax and then detumesce but intermingle with a back-and-forth motion. Themes may be the same, but the impulse is mutuality, mirroring. Again, for example, sonnet 3 exchanges a masculine constellating ego for parallel involvement, concluding: "somehow, each of us will help the other live, / and somewhere, each of us must help the other die." "(The Floating Poem, Unnumbered)" reinscribes a sonnet in the middle of a sequence. Titled only parenthetically, and unnumbered, it is written to portray fluidly its openly erotic content. Here is an eroticism of myriad gesture, porous and surfaced. The interiority here vastly belies Freud's assessment, becoming mutual sensual entrances for each to each, mirroring surfaces that are responsive in kind. The sonnet's conclusion—"whatever happens, this is"—recalls the intent of the speaker in "Diving into the Wreck."

The sensual moment in "Diving" occurs when the speaker seeks "the treasures that prevail" amongst the ruins, and "stroke[s] the beam of [her] lamp / slowly along the flank," signaling a change from her previous self-image as a "half-destroyed instrument / that once held to a course." The course has changed, and Rich is charged with a feminist mandate, depicting with incredible clarity a marked place and mode which distinguishes her from the unified, tumescence-detumescence, originary logocentric source. She has found a space for herself, acting on an earlier premise, articulated in "When We Dead Awaken: Writing as Re-Vision," that "the word 'love' is itself in need of revision" (Lies 47). In The Dream of a Common Language, Rich finds that poetry is also a word in need of revision, its "true nature" now seen as "the drive to connect" (7). So, with both love and poetry in transition Rich, mirroring, finds in "Origins and History of Consciousness" that "It was simple to meet you, simple to take your eyes / into mine, saying: these are eyes I have known / from the first . . . / It was even simple / to take each other's lives in our hands, as bodies." Acting as a subject with another subject, a play of signifiers, mutual and similar, Rich concludes her last sonnet by "staking out the circle" of her choice, living the life of her choice—in re-vision:

> I choose to be a figure in that light,
> half-blotted by darkness, something moving
> across that space, the color of stone
> greeting the moon, yet more than stone:
> a woman. I choose to walk here. And to draw this circle.

Rich's circle includes a love. But the rapport they share excludes any merely specular interest; one body is never fragmented for the delight of another. Rich's discourse asserts a comprehension different from binary logic. No longer "split at the roots," she shall never again dance with Robert Bly; they are not opposite, but they differ.

Christiane Makward suggests that the symbolic functions necessarily "on the basis of the repression of women's bodies. Language is said to function through male control of women's bodies at the cost of female silence and submission. The corollary of this conception of language is that the feminine is said to be, by definition, undefinable, unspeakable and silent . . . [though] women continue to write and speak and agitate" (Eisenstein 96–97). Rich does write the woman, subverting patriarchy in content and form, revitalizing the sonnet, while telling a woman's story. In form and content, Rich subversively reshapes, by inserting a marginal position into public discourse. This position is hers. On the other hand, Bly's recent collection, which also is explicitly sexual, cannot be described in terms of justice, since his portrayal of sexuality from a male vantage is typical.

How the subject articulates itself publicly is of great import, since those articulations allow both cognition and recognition. Now, Rich's story, inserted into the "book of myths," subverts masculinist discourse through the process of *inclusion*. Since sexism benefits no economy, a feminist project that would duplicate sexism, though reversing the positions of power, is less radical than an investment of public language with the specificity of its undervalued, thereby enlightening, perspectives, and indeed causing transformation. There is little consolation in a domination reversal, which perpetuates co-optation. Opportunistic gestures by anyone wishing to situate her- or himself within the power system are appalling. Both Bly and Rich, political and poetic activists, intend to reverse such co-optation through language. While Bly enlarges the perceptual frame, though from a position undeniably within patriarchy, Rich reshapes the marginal status of female specificity. Both have greatly altered the vocabulary of contemporary American poetry.

Notes

1. In *Your Native Land,* her most recent book to date, Rich makes peace with her father after his death. See, for example, poem 22 in "Sources."
2. For a variety of revisionist readings of Jung from feminist perspectives, see the essays in Lauter and Rupprecht. Such "revision is necessary," the editors explain in their introduction, "because of Jung's tendency, despite the remarkable range, complexity, and fluidity of his system, to think in terms of rigid oppositions. For example, he posited that Eros, or the principle of relatedness, was not only associated with females but was dominant in the female psyche; conversely, the analytical principle, or Logos, was dominant in males. Despite all our efforts toward individuation, he said, Eros would remain weaker in most males and Logos weaker in most females. Thus he set arbitrary limits on the development of both sexes and reinforced the stereotypes of man as thinker, woman as nurturer. By associating men with thought, the cultural category with the higher value in the twentieth century in most Western societies, he helped to perpetuate the inequality of women" (5–6).
3. In various essays, I have tried to analyze Bly's attempt to incorporate the archetypal feminine into his poetry and his psyche. See, for example, "Criticism and the Incorporative Consciousness," "Relationship and Change," and, especially, " 'Walking Where the Plows Have Been Turning.' "

Works Cited

Barthes, Roland. *Mythologies.* New York: Hill and Wang, 1972.

Beck, Evelyn T., ed. *Nice Jewish Girls: A Lesbian Anthology.* Trumansburg, N.Y.: The Crossing Press, 1982.

Bly, Robert. *Silence in the Snowy Fields.* Middletown, Conn.: Wesleyan Univ. Press, 1962.

———. *Loving a Woman in Two Worlds.* Garden City, N.Y.: Dial Press, 1985.

———. "Being a Lutheran Boy-God in Minnesota." *Growing Up in Minnesota: Ten Writers Remember Their Childhoods.* Ed. Chester G. Anderson. Minneapolis: Univ. of Minnesota Press, 1976.

Bulkin, Elly. "An Interview with Adrienne Rich." *Conditions* 1 (1977): 50–65, 2 (1977): 53–66.

Cixous, Hélène. "The Laugh of the Medusa." *Signs* 1.4 (1976): 875–93.

Crowder, Diane Griffin. "Amazons and Mothers? Monique Wittig, Hélène Cixous and Theories of Women's Writing." *Contemporary Literature* 24.2 (1983): 117–44.

Eisenstein, Hester, and Alice Jardine, eds. *The Future of Difference.* New Brunswick, N.J.: Rutgers Univ. Press, 1985.

Gelpi, Barbara Charlesworth, and Albert Gelpi, eds. *Adrienne Rich's Poetry.* New York: Norton, 1975.

Harris, Victoria Frenkel. "Criticism and the Incorporative Consciousness." *Centennial Review* 25.4 (1981): 417–35.

———. "Relationship and Change: Text and Context of James Wright's 'Blue Teal's Mother' and Robert Bly's 'With Pale Women in Maryland.' " *American Poetry* 3.1 (1985): 43–56.

———. " 'Walking Where the Plows Have Been Turning': Robert Bly and Female Consciousness." In *Robert Bly: When Sleepers Awake,* ed. Joyce Peseroff. Ann Arbor: Univ. of Michigan Press, 1984: 208–22.

Irigaray, Luce. *This Sex Which Is Not One.* Trans. Catherine Porter. Ithaca: Cornell Univ. Press, 1985.

———. *Speculum de l'autre femme.* Paris: Editions de Minuit, 1974.

Kristeva, Julia. "The Subject in Signifying Practice." *Semiotexte* 1.3 (1975): 19–26.

———. *La Revolution du langage poetique.* Paris: Editions du Seuil, 1974.

Lauter, Estella, and Carol Schreier Rupprect, eds. *Feminist Archetypal Theory: Interdisciplinary Re-Visions of Jungian Thought.* Knoxville: Univ. of Tennessee Press, 1985.

Marks, Elaine, and Isabelle de Courtivron, eds. *New French Feminisms: An Anthology.* Amherst: Univ. of Massachusetts Press, 1980.

Ragland-Sullivan, Ellie. *Jacques Lacan and the Philosophy of Psychoanalysis.* Urbana: Univ. of Illinois Press, 1986.

Rich, Adrienne. *Of Woman Born: Motherhood as Experience and Institution.* New York: Norton, 1976.

———. *On Lies, Secrets, and Silence: Selected Prose, 1966-1978.* New York: Norton, 1979.

————. *The Dream of a Common Language.* New York: Norton, 1978.

————. *Diving into the Wreck.* New York: Norton, 1973.

————. *Your Native Land, Your Life.* New York: Norton, 1986.

Theory and
Disruption

Imaginary Images:

"H. D.," Modernism, and

the Psychoanalysis of Seeing

ELIZABETH A. HIRSH

"The Image" which was once standard operating equipment in most critical vocabularies has lately fallen into disuse, and the impact of psychoanalytic theory is largely responsible for its decline. Two theoretical texts that have fueled our skepticism about such critical language are Lacan's utterances on the Imaginary and Irigaray's critique in *Speculum de l'autre femme* of the "oculocentrism" of Western theoretical discourse (including, of course, both Freud and Lacan). In great part, the force of these and other psychoanalytic articulations on *feminist* criticism in America has been to evict our native "images of women" criticism in favor of more or less frenchified inscriptions of "difference." In doing so, they link the sense of sight, the eye, to the constitution of the ego or "I," and indict both as instruments for the repression of (feminine) difference.

Lacan theorized the genesis of the ego as a series of alienating identifications inaugurated by the subject's assumption of his own specular image during the mirror stage. In part his theory develops Freud's suggestion in *The Ego and the Id* that "[t]he ego is first and foremost a bodily ego," which, Freud says, "may be considered a mental projection of the surface of the body," as well as Freud's consistent characterization of the ego as the first psychic organization and agent of psychic synthesis. For Lacan, it is "the total form of the body" which provides the nucleus of the ego, and this "total form" first emerges in the mirror stage. In his theory the specular image functions as a kind of prosthesis, a pseudototality that permits the subject, by a fantasmatic detour, to evade the lack congenital to his humanity. At the same time, in subject-ing him to the gaze that returns his look in the mirror, the mirror stage prefigures the moment when castration will propel the subject into the order of the Symbol (and vice versa). But despite this interesting turn of events, and especially in Lacan's early work, the image as such remains tainted with associations of narcissistic bad faith, insofar as it spells the "scotomization" of absence or lack. "Our experience shows that . . . the function of *méconnaissance* . . . characterizes the ego in all its structures," Lacan writes, invoking Anna Freud's *The Ego and the Mechanisms of Defence*.[1] The ego is in essence a defensive formation that shares in the paradoxical nature of the symptom as Freud defined it, a structure that at once masks and betrays—betrays by masking—the lack it is meant to re(ct)ify. Thus, as paradigm of the ego, the image is also a pseudopresence in the sense that it can escape its status as substitute only fantasmatically, that is, in "the function of *méconnaissance*." The disavowal embodied in the symptom recapitulates the *méconnaissance* of the mirror stage. The genetic relation that obtains between image, ego, and symptom in Lacanian theory is most readily apparent in the case of the fetishist, which Lacan uses to elucidate his distinction between the Imaginary and Symbolic orders: "The imaginary is decipherable only if it is rendered into symbols. Harry's [a fetishist's] behavior at this moment is not; rather, he is himself drawn in by the image. This imaginary captation (*captation of and by the image*) is the essential constituent of any imaginary 'reality' . . . experience in analysis proves that instead of giving reality to the symbol, the patient attempts to constitute *hic et nunc*, in the experience of the treatment, that imaginary point of reference which we call bringing the analyst into his game."[2]

Irigaray concurs in indicting the eye even as she diverges from Lacan in attributing the prestige of the (Symbolic) Phallus to, precisely, its *visibility*. Jane Gallop and others rightly stress that the visibility in question here is not, to begin with, empirical or perceptual, but rather metaphoric and ideal; what is at stake is a certain sense of form, a certain construction of space, a certain positionality of "subject" and "object."[3] Where in Lacan's genealogy of the ego an other (the mirror image exterior to the subject) passes itself off as a self, in Irigaray's exposé a self-sameness (the Law of the Symbolic Order) passes itself off as an Other. In both operations, cognition implies seeing—empirical and ideal—and seeing connotes the containment of feminine difference by an image of the self-same.

The psychoanalysis of cinema exploits these insights in demonstrating that within the conventions of classic cinema, "images of women" are likely to function as sites of epistemological crisis or self-verification, as prostheses or fetishes, in a masculine Imaginary. In fact, one contemporary filmmaker, Peter Gidal, suggests that within the order of cinematic rep-

142

resentation as it now exists there is no way to photograph women that is not in effect pornographic, since *images* of women can never be images of *women*. To students of theory, the form of such an argument is by now familiar.

It is probably because the term connotes a cognitive, cognizable totality that in literary criticism representations of woman (and other kinds of representations) have been called "images." A literary "image" of a woman suggests a coherent account of a recognizable identity whose intelligibility is implicitly modeled on that of a visual *Gestalt*. Of course, "image" and its derivative "imagery" have also commonly designated any language that evokes imaginative perception or sensation, typically as part of a figurative structure—a synedoche which itself implies the subordination of the sensory manifold under the hegemony of a single sense, the eye.

To students of Modernist literature, the word "Image" often bears a capital "I" that marks it with the copyright of that famous egotist Ezra Pound, chief entrepreneur of literary Modernism and proverbial parent of the poetic school that his friend T. S. Eliot called "the *point de repère* for the beginning of modern poetry," namely, *les Imagists*. Eliot said, incidentally, that this designation was conventional, a convenience, but in any case it reinscribes a kind of Imaginary etiology in which everything begins with an image, a moment of coherence, plenitude, originality.

As a critical *point de repère*, Imagism's Image has recently become a contested site in conflicting interpretations of literary Modernism. Poststructuralist critics have tried to reclaim the Image as rubric from the clutches of a visualist and spatialist reading of Modernist aesthetics, inherited, they suggest, from the New Critics, in favor of their own temporalizing and antiformalist readings. They point out that in deploying terms like "spatial form" New-Critical criticism privileged the classicizing, reactionary strains of High Modernism, recuperating Modernist texts as "timeless" artifacts and self-sufficient objects of aesthetic contemplation. In this interest, lyric is privileged, reference suppressed or subordinated to the requirements of abstract form. Obviously, this also entails a privilege granted to the mind's *eye*. Instead, critics like Paul Bové, Joseph Riddel, and William Spanos offer readings that mobilize, for example, Heideggerian notions of interpretation and historicity, the indeterminacy of Derridean spac*ing*, the constitution of identity in *différance*. In some cases deconstructive or destructive impulses are attributed to the practices (if not to the theories) of the Modernist writers themselves, in some cases the deferred action of interpretation is invoked, but in every case one effect of such rereading is to obscure—perhaps I should say, to defer—any distinction between the "Modern" and the "post-Modern."[4]

Because Pound's Image has so often been taken as paradigmatic of the Modernist poetic epiphany, it presents an ideal site for the deconstruction of this imaginary periodization. For example, Joseph Riddel argues that the real force of Imagism was to effect a quasi-Nietzschean *undoing* of any poetics based on an Imaginary image, on the image misrecognized as plenitude and origin.[5] In what follows my concern will be to indicate, in connection with the work and reputation of H. D., that feminist issues are implicated in this conflict about Modernism through their implication in the problem of the Image, whose dimensions feminism and psychoanalysis have been redefining. The same problematic therefore provides an entrée to the complex affiliations and disaffiliations of femininity and Modernism, and of feminist and post-structuralist modes of "criticism"— always blithely assuming that there can be such things.[6]

H. D. was in a unique position to appreciate the special relation that women have always had to images—mirror images, photographic images, literary Images. Born—or rather baptized—Hilda Doolittle, she was rechristened "H. D." by her friend Pound, who appended this signature to her earliest publications, along with the epithet that until recently defined her reputation: *Imagiste*. Critical legend made "H. D." "the perfect Imagist," not only *an* example but *the* example, the exemplar, the figure in whom Imagism recognized itself. And since, as Eliot says, *Imagisme* is itself widely recognized as the *point de repère* for the beginning of modern poetry, "H. D." has been accorded a certain place in the history of literature—but only insofar as she exemplifies, perfectly, *fully adequately* and with nothing left over, a certain *theory* of the Image, which is not her own. For, as one historian of Imagism remarks, "H. D. was no theorist."[7]

"H. D." was no theorist—only an example of a theory, an image, her images, offered in evidence for a male-authored truth. A naive reading practice thus reinscribed *as history* the theory of the Modernist Image as effecting, in a timeless moment of aesthetic perception, an adequation of seeing and knowing, appearance and reality, inside and outside. But such effects are not limited to the discipline of literary criticism. For Irigaray, the constitution of knowledge, aesthetic or scientific, always entails the erasure of female images as such, their fetishization as evidence or incarnation within an order of visibility. In a brilliant essay, Joan Copjec traces comparable developments in the intellectual and institutional history of psychoanalysis. Insofar as psychoanalysis begins with the theory and treatment of hysteria, with Freud's revision of Charcot, it begins by making (mute) female images "speak" theoretical truths—a phenomenon answerable to Pound's formula "the Image is itself the speech." (Copjec associates it with his anti-Symbolist claim that "the natural object is always the *adequate* symbol.")[8] This appropriation is literally registered in the photographs of the *Iconographie photographique de la Salpetrière,* beautiful images which through the discipline of Charcot's theoretical labels become illustrations of beautiful truth. Copjec makes the case that the alienating image of Lacan's Imaginary intrudes itself *as* alien into any attempt, phenomenological or poetic, to make the image of seeing or perception coextensive with (its) meaning. And yet, I would add, for Lacan as for Charcot "the cure" works in essence by making the fascination of the (female) image yield to the Law of the word/Symbol (the "nom du père"). This suggests that psychoanalysis may be seen as at one level antivisualist—contra Stephen Heath[9]—and at the same time or at another level phallomorphic, that is, tied precisely to an order of ideal visibility which—contra Jacqueline Rose[10]—it simultaneously unveils and upholds.

The essential form of Charcot's Svengali-like gesture is repeated in the moment when Pound signs (for) "H. D., Imagiste." Nevertheless, "H. D." clearly embraced this "H. D.," and if her feelings about the "Imagiste" were mixed, it is also clear that she liked the visibility it brought her and in general liked being an Image—almost as much as she *dis*liked theorizing. Certainly she sought out the eye of the camera. Yale's Beinecke Library houses nude photographs of "H. D." and her longtime friend Bryher (taken by Bryher's husband, Kenneth MacPherson), and of "H. D." striking the traditional poses of the Greek goddesses whom she tried, in so many ways, to emulate.[11] In addition, "H. D." appeared in three films, playing with Paul Robeson during the 1930s in *Borderline;* she wrote for the film journal *Close-Up,* which Bryher coedited; and at one point she seriously considered a career as a film actress, inspired, perhaps, by her strong identification with Greta Garbo. (Dietrich's was another image with which she identified.) The truth is, "H. D." always had a taste for stardom, a ready capacity for transference, and a love of images—both her own and others'. These qualities pervade her writing from first to last.

Between the first ("Imagist") and the last ("post-Imagist") writings of "H. D." there intervened the person and the doctrines of Freud. So crucial was their effect on her subsequent development as a writer that "H. D."'s later writings might more aptly be termed "postanalytic." Indeed, a remarkable number of these post-Imagist writings of the 1940s and 1950s are, like so many Modernist texts, structured around images. More striking is the fact that these images themselves depict not only instances of seeing but tableau-like scenes of dramatic revelation, often involving the literal drawing back or lifting of a curtain. These tableaux evoke the Modernist "moment" of seeing-knowing, and in this way often function as the implied point of origin and *telos* of a narrative which gradually recovers or reconstructs them though a process of recollection, inference, association, and correction. Narrative structures vehiculate imagistic ones in a textual interface whose model is clearly psychoanalytic. But at the same time, countertrends are at work in the text which suggest that analysis is interminable, seeing uncertain, unveiling veiling. Thus the image can never be the site of an adequation or epiphany, nor any sort of proving ground, one way or the other, but is at once a place where the eye rests and the site of an unending inquiry. For this *second* trend in "H. D." 's work, which might be called "post-Imagist," the most important model is, again, psychoanalytic.

"H. D." 's "Imagist" and "post-Imagist" moments thus correspond approximately to the two "Modernisms"—the "spatializing" or "New Critical" and the "temporalizing" or post-structuralist that would "cure" it—as well as to the two "Psychoanalyses" proffered by Stephen Heath and Jacqueline Rose respectively, and finally to "the two feminisms," American and French, as we have grown accustomed to thinking of them. In considering the historical and theoretical relation of femininity and (post-) Modernism I think it important to bear in mind not only the authoritarian ideology of much Modernist writing but also the fact that some of the most authoritarian texts of Modernism are antiformalist, vitalistic, and mimetic with a vengeance—Futurism being an obvious case in point. Perhaps in their very opposition the contemplative, idealizing elevation of abstract form and the overt aggression of an iconoclastic mimesis both swear allegiance to the eye/I. And as Jane Gallop observes, "writing a non-phallomorphic text" is a rather "common modernist [in Anglo-American parlance, post-Modern] practice" which in my terms may be post-structuralist but proto-feminist.[12] That is why Irigaray *adds* to her deconstruction of phallomorphism another discourse, marked by what Gallop calls "the gesture of a troubled but nonetheless insistent referentiality," an illusion of reference embodied partly in a vulvomorphic imagery that has often led to her misrecognition as "Essentialist." But as Margaret Homans observes, "Irigaray does not so much answer as rewrite the question of essentialism."[13]

To write (in French, *écrire*) and write again ("rewrite"), rather than to answer, a question—the question of "essentialism," the question of female identity—also aptly describes the project of "H. D." 's *Helen in Egypt,* a three-hundred-page pseudo-epic written partly as a rejoinder to Pound's *Cantos.* The *Cantos'* pantheon of Real-Life Heroes—manly figures drawn from the annals of history—finds its correlative in the realism, the essentialism, of Pound's Image, and later in the "ideogram," where a collocation of particulars theoretically forces some more general truth to appear, as it were, "in person"—not as an abstraction but as it, in itself, really is. As if by way of contrast to this factual atomism, "H. D." devises a heroine whose status as nothing more nor less than a textual effect is insistently emphasized. "She herself is the writing," we are repeatedly told, her identity palimpsestically inscribed by several hands in several variant narratives. In this sense the text takes as its subject the condition of its own existence as fiction or myth, a problem it will ultimately assimilate, through the "figure" of Helen, to the problem of femininity itself. For if Helen is writing, she is also and emphatically Image—the most beautiful woman in the world, after all—the Image of beauty and for "H. D." therefore the Image of Imagism. In her text we see Helen diversely reflected in the eyes of several men, each of whom narrates a history that constructs a tableau in which he "sees" and "inscribes" his very own "Helen." Thus, "H. D." 's Achilles, Theseus, and Paris might be compared to Stesichorus, Homer, Euripides, Goethe, and their anonymous precursors, each of whom narrated a tale of "Helen." Collectively these male figures repeat "inside" the text the process of mythmaking that constitutes its "outside" or context, that is, of mythmaking conceived as a culture's collective writing and rewriting of a tale which thereby acquires the force of (psychological and cultural) fact. For "H. D." as for Freud, myth is the collective correlative of individual phantasy.

The title of the poem refers to a pre-Homeric variant of the Helen myth by Stesichorus of Sicily, which claims, as "H. D." 's copious gloss to the poem says, that "Helen was never in Troy. She had been transposed or translated from Greece into Egypt. Helen of Troy was a phantom, substituted for the real Helen, by jealous deities."[14] The purpose of this variant was to vindicate "the real Helen" by making her remain faithful to Menelaus throughout the Trojan War, stowed away in Egypt under the protection of its virtuous king, Proteus. This *division* of the female image is a familiar expedient which becomes an implicit target of "H. D." 's satire. But even in *her* text, Helen, swamped as she is by masculine narratives that contradictorily define her and unable to construct an image or truth-scene of her own, is a thing of naught, a blind reflection of the sighted male. Thus the multiplicity or fragmentation of Helen's text/ identity is not initially posed as an antidote to her captation by a collective masculine Imaginary but rather as the result of it.

In response there emerges what might be called the Helen of "American feminism"—the "images of woman" Helen—in quest for an authentic self-perception, a true account of her being and experience. At the beginning of the poem, Helen is in Egypt, believing herself the virtuous and maligned woman of Stesichorus's *Palinode,* but only because she has repressed all memory of her involvement with Paris and the war, which she will shortly begin to recollect. The action of the poem is wholly "interior" or interpretive, comprising Helen's laborious efforts to reconstruct crucial scenes from her past so as to arrive at an accurate account of her personal history and thereby a determination of her true identity, evident, as it were, in these scenes. At this level the text presses toward the amnesiac Helen's recognition of the complementary duality of her own nature as both human and divine, and toward the derivation of her contradictory identities from a single source, the "great white mother goddess" of comparative mythography, whose power as (m)other can oppose that of the death-dealing patriarchal order. But finally "H. D." 's text will simply not sustain any such attempt to add up the two (or the several) Helens, the good and the bad, the real and the apparent, into some kind of well-balanced totality. Instead, "H. D." multiplies Helens, images, variant myths and narratives, superimposing these in such a way that there can no longer be any question of which represents "the original" or authoritative *one.* As in the echoing *antre/entre* of Irigaray's *Speculum,* the echoing, querying voice(s) of the text—chiefly of "Helen" and of the narrator who doubles her—effect a spatiotemporal dislocation that moves us, together with "Helen," into an imaginative space where feminine images proliferate beyond any horizon of truth, or of deceit.

"H. D." 's conception for *Helen* was informed by the second part of Goethe's *Faust,* in which Mephistopheles calls up the ghost of Helen of Troy at Faust's bidding, because he, Faust, wishes to marry the most beautiful woman in the world, even if only in a kind of make-believe. Evil as he is, Mephistopheles can't resist tormenting Helen, a phantom brought back from the dead, a mere semblance who, happily oblivious to her lack of ontological status, believes herself to be real. Mephistopheles can't tell Helen the truth outright, but he undermines her by hinting at it, recollecting the Stesichorus myth about the phantom Helen and demanding of her a question he knows she can't answer: which was the real? The effect of the bizarre scene is wonderfully pathetic, a triumph and an allegory of art in which we *feel* for Helen even though we know she exists only as a figment of the Imagination, that is, doesn't exist. A triumph, then, like Mephistopheles', of *trompe l'œil.*

Substituting for the real but absent Helen, Goethe's/Mephistopheles' phantom shares the same status of nonentity as the simulacrum of Stesichorus, the statue-image which is called, in both Goethe and Euripides, *eidolon*—"painted image" or "cloud image"; she remains equally subject, as his creation and mouthpiece, to the requirements of the male artist/

magician. To the extent that Goethe recognizes a kind of pathos in the situation of the woman/phantom his conception begins to approach that of *Helen in Egypt*, for as I have suggested it too is an allegory of art, an allegory of the woman as artwork, but one told, as it were, from the point of view of the work. As such it becomes also an allegory of feminine identity or self-knowledge. For the "Helen" of *Faust* there can be no solution for the usurpation of her identity; for that of Stesichorus and Euripides, the solution lies in distinguishing between the true and the false, the chaste and whorish, Helens (with much play, in Euripides, on the power of appearances to deceive); but for the "Helen" of *Helen in Egypt* the "real"/chaste Helen is no less an image, a projection/reflection of male wants, than her phantom counterpart.

The problem of feminine identity cannot, thus, be formulated in terms of a decision to be taken between the one/true and the false/double woman—whether from a masculine or from a feminist perspective. What, indeed, would or could it mean to recover a true "Helen" within a context where identity itself is conceived as a fictional/mythic projection? The question Mephistopheles puts to Helen—which was the real?—expresses the same desire for a determination of female identity expressed in Freud's famous question, "What does a woman want?" But as Irigaray says, "It is . . . useless to trap women into giving an exact definition of what they mean . . . they desire at the same time nothing and everything." Thus, "in a culture that claims to enumerate everything, cipher everything by units, inventory everything by individualities," woman will represent "a mystery," being, in Irigaray's words, *"neither one nor two."*[15] Initially "trapped" by the dualistic/monolithic form of the question that Achilles (echoing both Mephistopheles and Freud) puts to her—"Which was the real?"—the "Helen" of *Helen in Egypt* struggles painfully to satisfy his demand for the truth with an answer/statement that will "stop" the question, close and complete its gaping form. But this proves futile, as in the course of Helen's interior quest what emerges is rather a bewildering multiplicity of selves, a multiplicity obscured by the singularity of the proper name "Helen." Ultimately, it is only in the homecoming of her own quest(ion)ing, only in the shelter of such an opening, that the heroine's identity rests: an (ir)resolution that contrasts with the restoration of family and state in which the questing of masculine heroes, however elaborately digressive, must finally conclude.

Thus if the Stesichorus myth is an alternative to the dominant tradition of Homer, the myth of feminine identity represented in *Helen in Egypt* must be considered an alternative to that alternative. As Froma Zeitlin and others have shown, in Homeric tradition the figure of Helen bears connotations of eroticism, disguise, and deception that associate her with the art of poetry and more simply with art as such, but she also bears the suggestion of divinity and thus of a "truth beyond fiction."[16] Stesichorus then "analyzes" this ambiguity into a clear and distinct duality that erects an absolute distinction between truth and trope, rehabilitating the figure of Helen by stripping her of her figurality, transferring or projecting all her erotic/poetic properties onto a "bad"/external simulacrum of the real woman. He proposes, in short, that Helen should recover her good or proper "name" by forswearing all the potency implied by her status as image, imposter, or mime. But Stesichorus cannot escape the irony that in formulating his *Palinode* he must himself have recourse to the arts of fiction or rhetoric, the art, thus, of the sophists who Plato said exhibited "painted images" or *eidola* of things in order to make the speaker seem wise; according to Plato, in fact, the sophist Gorgias set out to rehabilitate the figure of Helen using the power of rhetoric alone, simply to prove that it could be done.[17]

The *eidola* or tropes of the sophist and the *eidolon* or cloud image of Helen devised, in one version of the Stesichorus myth, by Zeus, the cloud-gatherer, are both fashioned to deceive; yet the Greek word *eidos*, from which *eidolon* derives, is also and more famously translated from the text of Plato as "form." In fact, the word *eidolon* has what Freud called an "antithetical sense" and can mean both form and image, can designate a sacred manifestation or icon of a god, or can have the sense of a forgery, a "mere" copy or image. In *Helen in Egypt,* the heroine's anamnesis is paralleled by that of her leading man, Achilles, which culminates in the recovery, in effect the uncovering, of a certain *eidolon,* the memory of an image. Here the so-called *eidolon* is a wooden doll representing Achilles' mother, the goddess Thetis, which was cherished by the boy in her absence but which he abandoned when his military training began. In the mythic idiom of the poem, the repudiated mother-substitute or Thetis-*eidolon* is associated not only with the Helen-*eidolon* of Stesichorus but also with the figure of Helen Dendritus, described by Robert Graves as "an orgiastic goddess" whose cult was centered at Sparta and whose ritual involved the use of wooden dolls, often hung from fruit trees, that helped to increase fertility. In "H. D." 's psychologizing of "Helen," Helen Dendritus becomes a repressed aspect of the heroine's identity that must be recovered along with the lost memory of her part in the Trojan War, and it is Achilles' recovery of the primal *eidolon*—also the title of the final book of the poem—that links "Helen" 's recovery with that of the repudiated mother (and with the repudiated divinity or potency of the mother-as-goddess).

But insofar as the Thetis-*eidolon* is itself a substitute, a doll-signifier that usurps the potency of "the real" in Achilles' psychic economy, its unveiling, like the psychomythic archaeology of "Helen" 's identity, can only lead to further revelations, further questions. And if the "veil" or "garment" of style is traditionally the trope of rhetoric, the trope of tropes, *Helen in Egypt* literalizes this trope by making "Helen" 's veil her defining attribute in the poem, a metonymy of the figure of "Helen" herself. More precisely, as a (literal) "image" (*eidolon*), the veil plays a crucial part in the plot and scenography of the poem, including several dramatic scenes recollected by Paris, Achilles, and Helen, while as symbol or signifier ("veil") it suggests the deceptive and alluring properties associated with the Helen-*eidolon*. Indeed, if the *eidolon* proves to be a "veil," the veil in turn proves to be an *eidolon*. Thus *Helen*'s reinscription of the Image as veil*ing* must be distinguished not only from the imaginary self-evidence of a Poundian Image but also from any concept of reading as explication. As Irigaray demonstrates in her retraversal of Plato's cave allegory in Part III of *Speculum*, the traditional structure of *allegoresis* and of trope in general depends upon distinguishing, deciding between, an outside—the literal sense or vehicle—and an inside—the figurative, non-sensible "sense," or tenor—in order to arrive, through such judicious deliberation, at the unveiling of a singular truth-scene. "Interpretation" on this model is thus a process that pleasurably recapitulates the primordial self-constitution of the specular ego in the action of *placing outside*, the articulation of a (bad or inessential) outside and a (good, essential) inside, meaning or truth. But *Helen* not only calls into question any distinction between (its) "inside" and "outside"; as allegory, it emerges only in/out of this quest(ion)ing. Thus, *Helen*'s "allegorical" "veil," though in one scene torn or rent, is otherwise represented as many-folded—endlessly self-implicating and finally inexplicable.

It is because of "H. D." 's tendency to read psychoanalysis as an interminable dialectic of (un)veiling that her writing can be characterized by Joseph Riddel as anticipating Lacanian psychoanalysis.[18] But Riddel's brilliant reading of "H. D." is inscribed wholly within the same Lacanian problematic that simultaneously subordinates the female image to the phallic "word" and upholds the form of the phallus in its place. Thus, when Lacan speaks of the "kaleidoscopic" structure of imaginary space, he underlines both the formal/aesthetic properties of that beautiful (*kalos*) form (*eidos*), the ego, and its purely spectral (*skopein*) or illusory nature.[19] It is, again, the subject's narcissistic interest in the integrity of his own form that ultimately impels him to "imagine the [Phallic] Symbol" and so pass beyond the state of "captation to the Image." Irigaray's analysis of

151

the cave allegory is in effect an extended allusion to Lacan's account of the passage from the Imaginary to the Symbolic, in which she indicates that like the *eidos*/form of Platonic philosophy, the Lacanian Phallus is ironically yet definitively set *beyond* the field of vision—"the [Phallus] can play its role only when veiled" (that is, only *as* trope or signifier), according to Lacan[20]—precisely in order that it should function in that "beyond" as the truth-reserve, the guarantee of the visible/knowable/re-presentational world. For Irigaray, the difference between the Imaginary Ego/*eidolon* and the Symbolic Phallus/*eidolon* therefore doesn't amount to much: the formality of the Symbolic Order and the singularity of its Phallic *differentia* continually returns (in) the Symbolic to the specularity of male narcissism or "hom(m)osexualité," as Irigaray puts it.

I would suggest therefore that the critical psychoanalysis developed by Irigaray provides a more appropriate counterpart than Lacan's to *Helen*'s assimilation of the problem of the text to the problem of female identity. Unlike the phallic structure of Lacanian trope (and the tropological structure of the Lacanian Phallus), which privileges absent sense, *Helen*'s "veiling" resembles the Derridean "hymen" of *Spurs*, that indeterminate place/ word ("hymen" signifies both marriage and virginity) that separates/joins inside and out.[21] The hymen/veil also epitomizes the problem of Helen's female identity: chaste? (in-tact?) or (de)spoiled? These are the two narrow parameters that traditionally have defined feminine (im)possibilities.

Where Irigaray draws from Lacan a critique of formalism that reflects on his own psychoanalysis, *Helen*'s reworking of the Image/*eidolon* draws out Pound's critique of representation in a way that implicates his own aesthetic. Just as the traditional structure of a well-made trope is divided into an essential/inside and an inessential/outside part, more recently called a tenor and a vehicle, so, for Pound, trope in general was divided into two kinds, which he called decorative metaphor and interpretive metaphor. To eschew decoration was of course among the cardinal principles of Imagism, which from the first exhorted its followers, "don't be viewy," and "use no word which does not contribute to the presentation" of the object, "whether subjective or objective." But for Pound "interpretive metaphor" was another matter. Whereas decorative metaphor merely *copied*, re-presented, or embellished a preexisting sense—belonged, in short, to the despised order of "mimesis"—interpretive metaphor *created* the sense which it incarnated, and was in this sense presentational, admitting of no distinction between vehicle and tenor. In Saussurian terms, it was a motivated sign. Pound's commentary on Fenollosa argues, in a manner reminiscent of Shelley's *Defense of Poetry*, that the self-renewing processes of language as such are, in the interpretive sense, metaphoric;

in contrast to the arbitrary phonetic symbols of the West, the Chinese ideogram "bears its metaphors on its face" and so prevents their unheeded degeneration into abstraction or a merely conventional relation between symbol and symbolized, their degeneration, that is, into dead or decorative metaphor. Thus it is of the essence of interpretive metaphor to embody an act of cognition and not recognition; to incarnate new knowledge rather than to repeat or vary something already known; and this epistemological value is inseparable from its phenomenological mode of being as a full yet significant presence. Ideogrammic metaphors are "interpretive," oddly enough, because they require no interpretation or reading, being self-evident, visible, pictorial; they embody and do not refer or represent. And even when Fenollosa says that the ideogram is a visible bridge to the invisible—a more traditional definition of metaphor or analogy—this "invisible" is that which inheres in the directly observable relations of the ideogrammic structure, what Hugh Kenner calls its "intelligible form."[22] Seeing, the discernment of form, remains the privileged metaphor of cognition and of metaphor *as* cognition, while in all essentials Pound's characterization of the ideogram—ontology, epistemology, and aesthetics—remains wholly consistent with that of the Image. Decoration suggests that which distracts and (merely) amuses the eye, contributing nothing to knowledge; while the ideogrammic method is a mode of writing that permits the antidecorative principle of Imagism to be applied to a long poem. Both Imagism and the ideogram express Pound's deeply felt aversion to "decoration" as the antithesis, the obscurer, and potentially the corrupter of (good) form.

It is largely as such, no doubt, that decoration has long been associated with the feminine; psychoanalysis suggests that woman's love for self-adornment is a form of self-disguise or veiling that proceeds from her inherent "lack," and Irigaray identifies this "lack" as, above all, the lack of (a) (good) form. Pound, of course, deplored not only decoration but also the effete serenity of Greek "form," which especially in his Vorticist phase he regarded as a sham of true, dynamic form. To the Vorticists the color and primitive energy of Egyptian art represented the opposite of the Greek aesthetic, and in many accounts of Pound's poetic development Vorticism therefore marks an essential transition from the static confines of the Image to the dynamic inclusiveness of the *Cantos*' (theoretically) ideogrammic method. The opposition between Greek and Semite which in this way was so important to Vorticist rhetoric is called into question by the elusive figure of "Helen" in Egypt as by James Joyce's equally elusive "Jewgreek" or "greekjew," Leopold Bloom; in both figures, "extremes meet."[23] But the impact of this meeting in *Helen in Egypt* is not that of a marriage or dialectic of force and form, a formula that some critics have recently proposed as capturing the essence of Modernism.[24] Rather, just as *Helen*'s undecidable veil/*eidolon* reinscribes the Poundian Image, its/her Egyptian "hieroglyphics" transmute the "ideogrammic method" into a mode of writing that oscillates perpetually between symbol and image, decoration and genesis, spectacle and sense.

For "H. D.," dreams and visions were "the hieroglyphics of the Unconscious," and thus the ancient ground of consciousness and the ego, which in this scheme would correspond to the rational "form" of the Greeks. Freud called dream interpretation "the royal road to the Unconscious," and the phrase "hieroglyphics of the Unconscious" suggests a script to be deciphered, an art of interpretation which in Lacanian terms must depend upon the opposition of image and symbol/signifier. It is in connection with Freud's *Interpretation of Dreams* that Lacan insists there can be, strictly speaking, no such thing as picture writing: "Freud shows in every possible way that the value of the image as signifier has nothing whatsoever to do with its signification, giving as an example Egyptian hieroglyphics . . . even in this writing, the so-called 'ideogram' is a letter."[25] The *interpretation* of dreams and the unconscious, whether regarded as terminable or interminable, thus entails the same sort of *Aufhebung* that, in the passage from the Imaginary to the Symbolic, conscripts the (female) image in service to the "nom du père." In this sense Lacan's distinction recapitulates the passage from polytheism, the worship of images, to the unified rule of the father-god and concomitant banning of images, as described by Freud in *Moses and Monotheism*.

The very term "hieroglyphic," however, inscribes an uncertainty concerning its own nature similar to that of the *eidolon,* for the *glyphē* in question here, from Greek *glyphein* 'to carve' can designate either a symbolic "figure" or character carved in relief *or* an ornamental groove in a Doric frieze, that is, a purely decorative element that bespeaks no other value. Both antithetical senses speak together in *Helen in Egypt,* a text that might just as well be named "Egypt in Hel(l)en(e)," where the gaudy hieroglyphs of Egypt are associated not only with an art of interpretation but also with a script of "silent," purely decorative images that "H. D." identified as a particularly feminine art.[26] Thus in one moment the variable Helen longs to be like Achilles, master of the "Star Script," in "untangling the riddle" of her identity; but in another, she "flings away knowledge," preferring instead to dwell on/in the beauty of the holy picture-writing, preferring pleasure to desire. Not incidentally, "H. D." (like Dorothy Richardson) regarded the silent cinema as a feminine medium which lost this character when it began to "talk." "The screen image, a mask, a sort of doll or marionette was somehow mechanized," she wrote in *Close-Up;* "I didn't really *like* my old screen image to be so improved (I might almost say imposed) on. . . . Haven't we been just a little hurt and disappointed that our dolls have grown so perfect?"[27] The light-writing or photography of the silent cinema also came to be associated too with the protracted hallucinations "H. D." experienced while visiting on Corfu, and which later served as partial inspiration for *Helen.* Moreover, the silent script beheld in *Hellas* became a kind of mother tongue akin both to the silent cinema and to the decorative images painted by "H. D." 's mother, Helen Wolle, amateur creations whose decorative purpose and domestic content were ridiculed by the youthful Pound.[28]

It was not only the conventional character of Helen Wolle Doolittle's paintings but also their representational or referential nature that Pound disdained, as he would later disdain photography, cinema, and "decorative metaphor." Riddel says that Pound's "presentational" poetic consisted essentially in removing the "re" from "representation" through the elevation of interpretive metaphor. But in his well-founded determination to displace the orthodoxy of Kenner's Modernism, Riddel does not acknowledge the degree to which the radical force of Pound's gesture was contradicted by its historical and ideological context. After all, Kenner's Pound is also to a great extent Pound's Pound. For the illusion(ism) of referentiality, the illusion of the presence of something actually absent, Pound sought to substitute the real presence of the Image/ideogram as form, a form incarnate in the text as perfected through the poetic regimen of "Imagism." "H. D.," the living doll, the spitting Image of Imagism, responds with a "hieroglyphic" text that, on the one hand, reinterprets the Image in light of psychoanalysis, as a mode of hermeneutic veiling that restores the centrality of reading, and on the other, suggests a purely decorative or "silent" picture writing that favors the pleasurable illusion of a feminine presence over the desire for knowledge.

In this way, "H. D." 's writing touches that of Irigaray and also constantly touches or implicates itself, not as verbal artifact but in its own (un)veiling. Lacan indicates that subjectivity is structured by two glances— the glance of specular self-recognition and the glance that spots a hole— one constituting and the other forever breaking a psychocorporal totality. Yet, as a developmental fiction the Imaginary folds back on itself, implicitly barring the possibility of identifying any such "moment of origin" for the subject.[29] Thus, charges of Imaginary captation leveled against this position or that one necessarily implicate themselves, as we all are implicated, in the Imaginary, that is, by believing in it. Feminism should analyze but cannot purge itself of Imaginary effects because feminism depends on

Imaginary effects for its putative existence and perpetually reinscribes them. This is a situation I see reflected in the text of *Helen in Egypt.*

Finally, psychoanalysis motivates but will not necessarily authorize such a reading practice. But perhaps feminist psychoanalysis will always have to be "wild." That was Freud's term for psychoanalysis undertaken by amateurs, a practice he regarded as a grave danger both to the patient and to the doctrine of psychoanalysis. Perhaps "H. D." 's wild inventiveness with psychoanalytic doctrine was attributable to the fact that she was Freud's patient and "student," as he called her, but was not actually psychoanalysed by him. Freud told her he saw "from signs" that she did not want to be analyzed, and perhaps this was because, as "H. D." herself said, "[his] explanations were too illuminating, it sometimes seemed."[30]

Notes

1. Jacques Lacan, *Écrits,* trans. Alan Sheridan (New York: W. W. Norton & Co., 1977), 6.
2. Jacques Lacan and Wladimir Granoff, "Fetishism: The Symbolic, The Imaginary and the Real," in Sandor Lorand and Michael Balint, eds., *Perversion: Psychodynamics and Therapy* (New York: Random House, 1956). See also Lacan's "Reflections on the Ego," *International Journal of Psychoanalysis* 34 (1953), 11–17, where he connects the body *imago* or "imaginary Anatomy" with the "laws of *gestalt,*" which he says are "exhibited" in the forms taken by hysterical symptoms. "[T]he fact that the penis is dominant in the shaping of the body-image . . . may shock the sworn champions of the autonomy of female sexuality," he writes, "[but] such dominance is a fact and one moreover which cannot be put down to cultural influences alone" (13). The "relation of the subject to his own body" (12) is mediated by his identification with this penis-shaped *gestalt* or *imago,* which Lacan here goes on to associate with both the mirroring function of the cerebral cortex and "Aristotle's idea of *Morphe,*" an idea "discarded by experimental science" which "[w]e psychoanalysts are here introducing" in terms of the theory of narcissism. Additional comments on the relation between the Imaginary, the Symbolic, and the Real are scattered throughout Lacan's writings, but on the role of the mirror stage see especially "The Mirror Stage as Formative of the Function of the 'I' " and "Aggressivity in Psychoanalysis" in *Écrits.*
3. Jane Gallop, "*Quand Nos Lèvres S'Écrivent:* Irigaray's Body Politic," *Romanic Review* 74 (1983), 77–83.
4. *Boundary 2* has published several articles that propose or propound such post-Modern rereadings of Modernism. See, for example, William V. Spanos, "Heidegger, Kierkegaard and the Hermeneutic Circle: Towards a Postmodern Theory of Interpretation as Dis-closure," *Boundary 2* (Winter 1977), 115–48;

" 'Modernism' in Western literature—and the New Critical and, more recently, Structuralist hermeneutics it has given rise to—is grounded in a strategy that spatializes the temporal process of existence. . . . It is no accident that the autotelic and inclusive circle, that is the circle as image or Icon, is the essential symbol of high Modernism . . . and of the New Criticism and Structuralism" (116). Spanos attempts a reading that substitutes a post-Modern-Heideggerian hermeneutic circle for the Modernist circle as image. See also the Winter 1976, Fall 1979, and Spring/Fall 1984 issues of *Boundary 2;* Paul Bové, *Destructive Poetics: Heidegger and Modern American Poetry* (New York: Columbia Univ. Press, 1980); Joseph Riddel, *The Inverted Bell: Modernism and the Counter-Poetics of William Carlos Williams* (Baton Rouge: Louisiana State Univ. Press, 1974) and "A Somewhat Polemical Introduction: The Elliptical Poem," *Genre* XI (Winter 1978), 459–77: "the theory of the lyric is indeed the model for modern poetry, because it is a theory that undoes its own closure and therefore all the spatial metaphors which reify its 'form' " (466), and "[a]fter de Man and Derrida, it is probably wise to use the terms modern and postmodern with caution, if not to abandon them altogether" (470).

5. Joseph Riddel, "Decentering the Image: The 'Project' of "American' Poetics?" in Josué V. Harari, ed., *Textual Strategies* (New York: Cornell Univ. Press, 1979), 322–58, and " 'Neo-Nietzschean Clatter'—Speculations and/on Pound's Poetic Image," in Ian F. Bell, ed., *Ezra Pound: Tactics for Reading* (London: Vision and Barnes and Noble, 1982), 187–220.

6. No one writing on femininity and Modernism can disregard Alice Jardine's *Gynesis: Configurations of Femininity and Modernism* (New York: Columbia Univ. Press, 1985). If my suggestions here contradict hers there, it is largely because we are writing about different things: she about the contemporary French scene, I about the Anglo-American one as it developed in the teens and twenties and has been subsequently approached by (Anglo-American) readers. As Jardine notes, what is "called 'modernity' in France" is "more problematically in the United States [called] 'post-modernism' " (22). Thus, what she calls "modernity" I call "post-Modernism" or "post-structuralism," and what I call "Modernism" she does not discuss because it is not the concern of her book to do so. Still, a curious disjunction emerges in our different mappings of the opposition narrative/space: following precedents, Jardine and I both associate the former with masculinity and the latter with femininity, but while she sees in French "modernity" a breakdown of (paternal) narrative(s) and a privileging of new (feminine) space(s), I see in Anglo-American "post-Modernism" (which is, after all, an appropriation of French "modernity") a privileging not of narrative but of a temporality (still coded "masculine") irreducible to the category of space (still coded "feminine") and in many ways opposed to it. Perhaps insofar as "theory" theorizes (the Woman, *écriture,* and cognate phenomena), that is, offers itself or is read *as* theory (truth, knowledge), it entails the subordination of the image to (a master) narrative, while insofar as it writes, marks, inscribes (the Woman, *écriture,* etc.), it privileges the Woman/

space. Of course, it is not clear that a discourse can do one without doing the other, that there can be *écriture* without a theory of *écriture*.

7. Stanley K. Coffman, Jr., *Imagism: A Chapter for the History of Modern Poetry* (Norman: Univ. of Oklahoma Press, 1951), 163.

8. Joan Copjec, "*Flavit et dissipati sunt*," *October* 18 (Fall 1981).

9. Stephen Heath, "Difference," in *Screen* 19, no. 3 (Fall 1978), 51–112.

10. Jacqueline Rose, "Introduction," in Jacqueline Rose and Juliet Mitchell, eds., *Feminine Sexuality: Jacques Lacan and the Ecole Freudienne* (New York: W. W. Norton & Co., 1980.)

11. I am indebted to Susan Friedman for telling me about these photographs, which I have not had the opportunity to see myself.

12. Gallop 83.

13. Margaret Homans, "Reconstructing the Feminine," *Women's Review of Books* 3, no. 6 (1986), 12–13, 13.

14. H. D., *Helen in Egypt* (New York: New Directions, 1961), 1.

15. Luce Irigaray, *This Sex Which Is Not One*, trans. Catherine Porter (Ithaca: Cornell Univ. Press, 1985), 29, 26.

16. Froma I. Zeitlin, "Travesties of Gender and Genre in Aristophanes' *Thesmophoriazousae*," in *Critical Inquiry* 8, no. 2 (1981), 301–27. Zeitlin reads Helen as an expression of Greek ambivalence toward both art and the feminine.

17. Zeitlin 324.

18. Joseph Riddel, "H. D.'s Scene of Writing—Poetry as (and) Analysis," *Studies in the Literary Imagination* 12, no. 1 (1979), 41–59.

19. Lacan, *Écrits*, 27.

20. Lacan, *Écrits*, 288.

21. Jacques Derrida, *Spurs: Nietzsche's Styles*, trans. Barbara Harlow (Chicago: Univ. of Chicago Press, 1978).

22. Hugh Kenner, *The Poetry of Ezra Pound* (London: Faber and Faber, 1951).

23. Quoted from *Ulysses* by Jacques Derrida in *Writing and Difference* (Chicago: Univ. of Chicago Press, 1978), 153.

24. See, for example, Sanford Schwartz, *The Matrix of Modernism* (Chicago: Univ. of Chicago Press, 1985).

25. Lacan, *Écrits*, 159.

26. Susan Stanford Friedman and Adelaide Morris also emphasize the feminine character of the Image as it was reinterpreted by "H. D." See Susan Stanford Friedman, *Psyche Reborn: The Emergence of H. D.* (Bloomington: Indiana Univ. Press, 1981) and Adelaide Morris, "The Concept of Projection: H. D.'s Visionary Powers," *Contemporary Literature* 25, 4 (1984), 411–36. And for a discussion of "H. D." 's and *Helen's* textual "femininity," see Rachel Blau DuPlessis, *H. D.: The Career of That Struggle* (Bloomington: Indiana Univ. Press, 1986).

27. H. D., "The Cinema and the Classic, Part III," in *Close-Up* no. 5 (Nov. 1927), 19–20.

28. H. D., *Tribute to Freud and Advent* (New York: New Directions, 1956, 1974).

29. Jacqueline Rose argues that Lacan's later writings exhibit a shift of emphasis from the early notion of the ego as *Gestalt* to a latter one which retheorizes

the ego/image as a structure of linguistic insistence or repeated difference—
thus hardly distinguishable from the Symbolic. Rose, "The Imaginary," in Colin
McCabe, ed., *The Talking Cure* (London: Routledge and Kegan Paul, 1981).
30. H. D., *Tribute to Freud,* 30.

Rereading J. S. Mill:

Interpolations from the (M)Otherworld

CHRISTINE DI STEFANO

[T]he existence of two sexes does not to begin with arouse any difficulties or doubts in children. It is self-evident to a male child that
a genital like his own is to be attributed to everyone he knows, and
he cannot make its absence tally with his picture of these other people.

SIGMUND FREUD
Three Essays on the Theory of Sexuality

For what is important is to disconcert the staging of representation
according to *exclusively* "masculine" parameters, that is, according
to a phallocratic order. It is not a matter of toppling that order so as
to replace it—that amounts to the same thing in the end—but of
disrupting and modifying it, starting from an "outside" that is exempt,
in part, from phallocratic law.

LUCE IRIGARAY
"The Power of Discourse and
the Subordination of the Feminine"

Introduction

Rereading philosophy, as Luce Irigaray has argued for her counterspecular
enterprise, is a psychoanalytic interpretive undertaking, aimed at and within
a symptomatic discourse, one which both reveals and conceals underlying
patterns of meaning, motivation, and desire. In spite of its claim to metadiscursive status, philosophy is a signifying practice like any other. But
also not exactly like: insofar as philosophy constitutes the discourse *on*
discourse, it "sets forth the law for all others" (Irigaray 74). Hence, the
feminist disruption of philosophical discourse is a crucial, but no longer
intellectually privileged, part of critical activity directed at and within a

wide range of signifying practices, including those of both "high" and "low" culture. Gendered configurations in and across their multidisciplinary array are what concern us *as feminists.*

Like philosophy, political theory also carries metadiscursive claims about itself: political theory is the discourse on *political* discourse and practice. It too is a signifying practice like any other, even as it carries a self-privileging claim to metastatus. Like philosophy and literature, political theory is replete with texts that inscribe gender, with representational systems that are self-representative of a masculine subject (Di Stefano, 1984). Liberal political theory, I want to argue, is one such system. As such, it is a symptomatic discourse which carries its own disruptive excess in the figure of the (m)other.

In Search of the Missing (M)Other: Preliminaries

Who is this (m)other? From a psychoanalytic perspective, she occupies a crucial, privileged position on the overdetermined terrain of masculine gender identity acquisition (Chodorow, Dinnerstein). This position in the pre-Oedipal familial configuration and drama is simultaneously charged, central and highly problematic, most especially for the masculine neonate. The pre-Oedipal (m)other is the posited *negative* ground of a constructed and apparently "positive" masculine identity, which proceeds on the basis of accumulated negative counterfactuals. This (m)other of negative counterfactual comparison may be called on to aid in the criticism or deconstruction of masculine privilege and signification in "male-stream thought" (O'Brien). She embodies the protected sham at the core of the acquired masculine incentive and power "to eradicate the difference between the sexes in systems that are self-representative of a 'masculine subject' " (Irigaray 74).

In those literary and theoretical discursive systems which have been produced and reproduced within a hegemonic masculine framework, this (m)other inhabits a subtextual or unconscious terrain. Coppélia Kahn has referred to this terrain as a maternal subtext and described it as "the imprint of mothering on the male psyche, the psychological presence of the mother in men whether or not mothers are represented in the texts they write" (Kahn 36). More often than not, the (m)other occupies no visible legitimate space within the discourse of modern political theory: what we encounter in that discourse is a Missing (M)Other Syndrome of huge and fascinating proportions.[1] The (m)other of masculine projection and exclusion, simultaneously present and absent, serves as an unacknowledged referent of meaning within masculine discourse; as such, she threatens to decenter and undermine the very discourse that has created her. In this sense, the maternal subtext can take on a critical dynamic of its own in the hands of feminist readers, for it provides an immanent point of contact with discourses that seek, on the one hand, to produce their subjects in a singular (masculine) mold, and on the other, to maintain a pseudodifferentiated feminized Other as the projected counterfactual mirror image of the masculine subject. Rereading literature, film, philosophy, or political theory (among other discourses and signifying practices) in the name of the (m)other reveals and disrupts this patterned privileging of masculine experience and meaning.

It is important to keep in mind that the (m)other revealed by psychoanalytic theory and the masculine imagination is a complex representational figure, simultaneously "real" and fantasized. To treat her in any but the complex fashion entailed by this understanding is to fall prey to one of the following two errors, naturalism or idealism. The naturalistic fallacy issues in biological explanations for women's mothering, along with an underdeveloped historical and cultural appreciation for the wide varieties of maternal practice and experience. The idealist fallacy, on the other hand, treats the mother as nothing but the fantasized projections of her offspring. The "real" mother is that woman who most probably birthed us and cared for us during our early, vulnerable, and formative years. She provided the original ground of our difficult strivings for (and resistance to) identity. The fantasized mother is the mother of huge proportions—terrifying in her power and wrath, overwhelmingly seductive in her promise of a recaptured "oceanic feeling." Understood in these terms, the representational Missing Mother is a complicated figure; she must be handled with care. It is for this reason that she is now often designated as "(m)other."

A focus on the (m)other in these terms and for critical reinterpretive efforts aimed at and within masculine discourses must be clear on several potential misunderstandings with distinctive antifeminist implications.[2] Feminists who invoke the (m)other must simultaneously disengage from and criticize the following attitudes and positions: that mothering is unproblematic for women and should not be critically exposed as an often limiting and imposed "choice"; that most women ought to be, or will continue to be, maternal care-givers; that mothers are more privileged (in terms of critical cognitive perception) or "correct" than women who choose not be mothers; that mothering exhausts the full range of "womanly" practices that feminism needs to pay attention to in its critical and reconstructive efforts; that mothers cause/are responsible for masculine identity and behavior.

In the face of such potential and antifeminist abuses, why focus on mothers at all? E. Ann Kaplan's position is similar to my own: "Motherhood thus becomes one place from which to reformulate our position as women, just because men have not dealt with it theoretically or in the social realm. . . . Motherhood has been repressed on all levels except that of hypostatization, romanticization, and idealization. Yet women have been struggling with lives as mothers—silently, quietly, often in agony, often in bliss, but always on the periphery of a society that tries to make us all, men and women, forget our mothers" (322). A focus on the maternal subtext in political theory, then, is aimed at this collective forgetfulness. Rereading is, among other things, a strategy of remembering.

The View from the (M)Otherworld

What I propose to offer, in the brief space of this essay, is a short series of interpolations on several works by John Stuart Mill. These interpolations—or interruptions—are elaborated from the standpoint of the (m)other. What will be missing in this essay is a full rendering of the texts to which these disruptions are directed.[3] Those who are not familiar with Mill's political theory should not give up at this point. Much of this discourse is familiar to us already: it is the commonplace fare of liberal political discourse in this country today, including (and especially) that of liberal feminism. The key components of liberal discourse include the elaboration and defense of a public/private distinction; an autonomous individual whose (threatened) freedom and protection is secured through political means; and a politics which is concerned with the public adjustment of actual and potential conflicts between and among such individuals. Finally, the "legitimacy" of the political order is grounded in the "free" and "rational" consent of these individuals.

Turning now to the political theory of John Stuart Mill, let us see what the (m)other has to show us. Where do we look for her and how do we find her? A logical starting point would be in the *Autobiography,* but there she is nowhere to be found, except in the sheer excess of her absence. Here is Mill's touching account of his birth: "I was born in London, on the 20th of May, 1806, and was the eldest son of James Mill, the author of the *History of British India*" (*Autobiography* 2). As far as his *real mother* is concerned, Mill makes no explicit mention of her anywhere in his published writings. With some perseverance, we finally track her down in his feminist tract, *On the Subjection of Women*. The following "hypothetical" description of the beleaguered husband fits perfectly with several accounts of the elder Mill's feelings about his wife, which were not kept quiet either within or outside of the immediate family circle:

> A man who is married to a woman his inferior in intelligence finds her a perpetual dead weight, a drag, upon every aspiration of his to be better than public opinion requires him to be. It is hardly possible for one who is in these bonds, to attain exalted virtue. If he differs in his opinion from the mass—if he sees truths which have not yet dawned on them, or if, feeling in his heart truths which they nominally recognize, he would like to act up to those truths more conscientiously than the generality of mankind—to all such thoughts and desires, marriage is the heaviest of drawbacks, unless he be so fortunate as to have a wife as much above the common level as he himself is. (114)

As we know, Harriet Mill, John's mother, played the scapegoat, as the all too visceral reminder of her husband's failure to live up to his hypocritical ideal of sexual asceticism. James Mill, who, according to his son, viewed "the physical relation and its adjuncts" as "a perversion of the imagination and feelings . . . one of the deepest seated and more pervading evils in the human mind" (*Autobiography* 75), managed, somehow, to father nine children. Harriet Mill must have stood as a constant source of mortification to her husband and eldest son, a pregnant reminder of her husband's illicit desires and behavior, which had little legitimate space within the frame of his rationalist Utilitarianism.

John Stuart Mill's case against his own mother as a stupid, simple woman undeserving of love and respect (Mazlish)—a carryover from his father's attitude—is refracted throughout his work in his overidealization of intellect, which influenced his ideas about which people should have the vote (only the educated); his idealist account of history and human motivation ("it is what men think that determines how they act"); and his negative portrayal of a brutish working class (*Considerations* 14). These themes are especially pronounced and visibly interrelated in his *Considerations on Representative Government*. Throughout his life and writings, he denied a denigrated mother who surely existed and worshipped a brain that probably did not. The genius brain belonged to Harriet Taylor, lifetime friend, lover of sorts, and colleague, eventually his wife. Harriet Taylor was undoubtedly a bright and intelligent woman; certainly her feminism was more sophisticated and developed than Mill's.[4] But it is also clear that Mill exaggerated her intellectual acumen. Harriet Taylor's desexualization and inflated genius would seem to be related much in the same way as Harriet Mill's unavoidable sexuality is tied in with her reported simplemindedness. John Stuart Mill, mirroring his own culture, seems to have had some real-life difficulties in dealing with women as flesh and blood and brain creatures combined. Instead, he resorted to split images. These split images, which weigh heavily on the (m)other, are refracted throughout his political theory in a variety of more subtle and insidious ways.

The wife and (m)other who is "a perpetual dead weight, a drag" (*Subjection* 114) appears in a key and strange passage from *Considerations on Representative Government.* In this particular section of the text, Mill is arguing for a conception of politics that is capable of accommodating the twin needs of order (stability) and progress (change). On his reading, stability itself must be understood as a form of energetic progress, since it is secured by means of ongoing efforts directed against a perpetually encroaching and threatening decay. We must always remember, writes Mill, "that there is an incessant and everflowing current of human affairs toward the worse, consisting of all the follies, all the vices, all the negligences, indolences, and supinenesses of mankind; which is only controlled and kept from sweeping all before it by the exertions which some persons constantly, and others by fits, put forth in the direction of good and worthy objects. . . . A very small diminution of those exertions would not only put a stop to improvement, but would turn the general tendency of things towards deterioration which, once begun, would proceed with increasing rapidity and hence become more and more difficult to check" (22–23). Here, I argue, lies Mill's overall worldview. Immorality is equated with passivity; passivity with decay. Evil can only be controlled by constant exertion directed against the exponential drag effect of decay. Life is a constant struggle against the quicksand of regression, a feminized drag effect evocative of the annihilating (m)other. If civilized Victorian man succumbs to her on occasion, that is only further proof that he must continue to deny, fear, and despise her—through constant vigilance and exertion.

"Politics" for Mill is part of the human cultural enterprise which is strictly set apart from, but also susceptible to, incursions from an irrational and diabolical—and, as we will see, feminized—Nature. The political arena of his liberalism bears the unmistakable representational imprint of a set of needs and practices premised on the denial and fear of the (m)other. Mill's liberalism, most familiar to the readers of *On Liberty,* houses an individual who bears the distinct features of masculine identity: the liberal Everyman is a unitary, disembodied subject whose ego boundaries are strictly drawn and carefully maintained. Without such boundaries, Mill would have been unable to construct and elaborate the public-private distinction which is at the heart of his passionate defense of tolerance in *On Liberty*. The field-independent (autonomous) subject of this work is effectively and affectively capable of maintaining a discrete sense of identity vis-à-vis "fellow" human beings and his society, to whom and to which he is cautiously related. Such an identity, as Mill understood clearly, stood to be threatened in the absence of a self/other demarcation and by means of incursion into its "space" by the undifferentiated and uncivilized proletarian mob. *On Liberty* may be understood to provide such a demarcation and consequent protection.

In short, *On Liberty* is preoccupied with the liberty of a well-differentiated masculine subject who requires a protected zone of thought, expression, and action for his survival and well-being as a masculine subject. Within this protected, but ever-vulnerable, zone, the liberal masculine subject is constituted as a self-sufficient and sovereign entity. His ventures into the sociopolitical arena are maneuvered from this zone. In the absence of specific exceptions, this individual must be protected; that is, left alone. The burden of proof effectively falls on those who would curtail this individual, as Mill's discussion makes clear: "the sole end for which mankind are warranted, individually or collectively, in interfering with the liberty of action of any of their number is self protection" (13). While few of us would quarrel with self-protection as a bottom-line ethical maxim, the real question here has to do with the kind of self that merits and requires protection. Mill's abstract morality of right, centering around a presumed antagonistic relationship between the individual, other subjects, society, and nature, assumes a specifiably masculine aura, one that emerges out of and recapitulates the scene of oppositional conflict with the (m)other.

On this reading the return of the (m)other threatens to clutter the liberal subject's carefully manicured identity and to impede his access to privately generated rights. She poses a fundamental challenge to the nature-culture distinction by straddling it and she threatens to release the lid of the Pandora's box of repressed nature and desire. Effaced maternal origins inhabit the unconscious substratum of the liberal conception of inviolable, centered, unitary egos which are self-generated and self-contained. Egos such as these embody the masculine fantasy of omnipotence and self-sufficiency. In Mill, the denial of maternal origins is never completely successful. (How could it be?) The liberal subject is precariously balanced on the edge of massive, irreparable, chaotic regression. And so we are bound to encounter the repressed (m)other in huge and threatening proportions, ready to swallow up everything in her vindictive wrath. We find this revolting (m)other in "Nature," the flip side of the stupid and powerless (m)other, who is finally getting even: "Nature impales men, breaks them as if on the wheel, casts them to be devoured by wild beasts, burns them to death, crushes them with stones . . . starves them with hunger, freezes them with cold, poisons them by the quick or slow venom of her exhalations, and has hundreds of other hideous deaths in reserve" (463). Mill's linkage of feminized Nature with death and destruction reaches its apex in his description of reproductive sex, effectively "sealing" the association between the (m)other and death. In the same essay, he describes sex as "that clumsy provision which she [nature] has made for that perpetual renewal of animal life, rendered necessary by the prompt termination she puts to it in every individual instance" (463). Mill's wedding of sex and death is embodied in the figure of the (m)other who is rebelling, as she must and will, against her civilized, liberal repression.

These observations from the (m)otherworld prompt a political hermeneutics of suspicion as we approach Mill's feminist essay, *The Subjection of Women*. What we begin to notice in this work is that Mill, in extending his claims for the protection and freedom of liberal men to liberal women, enacts the masculine prerogative of privileged, selfsame identity. For the unitary disembodied subject housed by liberal theory is no abstract subject, appearances to the contrary. His motivation to separate from nature, to observe a "methodologically individualist" terrain; to cultivate a disembodied Reason; to protect himself and similarly constituted subjects from incursion into private "space"; to formulate abstract principles of rights which can be applied, context-blind, to any scene of social conflict—all of this may be traced to a substratum of experiences, fears, and needs which are masculine and, as such, embody the fantasy of clean and ultimate release from the (m)other. This privileging of the masculine subject is endemic in the political theory of J. S. Mill, which aims for a blind and coherent systematicity which is apparently (but only apparently) context-free. Those who "suffer" from the specificity of context-dependence—men and women of the working class and women in general—must make themselves over into the image of the liberal Everyman in order to benefit from the promise of liberalism. To the extent that they are masculinizable, women are accommodated within Mill's feminist framework. When they are not, notably in their embodied capacities as wives, mothers, and working-class laborers, Mill's feminism fails them completely. More precisely, Mill's feminism collapses on the terrain of *difference*.

167

As Zillah Eisenstein, articulating the socialist-feminist critique of Mill's liberalism, has argued, his feminism is a feminism for the exceptional (i.e., privileged) woman (137). But I would add that she is exceptional in terms that go beyond those of class and educational privilege. The exceptional woman, within the terms set by Mill, is also effectively transsexed and regendered, for the terms of her exceptional talent and drive are masculine terms. They include self-discipline (the conquest of inner and outer nature), an individualized and objective cognitive stance, and a clear demarcation between self and other. Mill's feminism, then, may be read as the symptomatic outcome of an unstable set of conflicting ideas about women and difference. That is, while this feminism is *predicated* on difference, it simultaneously *denies* it.

The exceptional woman of *The Subjection of Women* is the female who adopts a masculine posture in the world and toward the (m)other. Her achievement, like that of today's corporate feminist, is predicated on the existence of surrogate (m)others who will labor in her place. Mill tells us in one breath that human beings should "relish their habitual pursuits" (126): this means that we must have some meaningful freedom of vocational choice. In the same text, he informs us that those women who marry have effectively "chosen" a single profession, that of housemistress: "Like a man when he chooses a profession, so, when a woman marries, it may in general be understood that she makes choice of the management of a household, and the bringing up of a family, as the first call upon her exertions, during as many years of her life as may be required for the purpose; and that she renounces, not all other objects and occupations, but all which are not consistent with the requirements of this" (68). The absence of symmetry here between husband and wife is truly astonishing, in spite of Mill's sleight of hand with the concept of "choice." In this scenario, the exceptional woman with *unusual* talent and drive may opt out of her domestic duties, so long as she has made provisions for their fulfillment by other means (68); i.e., hiring others in her place. The underlying logic of this account is unmistakable: the unexceptional woman, especially if she is of modest or low economic means, had better not marry. Put another way, the unexceptional female had better avoid her social designation as a "woman."

Mill seems to have gotten himself into a potential paradox here. Taken literally and consistently pursued, his liberal feminism would annihilate the (m)other by transsexing women into masculine subjects. Without the (m)other, however, there is no masculine subject. He must have her. And so he does. Temporary, if unstable, peace is secured by means of the figure of the exceptional woman, who will adopt the posture of the masculine subject toward the (m)other. The rest of us, in our unexceptional ordinariness, keep the (m)otherworld safely populated. *The Subjection of Women,* I argue, functions at the subtextual level to remind us of our ordinariness and of the sexually differentiated *imperatives* of this ordinariness.

The figure of the exceptional woman, who has transcended difference, still presupposes and requires the grounds of her departure—the rest of us, some of whom will assume her domestic "duties." But this presupposition of the feminized Other is also entailed in another sense: without the (m)other, there is no masculine subject, for she provides the repressed primordial ground of his counterfactual identity. Small wonder, then, that the "feminist" woman must also be extraordinary. Best of all, she poses no threat to the liberal masculine subject. There will, by definition and necessity, never be very many of her; and the terms of excellence and achievement for the very few who do cross over to the "other side" are those of the masculine status quo.

Concluding Thoughts

Reading with and for the (m)other produces a cross-grained reading, one that is attentive to the text, yet oppositional. It is one strategy within the multifaceted feminist effort to develop "womanly" modes of thinking, speaking, writing, and political practice which are simultaneously rooted in and critical of feminine experience. Our relation to the (m)other is a complicated one. The hazards of invoking her are substantial. But the hazards of ignoring her are even more serious: to the extent that we collaborate in her repression, we are replicating the masculine course of action and confining ourselves to a limited and oppressive pool of existing representational resources. The (m)other provides us with a critical means of engaging masculine discourse on its own unsteady, yet largely hegemonic, terrain without getting lost in it; of "returning the masculine to its own language" (Irigaray 80) and perhaps finding our own voices in the process. When we invoke her, we take up our place as the constructed but ever-elusive Other with a view to disengaging that construction from its masculine moorings. To the extent that the (m)other is located and implicated in the "unconscious" of political theory (Flax), she holds significant clues to our understanding, interpretation, and refashioning of that discursive enterprise. More expansively still, she may join ranks with those others "whom society wastes in order to reproduce itself" (Kristeva 31) to question not only the asymmetrical distribution of social rewards and burdens but also the very terms of "human" need, desire, and achievement. In the case of the political and "feminist" theory of John Stuart Mill, the (m)other suggests that those terms are more specifically masculine than human.

By extension, contemporary liberal feminism is similarly vulnerable to the suspicion that the representational ground of its assimilative tactics preempts a more critical disclosure of and resistance to sexism. "How can the double demand—for both equality and difference—be articulated?" (Irigaray 81). This is the political question raised by the discursive and historical fate of the (m)other. Unless and until political theorists take up the full challenge of this question, it must be admitted, as Carole Pateman has recently asserted, that we really have no democratic theory at all.

Notes

Earlier versions and portions of this paper have been delivered to the Eastern Division Fall Conference of the Society for Women in Philosophy, Union College, Schenectady, New York, November 3 and 4, 1984; and to the Annual Meeting of the Western Political Science Association, Eugene, Oregon, March 20–22, 1986. I am grateful to the numerous participants from those sessions for their spirited questions, encouragement, and criticism.

1. On the treatment of women and mothers in political theory, see the following: Clark and Lange, eds., *The Sexism of Social and Political Theory;* Di Stefano, "Masculinity as Ideology in Political Theory"; Elshtain, *Public Man, Private Woman;* Flax, "Political Philosophy and the Patriarchal Unconscious"; O'Brien, *The Politics of Reproduction;* Okin, *Women in Western Political Thought;* and Saxonhouse, *Women in the History of Political Thought.*

2. The article which has really sparked quite a bit of debate on this issue is that by Ruddick, "Maternal Thinking." For an example of how it has been put to use by a political theorist, see Elshtain, "Antigone's Daughters." For a critique of the use of the mother as a critical standard in political discourse, see Dietz, "Citizenship with a Feminist Face."

3. Material for this paper has been taken from a larger and more extensive study of John Stuart Mill and several other political theorists—Di Stefano, "Gender and Political Theory."

4. See Harriet Taylor Mill, "Enfranchisement of Women." For various assessments of Harriet Taylor Mill see the following: Mazlish, *James and John Stuart Mill;* Rose, *Parallel Lives;* Rossi, "Sentiment and Intellect"; and Stillinger, "Introduction."

Works Cited

Chodorow, Nancy. *The Reproduction of Mothering: Psychoanalysis and the Sociology of Gender.* Berkeley: Univ. of California Press, 1978.

Clark, Lorenne, and Lynda Lange, eds. *The Sexism of Social and Political Theory.* Toronto: Univ. of Toronto Press, 1979.

Dietz, Mary. "Citizenship with a Feminist Face: The Problem with Maternal Thinking." *Political Theory* 13 (1985): 19–37.

Dinnerstein, Dorothy. *The Mermaid and the Minotaur: Sexual Arrangements and Human Malaise.* New York: Harper, 1976.

Di Stefano, Christine. "Gender and Political Theory: Masculinity as Ideology in Modern Political Thought." Diss., Univ. of Massachusetts, Amherst, 1984.

———. "Masculinity as Ideology in Political Theory: Hobbesian Man Considered." *Hypatia: Journal of Feminist Philosophy,* special issue of *Women's Studies International Forum* 6 (1983): 633–44.

Eisenstein, Zillah. *The Radical Future of Liberal Feminism.* New York and London: Longman, 1981.

Elshtain, Jean Bethke. "Antigone's Daughters." *Democracy* 2.2 (1982): 46–59.

———. *Public Man, Private Woman: Women in Social and Political Thought.* Princeton: Princeton Univ. Press, 1981.

Flax, Jane. "Political Philosophy and the Patriarchal Unconscious: A Psychoanalytic Perspective on Epistemology and Metaphysics." In *Discovering Reality: Feminist Perspectives on Epistemology, Metaphysics, Methodology, and Philosophy of Science.* Ed. Sandra Harding and Merril B. Hintikka. Dordrecht, Boston, and London: Reidel, 1973. 245–81.

Freud, Sigmund. *Three Essays on the Theory of Sexuality.* Trans. and ed. James Strachey. New York: Avon, 1965.

Irigaray, Luce. "The Power of Discourse and the Subordination of the Feminine." In *This Sex Which Is Not One.* Trans. Carolyn Burke. Ithaca: Cornell Univ. Press, 1985. 68–85.

Kahn, Coppélia. "Excavating 'Those Dim Minoan Regions': Maternal Subtexts in Patriarchal Literature." *Diacritics* 12.2 (1982): 32–41.

Kaplan, E. Ann. "Is the Gaze Male?" In *Powers of Desire: The Politics of Sexuality.* Ed. Ann Snitow et al. New York: Monthly Review, 1983. 309–27.

Kristeva, Julia. "The Ethics of Linguistics." In *Desire in Language.* Ed. Leon S. Roudiez, trans. Thomas Gora et al. New York: Columbia Univ. Press, 1980. 23–35.

Mazlish, Bruce. *James and John Stuart Mill: Father and Son in the Nineteenth Century.* New York: Basic, 1975.

Mill, Harriet Taylor. "Enfranchisement of Women." In *Essays on Sex Equality.* Ed. Alice Rossi. Chicago: Univ. of Chicago Press, 1970. 89–122.

Mill, John Stuart. *The Autobiography of John Stuart Mill.* Ed. John Jacob Coss. New York: Columbia Univ. Press, 1924.

———. *Considerations on Representative Government.* Ed. Currin V. Shields. Indianapolis: Bobbs, 1958.

————. "Nature." In *The Philosophy of John Stuart Mill: Ethical, Political, and Religious*. Ed. Marshall Cohen. New York: Random, 1961.

————. *On Liberty*. Ed. Currin V. Shields. Indianapolis: Bobbs, 1956.

————. *On the Subjection of Women*. Greenwich, Conn.: Fawcett, 1970.

O'Brien, Mary. *The Politics of Reproduction*. Boston and London: Routledge, 1981.

Okin, Susan Miller. *Women in Western Political Thought*. Princeton: Princeton Univ. Press, 1979.

Pateman, Carole. "Women and Democratic Citizenship." The Jefferson Memorial Lectures, Univ. of California, Berkeley, Feb. 1985.

Rose, Phyllis. *Parallel Lives: Five Victorian Marriages*. New York: Random, 1984.

Rossi, Alice. "Sentiment and Intellect: The Story of John Stuart Mill and Harriet Taylor Mill." In *Essays on Sex Equality*. Ed. Alice Rossi. Chicago: Univ. of Chicago Press, 1970. 1–64.

Ruddick, Sara. "Maternal Thinking." *Feminist Studies* 6 (1983): 342–67.

Saxonhouse, Arlene. *Women in the History of Political Thought*. New York: Praeger, 1985.

Stillinger, Jack. "Introduction." *The Early Draft of John Stuart Mill's Autobiography*. Ed. Jack Stillinger. Urbana: Univ. of Illinois Press, 1961.

Fathers, Daughters, Anxiety, and Fiction

CHERYL HERR

Influence and Anxiety

Since the 1973 publication of Harold Bloom's provocative volume *The Anxiety of Influence,* critical discourse about anxiety has centered on the problem that Bloom explores—the fathering through time and in conditions of great tribulation of "lesser" or "shadowed" writers like Keats by forepoets like Milton. Bloom finds the process by which the under-writer discovers a "clinamen" or gap in the super-writer at the heart of poetry-production as well as of identity-formation. Although attacked by many, Bloom's sophisticated study of literary relations opens up an extraordinary number of questions. Do literary traditions other than those of England and America conform to the same patterns of paternity and anxiety that Bloom charts? What similar spiritual and productive trials do writers of prose suffer from? Is the psychoanalytic sphere which Bloom theorizes the ultimately determining one, as opposed to the social sphere, the arena of history, which in the past decade ideological critics have undertaken with increasing vigor to understand? How does the model of father-son relations translate into the experience of the female writer,[1] or of the feminist writer of whatever gender? And how does the putative anxiety of the writer find expression in the widely varying representations of anxiety that form so large—and still so largely unexplored—a topic in literature?

Because it would be impossible to address all of these questions in a single essay, I have chosen to trace a single family line, as it were, from nineteenth-century England to contemporary America and France. Beginning with comments on the representation of anxiety in Freudian discourse and in James Joyce's *Finnegans Wake,* this essay charts the impact on

Donald Barthelme of Joyce-the-Father as well as of HCE-the-anxious-father. Then I explore the influence of Charles Dickens on Joyce, in particular of Dickens's anxious John Jarndyce on the embattled HCE. This line of inquiry turns to the father-daughter relationship in exploring both the life of Joyce's biological daughter, Lucia, and a novel by a writer much engaged with Joyce's work, Hélène Cixous. In her recent fiction *Angst*, a feminist aesthetic produces a fathered work that resists further fathering and, in the offing, attempts to stop the chain of anxiety within narrative representation. Along the way, the map of anxiety in literature enlarges to involve the social within and around Bloom's model of psycholiterary influence. The several models and dimensions of anxiety on which I draw suggest that a useful examination of the topic, in literature as well as in life, must be committed to a nontotalizing and aggressively feminist approach to self and affect.

I might add that the absence of attention to female writers in the first half of this essay is intentional; it mirrors the conditions out of which women have had to construct their own emotions as writers and as readers. After all, it has not been until recently that serious, empowering study has been made of women's affective states (other than "hysteria") and of the relationship between women's experiences of the world and the generation of their anxiety, their rage, their desire. Many feminists, finally able to address these issues in gender-specific ways, have concentrated on recovering women's history; my aim here is to reproject the historical ground in which human emotions were problematized, primarily by men who failed to notice or to acknowledge that all persons could not be assimilated to the same masculinist model of behavior. Some readers may want to skip over the first half of this essay, to turn directly to the portions on Lucia Joyce and Cixous; for my own part, following a male-to-female genealogy has unpacked the sense in which parenting, as historically and currently socialized, produces anxieties (and their cousin, resentment) in challengingly complex ways. What I have traced is a positive theorizing of resentment and anxiety as patriarchal social conditions—and the correlative absence of female voices within the standard and putatively gender-free theories.

The Father of Anxiety

Throughout his writings, Sigmund Freud moves again and again over the terrain of anxiety—its formation and determinants, its symptoms, its function. Initially committed to viewing anxiety as transformed libido, Freud

174

turned rather late to a reconsideration of this theory, which appeared in his small volume, *The Problem of Anxiety* (1925). "What we clearly want," he laments in an essentialist mood, "is to find something that will tell us what anxiety really is, some criterion that will enable us to distinguish true statements about it from false ones. But this is not easy to get. Anxiety is not so simple a matter." And Freud decides to "assemble, quite impartially, all the facts that we know about anxiety without expecting to arrive at a fresh synthesis" (Freud 132). It is as though Freud realized for the hundredth time that he still was uncertain about this emotion—and determined to work through his dilemma. Freud begins his inquiry confidently enough—"Anxiety, then, is in the first place something that is felt"—but he soon records a simple failure of vocabulary. The "unpleasurable character" of anxiety, he says, "seems to have a note of its own—something not very obvious, whose presence is difficult to prove yet which is in all likelihood there." Having established his inability to represent discursively for the reader a feeling that he has experienced, Freud turns immediately to the language of biology: he discusses what he calls the "motor innervations" or "processes of discharge" which "play a part in the general phenomenon of anxiety" and proceeds to explore the part played by birth trauma in initiating anxious feelings (Freud 132–33). What interests me here is the oscillation between scientific labeling and a perceived linguistic inadequacy. Never is Freud more intriguing than when he tries to convince himself and us of something that he does not know, that is, when he begins, however tentatively, to write fiction.

Freud's uneasy approach to a theory of anxiety finds tonal echoes in most discussions of this affect. Much more recently, Roland Barthes, in whose *A Lover's Discourse* what can only be called an anxious anguish repeatedly surfaces, writes, "If there is such a figure as 'Anxiety,' it is because the subject sometimes exclaims (without any concern for the clinical sense of the word): 'I am having an anxiety attack!' Anxiety, Anguish . . . just as this aria is identified, memorized, and manipulated through its *incipit* ('When I am laid,' *'Pleurez, mes yeux,' 'Lucevan le stelle,' 'Piangerò la mia sorte'*), so the figure takes its departure from a turn of phrase, a kind of verse, refrain, or cantillation which articulates it in the darkness" (Barthes 5). At the same time, Barthes displays Freud's tendency to evoke anxiety not as a figure or name or affect but rather as an objective reality. Barthes imagines a lover waiting for his beloved to return to their hotel: "The anxieties are already here, like the poison already prepared . . . they merely wait for a little time to pass in order to be able to declare themselves with some propriety. . . . Anxiety mounts; I observe its progress, like Socrates chatting (as I am reading) and feeling the cold of the hemlock rising in his body; I *hear it* identify itself moving up, like an inexorable figure, against the background of *the things that are here*" (Barthes 29). Still tossing us the notion of "figure" which is central to his concept of subjectivity and which maps the terrain of the Real, Barthes speaks of anxiety as a tangible but proliferating entity, something that demands that we define, measure, and then suffer as it just eludes our grasp. In a sense, anxiety might be taken as the Ur-figure for all representations; it is never what it seems to be; it insists that we recognize it (as we are reading, to echo Barthes's formulation above) and respect its integrity even beyond our own.

Although the effort to deal with anxiety continues to exercise contemporary writers as well as current psychologists, Freud remains the great theorist of this emotion partly because his writings do not limit themselves to a single explanatory model. On the one hand, Freud sought a universal *cause* for all forms of anxiety; on the other, he experimented with a semiotic model of its production. He noted the sense in which anxiety is both signified and signifier, both the thing under consideration and the trope for that phenomenon. Freud depicts anxiety, in conformity with this semiotic model, as a productive activity; anxious experience forms the self, whether we consider the definitive event to be the child's witnessing of the primal scene of parental copulation or the earlier pain of separation from the mother at birth. Freud's two models seem to me of great value in probing questions of identity and consciousness in twentieth-century fiction and its precursors. *Finnegans Wake,* Barthelme's *The Dead Father,* and *Bleak House* echo Freudian representations of anxiety and help to illuminate the historical nature of this emotion in their own anxious portrayals of it. The uses and feelings of women characters within those fictions sadly illustrate a manipulative stylization of the feminine when viewed against the projected foreground of writerly progeny like Cixous.

The Anxious Father in *Finnegans Wake*

In many respects, *Finnegans Wake* is explicitly about anxiety. Most if not all of the confrontations that take place in this narrative cast the contending characters into some equivalent of a panic attack. Accosted by the Cad in the Park, HCE manifests extreme distress, stammering, in a kind of anxiety of utterance, his innocence of any "municipal sin" (5:14) and worrying that a simple request for the correct time may result in his being murdered. ALP's chief characteristic in the lovely "Anna Livia Plurabelle" section may be rippling beauty, but her most persistent activities are her nervous efforts publicly to exonerate her husband and privately to distract him from his worries. Hence, ALP's "untitled mamafesta" (104:4), which has many provisional titles, and which is in some sense the Letter by which she hopes, anxiously, to free HCE from his anxiety, is called "The Augusta Angustissimost for Old Seabeastius' Salvation" (104:5–6). Just as we cannot ultimately separate the "mamafesta" from any other manifestation of ALP, so we find here, as in the Barthean passages quoted earlier, that her virtually non-gender-specific anxiety merges with or intensifies into a state of anguish which the name "Angustissimost" speaks; related affects echo one another's names and signal the mechanism by which culture produces emotions within a closed linguistic system that determines how and what we feel. Literature, especially works from the traditional canon, takes a privileged place within our culture's language and thus provides many of the terms through which we live. One of the messages explored in *Finnegans Wake* is the complex interarticulation of those terms within the dreams that our culture produces; much as dreams mediate the anxiety of the subject, so, it may be argued, fiction mediates the anxiety of the culture; the *Wake* insists that we recognize both processes. It may also be posited that whereas many literary works shut down the flow of distressing messages and failed mediations—recuperate this social static into comforting narrative closures—Joyce's writings relentlessly resist the management and containment that both individuals and the general culture exercise.

Hence, like their parents, Joyce's Shem and Shaun enact anxiety. They anxiously and hopelessly assert their independence from family and from each other; they also try to win their sister Issy's regard in an endless contest of words and will. Meanwhile, these activities are presented in a text that constantly transforms each unnamed siglum—that is, one of the shorthand figures that Joyce used in his notes to indicate various character-types—(McHugh, *Sigla* 10) into one after another named character: Λ becomes Shaun becomes Jaun becomes Yawn becomes Don Giovanni, St. Michael, Abel, Chuff, Judas, the Mookse, the Ondt, Othello, and Hermes Trismegistus. Notably, each such provisional name brings with it a rivalry that refigures a principal theme of the book—cultural contest—while insistently inscribing anxiety into narrated behavior. In fact, it would be difficult to imagine a narrative that more effectively produces interpretive anxiety in its most attentive readers as an echo of its own themes and structures. I would argue, in fact, that one of the major accomplishments of the *Wake* is its ability constantly to refresh the reader's initial distress at entering her or his culture, the code systems of which do not overtly cohere into a meaningful reality but are naturalized by the individual only through the maturing process. Reading the *Wake* refreshes, then, the failure of linguistic representation fully to contain the anxiety generated by this alternative primal scene of socialization, of forced entry into and by the culture.

Thus, critical approaches to the *Wake* vary enormously, as readers play out the competitions of the volume. Yet all readers do not discover in the *Wake* this work of the anxiety-production, nor do all readers agree on the affects represented in the narrative. Margot Norris, for instance, both tracks the presence of anxiety in the characters and argues that guilt and fear are the predominant emotions as well as in many respects the motive forces of this fiction. Her analysis of these feelings invokes the edenic and Oedipal paradigms through which she finds the fiction repeatedly depicting the Fall of the Father. This fall becomes the psychic equivalent of the supposed trauma in which the child first achieves knowledge of parental copulation and reproduction. As Norris playfully observes, the primal sin and the primal scene cannot be extricated (44–47); the *Wake* thwarts our discovery of an actual first event, a source for the character's guilt and fear, even while portraying many affects for which readers might justifiably seek a generative cause.

In Norris's influential assessment of Wakean psychohistory, we must, I believe, emphasize the encompassing term of anxiety, which, as Freud was uncomfortably aware, cannot be reduced to either guilt or fear. Joyce's text often gestures toward this ambiguous, amorphous emotional state by explicitly naming it. For instance, in chapter 4, the restless dreaming Earwicker is referred to as "he conscious of enemies, a kingbilly whitehorsed on anxious seat" (75:15–18). King Billy (William III), one of the historical mascots of the Northern Irish Orangemen, was the victor at the Battle of the Boyne in 1690. Adaline Glasheen notes that a lead statue of William, seated on a horse that was often painted white by patriotic Ulstermen, survived in Dublin's College Green until 1836, when a party of Catholics blew the king off his mount (Glasheen 309). HCE's enemies thus include not only those citizens of Dublin who seem determined to expose his ambiguous public sin but also the Catholic majority in Ireland; his anxiety emanates from his exposure to historical conflicts beyond his control, conflicts that regularly and repeatedly have transformed themselves from religious terms to political ones and then back again in a virtual parody of textual indeterminacy. But we must also note that HCE's anxiety defines him; his ubiquitous initials, which recur throughout the narrative in many covert forms, partake of his state of mind and form the only way in which the reader can know him at this moment in the fiction: "he conscious of enemies." Notably, HCE's problem here is not so much guilt as his anxious isolation in a place likely to be dangerous. It is fair to add that the religious debates in Ireland do not so much create his anxiety as they become one of the many situations into which his floating emotions insert themselves. The primal scene engenders specifically historical formulations at many points in the *Wake*.

HCE's consciousness of enemies in fact produces a "long list . . . to be kept on file of all abusive names he was called" (71:5–6). Although commentators on the *Wake* have been surprisingly quiet about the economic content of the work, this list of 111 names includes many that emphasize HCE's embattled economic condition. Hiding behind the "faminebuilt walls" of an impoverished Ireland, HCE is called "Beat My Price," "Twelve Months Aristocrat," "Salary Grab," "O'Phelim's Cutprice," "Ruin of the Small Trader," and "Woolworth's Worst" (71). These and other labels place him at every level of the social scale, from aristocrat through merchant down to workman. Like many passages in the *Wake,* the names suggest an economic hierarchy in relation to which HCE anxiously jockeys for position; his distress emanates in part from a profoundly social separation anxiety in that HCE seems to have no self-evidently correct structural position in his world. This displaced quality mirrors the affects associated with the loss of maternal plenitude in its most idealized state. From observing this complex of negative feelings and actual losses, it is a short step to explaining HCE's attributing his abusive names to his enemies in a process of projective identification: HCE resents his fellow citizens, so he portrays them as resenting him. He also compulsively resents himself and dreams his victimization again and again, without resolution. Framing, overdetermining, and undermining the personal side of HCE's experience, anxiety and resentment interact in the "faminebuilt" (71:2) setting of a history that constantly shifts from one temporal context to another. As recent readers of the *Wake* have noticed, any attempt to center the fiction's cause in HCE's alleged crime and in a fictive reproduction of some primal scene or original sin will come to grief. Joyce's master work constantly refigures its apparent cause, and hence the presumed origin of anxiety, from one historical or cultural position to another. The dream work also conflates anxiety with other emotions (guilt, fear, resentment) that cannot be thoroughly disentangled as readers seek to isolate motives, causes, and present conditions. The difficulties attending Freud's efforts to isolate anxiety in order to define it repeat themselves in the interpretive problems posed by the *Wake*.

In response to these multiple complexities, I think that we would be wrong to rest content in a now-predictable decentering, in a model of anxiety as displacement, deferral, or semiosis, for the narrative also teases us with frequent representations of pseudoprimal moments. Like Freudian children about to be frightened by an illicit view of the parental bed ("when we were jung and easily freudened"—115:22–23), in Book III readers of the *Wake* view the lovemaking of HCE and ALP (or, if you will, of Mr. and Mrs. Porter) from four different positions. Like Earwicker's self-exposure in Phoenix Park, which may or may not have happened, and which may or may not have been a simple answering of the need to urinate, this lovemaking has its ambiguous moments. For instance, when the parents awaken to the cry of one of their children, the anxiety of the various characters is spoken by the presiding figure of Mark, who, repeating the child's moment of psychic injury, is watching the parents in bed. "Do you not must want to go somewhere on the present? Yes, O pity! At earliest moment! That prickly heat feeling! Forthink not me spill it's at always so guey" (570:26–28). HCE's untimely urination in Phoenix Park, which was regarded publicly as self-exposure or worse, repeats itself here in a condensation of HCE's dream about the park event with his son's dream. Anxiety about wetting the bed or about having a wet dream prevails as the voyeurism of Mark and the childlike reader slides into a tour guide's view of the landscape (which is also the river ALP and the mountainous HCE); the vista of the parental bed is finally the terrain of history, which elicits Mark's cautious words: "Do not show ever retrorsehim . . . till that you become quite crimstone in the face! Beware! guaardafew! It is Stealer of the Heart! I am anxious in regard you should everthrown your sillarsalt" (570:33–36). The reader stands warned against viewing parental copulations without taking proper precautions against bad luck, against the "crimstone" of punishment (brimstone) and shame (crimson "in the face"); at the very least, we must throw some salt over our shoulders. Looking itself is dangerous, especially looking backwards. Among other things, this passage warns against the kind of returning or *turning back* that got Lot's wife and Orpheus into so much trouble. But *going forward* takes us from the prickly precursor of some bodily flow to the flowing Anna Livia, both on the following page and at the end of the *Wake*. The unknowable future, which triggers worry here, contaminates the ever-anxious and irretrievable past.

ALP's final monologue moves from her last efforts at helping HCE to her acquiescence to the primal father who is both HCE and Death. Saying yes to death, ALP testifies to the (male-centered) integrity of the familial unconscious when she enacts the anxiety dream that her child had experienced in Book III; her comforting of the child echoes her own final words: "Hear are no phanthares in the room at all, avikkeen. No bad bold faathern, dear one" (565:19–20). Like a traumatized child who thinks the father is harming the mother in bed, ALP the daughter/mother discovers death to be "cold mad feary father" (628:2) who is also her husband. In this regard, it is of interest that the word "avikkeen," which phoneticizes the Irish term for "my little son" (McHugh, *Annotations* 565), imbeds in its structure the word "keen," with its attendant paraphernalia of ritual mourning. ALP's mourning cannot be fully resolved, but it can be worked through to a large extent. Because HCE has been portrayed as the principal cause of ALP's anxieties, her deep resentment of the pain he has produced in her surfaces therapeutically in the last few pages of the book; but having witnessed a final time to the father's responsibility, having cut its losses and acknowledged a tentative source, anxiety no longer reproduces itself in *Wake*an narrative terms, and the text ends. This banishment of anxiety would be in keeping with the primal trauma theory, in which to recognize the origin is to relieve the symptom. And yet, sexual anxiety, the child's anxiety over bedwetting, worry over untimely ejaculation, and the sickness unto death serve throughout the narrative to unite character and society, the landscape and the flow of history. The behavioral model that seeks an original event to explain the ubiquitous presence of anxiety in human life cannot account for these many transformations. Rather, an alternative model, in which anxiety is both signifier and signified, in which it is the experience and the unknown (the primal unseen) of the text, must be evoked to account for the dimensions of anxiety repetition that exceed the admitted concern in *Finnegans Wake* with sons who see their parents' lovemaking, with the child's simultaneous insertion into the narrative of sexuality and the narrative of self.

Like Father, like Son: Barthelme

Barthelme's often-acknowledged debt to Joyce provides a ready transition from discussion of the centripetal HCE to discussion of the character of the Dead Father. Certainly Barthelme has thought a great deal about the influence of the Irish writer on his fiction; as Jerome Klinkowitz notes, the later author "once said that Joyce's *Finnegans Wake* should be taken as part of the landscape, around which the reader's life could be slowly appreciated, like one's home or neighborhood" (Bellamy 45).[2] In the interview that follows Klinkowitz's statement, Barthelme speaks even more to my point.

> Klinkowitz: In Richard Schickel's *New York Times Magazine* piece last year, you were reported as saying that "The principle of collage is the central principle of all art in the twentieth century in all

media." Would you care to expand and perhaps tell me how it specifically applies to fiction?

Barthelme: I was probably wrong, or too general. I point out however that New York City is or can be regarded as a collage, as opposed to, say, a tribal village in which all of the huts (or yurts, or whatever) are the same hut, duplicated. The point of collage is that unlike things are stuck together to make, in the best case, a new reality. This new reality, in the best case, may be or imply a comment on the other reality from which it came, and may be also much else. It's an *itself*, if it's successful: Harold Rosenberg's "anxious object," which does not know whether it's a work of art or a pile of junk. (Maybe I should have said that anxiety is the central principal of all art in the etc., etc.?) (51–52)

Whether the anxiety is that of influence, of interpretation, or of personal trauma, Barthelme's equation of anxiety and art attests to the condition of postmodern writing, its interminable having-been-fathered and its inherited efforts to make from that derivative status something original.

In *The Dead Father*, Barthelme's extremely funny novel about parent-child antagonism, the complex resentments shared by the Dead Father and his son Thomas represent the anxiety both of fathering and of being a son who wants to usurp the father's role. When the gigantic parent, whose death does not notably hinder his ability to walk, talk, and irritate his children, finally submits to burial by bulldozer, Barthelme's novel ends. When the father really dies, after all, he no longer produces anxiety in Thomas. (Another way of thinking about this, however, is to see the text of culture as coordinate with the paternal text so that when the story ends Thomas moves out of anxiety and out of narrative space; when the text ends, so does he.) But while the Dead Father is unburied, Thomas manifests *Wake*an nervousness; asked by the Father to "explain" himself, Thomas says rather that he always stutters in response to this request and asks the father to let him talk about, say, giraffes. Unfortunately, discussion of giraffe behavior, especially the herd's isolation of elderly male animals, offends the Dead Father, and Thomas agrees to provide the "basic data-tata" of his life (74). The predictable facts of his brutal schooling, his military induction, and his unfortunate marriages reinforce a key joke in the narrative. Thomas, anxious to kill off his parent once and for all, cannot at the same time dispose of the cultural systems that have produced the father's sons, and these vital cultural systems *are* the Father. As the Father tells us, his prodigious dissemination has created all of Western civilization—from the electric can opener to class hierarchy to warfare.

Hence, when Julie asks the Father whether he ever wanted to paint, he responds, "It was not necessary . . . because I am the Father. All lines my lines. All figure and all ground mine, out of my head. You take my meaning." Julie responds, "We had no choice" (28).

If the Dead Father thus writes all historical resentment and creates all anxiety, we might expect to find in him some central traumatic moment, some appropriately masculinist "click," that initiates the anxiety of culture, and Barthelme does not disappoint us. When Thomas succeeds in forcing the Father to relinquish his precious keys, the parent falls into a *Wake*an reverie of death-fear that includes the words: "AndI understand but list, list, let's go back. To the wetbedding. To the damp dream. AndI a oneoh-sevenyearold boy, just like the rest of them" (213). This earliest event recalled by the Dead Father figures as the anxious moment of his own movement into a selfhood which is also sonhood, a dissemination without engendering. It seems important, too, that the Father twice conflates a conjunction and the first-person pronoun: "AndI" suggests the Lacanian formulation "n + 1," which signifies, among other things, the movement of the individual consciousness into the prestructures of social life. Even the Father experiences himself as derivative and explained by something occurring in the unrecoverable past. Earlier, in a significant role reversal, Thomas tells the Dead Father a bedtime story. In this tale, a Great Father Serpent poses for a son a riddle which has for its answer the stammered word "murderinging." The Serpent writes the word, but the son pro- nounces it and wants to do the "murderinging" (60). In a typically *Wake*an maneuver, Barthelme makes us identify the Dead Father with both of the story's characters. This oscillation persists, for throughout the story Thomas increasingly bears the mantle of parenthood and the resentment of those he rules. Fathered by Joyce's writings, Barthelme's narrative finds its theme in the Bloomian anxiety of influence; *The Dead Father*, in its dual modeling of anxiety, shows us a world in which personal and communal dread endlessly anticipate each other in the social text, a fiction dominated by men.

Hence, I must take issue with readers like Robert Con Davis, whose essay on Barthelme argues that he "accomplishes nothing less than a major redefinition of what the father in fiction is" (69). Davis concludes that, "nearly abjuring comprehension, *The Dead Father* hurtles toward blissful transport" out of a narrative tradition bound to sense-making and structure (181–82). I remain unconvinced, however, because it seems to me precisely Barthelme's point that despite the play of language and meaning and all of the other destablizations of this postmodern text, the figure of the Father resonates endlessly in the reciprocal anxiety experienced by pater and offspring. Further, in the explicit terms of its obeisance to Joyce, Barthelme's novel makes no effort to cast off the presence of HCE as a determinant of fictional representation (though ALP leaves little or no trace) to transcend the presence of Joyce as an unavoidable, morbid, goading, engendering forebear. The most significant evidence for this position is that without the *Wake*, we could not red *The Dead Father* even as Davis encourages us to. If anything, Barthelme's ludic orientation toward the Father's presence and absence replays the Freudian grandson's *Fort!-Da!* efforts to control the Joycean narrative in which the later author must uncomfortably find his place.[3]

Dickens and Anxiety

Into this literary genealogy I would add Dickens's *Bleak House* because, as Mark Spilka has demonstrated, Joyce's debt to Dickens is much greater than has been suspected. Joyce's indebtedness to any great writer can be measured in part by his tendency to send-up the fathers who inscribed his aesthetic sensibility (can one reasonably argue that Joyce is as exercised by *any* literary foremother?), and Joyce parodies both Dickens's sentimentality and his proliferation of details. Even so, Joyce does not mask what he learned from Dickens about the handling of minor characters, textual coincidence, and eccentricity in all forms. Another reason to discuss this sublime encyclopedic text is that its panoramic analysis of social relations suggests that neither the public nor the private can stand alone as a full explanation of human behavior and emotion. And *Bleak House* presents us with one of literature's most delightfully anxious characters, John Jarndyce, while it depicts subjectivity in a way that influenced the conception of selfhood held by Freud's patients and by Freud himself.

A kind and fatherly guardian, Jarndyce participates quietly in many directly philanthropic activities and often shows us his chief peculiarity, which is his sensitivity to the changing weather. As he explains to Richard, "I am always conscious of an uncomfortable sensation now and then when the wind is blowing in the east" (49). He assents to Richard's diagnosis of rheumatism, but Jarndyce's problem is clearly more than physical. It is associated with his refusal to let people thank him for helping them. Ada recalls having heard that Jarndyce once disappeared for three months rather than suffer someone's gratitude. Jarndyce's efforts to keep his charities unacknowledged, his frequent retreats to his den or "Growlery," and his displacing worries into a seemingly rheumatic symptom form an obviously anxiety-produced avoidance pattern. But it must be emphasized that Jarndyce is a man whose personal wealth allows him to be indifferent to many of the workings of Chancery. About what is such a privileged person anxious? What relationship between personal psychology and social logic is Dickens asserting?

To answer these questions, we must look at Jarndyce's structural position in the story that Esther and an unnamed Editor struggle to compose. He is, of course, much like HCE and the Dead Father in being the exemplary symbolic parent, even more so because Jarndyce is in no sense a literal father. But Esther herself, perhaps because of her earlier engagement to Jarndyce, resists calling him by any paternal name. "[T]o me," she says, "he is what he has ever been, and what name can I give to that? . . . I feel towards him as if he were a superior being" (664). Nonetheless, Jarndyce acts as a surrogate father to his orphaned cousins, a surrogate spouse to Esther in her role as "Dame Durden," a friend to Rick, and a rival with Rick for Ada's affections. He is a kind of paternal putty, filling the social cracks and holes produced by the misfortunes of life in Dickens's London. Like HCE and the Dead Father, he is at once the necessary angel of the narrative and a response by the story to the historical anxieties that produced it.

Those anxieties are portrayed in *Bleak House* in character after character, but it must also be recognized that often anxiety appears to have been transformed into resentment; at least, the two emotions contend for prominence in the narrative. For example, Caddy Jellyby's anger over the trim tidiness of Esther and Ada expresses her jealousy of the natives of Borrioboola-Gha, who occupy her mother's attentions, and voices the resentment often felt by the Dickensian disfranchised toward the privileged members of society. Mrs. Pardiggle's children, better cared for than the Jellybys, express the same resentment toward her dominance over their minds and allowances as do the pitiful victims of Mrs. Pardiggle's businesslike, charitable tyranny. The man from Shropshire, whose agnomen expresses his pathetic alienation within the aggressive urban setting of London, eloquently explains the reasons for his resentment of Chancery. The ubiquitous and obnoxious Smallweeds all resent one another. And Richard signals the son's anxious distrust of the father when he resentfully argues that for all of Jarndyce's avoidance of the Chancery connection, the benefactor is nonetheless unavoidably implicated in its machinations. Richard questions: "If I have the misfortune to be under that influence, so has he. If it has a little twisted me, it may have a little twisted him, too. . . . You know it taints everybody. You have heard him say so fifty times. Then why should *he* escape?" (398). Richard asks us to ponder how it is that the ever-amiable Jarndyce can be both inside and outside society—

both a victim of Chancery's abuses, however remotely, and a being who has escaped the resentful attitudes that are a hallmark of the London milieu in *Bleak House*. Jarndyce's worries importantly represent this problem for us; his wind references attribute his distinguishing emotion to a natural or external cause. Yet it is not extrasocietal nature, some imaginary outside, that produces Jarndyce; he is rather a composite of cultural possibilities—or, better, of needs that are not met by the current system. To keep pace with his elaborately plotted and ever-mounting inscription into an uneasy society, we are presented with several ways to write his anxiety— the wind, the Growlery, panicky escape, philanthropic exertions, even the socially inappropriate expression of his tender passion for his surrogate daughter. These symptoms are both signifiers born from society's discontents and the signs, the emotions, that constitute Jarndyce's identity. In addition, the resentment that Jarndyce does not let himself express, resentment over his having to fill the gaps and sustain an authoritarian system that has broken him, finds expression only through the children whom he gathers around him and with whose plights he fully, endlessly empathizes.

To trace the character of Jarndyce through the text of *Bleak House* and to follow the tendrils linking his emotions to social forces is to adopt what is at the very least a semiotic model of anxiety, which obviates the findings of a specific *cause* and which de-emphasizes the force of psychological pressures in favor of social ones. Of course, we cannot ultimately undo the dialectic of psyche and society, and Dickens's narrative does not naively suggest that we can do so. Rather, as in *Finnegans Wake*, the alternative trauma-model of anxiety also figures in *Bleak House*. In this regard, readers have always recognized the paternal role of Chancery. The legal system as Dickens presents it in a profound sense fathers not only the wards of the court, Ada and Richard, but also the abandoned Esther and even the John Jarndyce of whose parentage so little is said in the narrative. The masculinist Wiglomeration of Chancery, as the reader is soon made aware, always causes a shift in the wind, a fact that neatly expresses Jarndyce's evident injury at being born in a cultural machine that remains inexplicable, repressive, and grimly efficient in its task of producing conformity at the cost of psychic health. Similarly, the fever that Jo brings with him out of Tom-All-Alone's and into Esther's home has as one of its symptoms a restless apprehension. That Chancery is the source of this illness is quite clear; the court literally constructs the despairing occupants of Tom-All-Alone's. Rewarding extensive comparison with the *Wake*, *Bleak House* replays again and again the coerced child's eager but puzzled confrontation with the parent; all of these variations find a locus in Chancery, the model parent in whose courts the primal scene is witnessed, in all senses, repeatedly. That scene, long before the era of deconstruction, was that of dissemination, the endless fathering of legal documents. In the courtroom of Chancery, productive engendering and semiotic activity play out the intertwining of Freud's two models of anxiety. Richard, the damaged child of Chancery, cannot forgive its primal semiotic sin, for in viewing the repetitious scene of his own begetting, Richard identifies himself as part of the social patrix (sans mother) and willingly acquiesces to his own destruction. He becomes, in effect, the delegated voice for a discontent, possibly emanating from deep inside the parenting system, that is so painfully at odds with legal discourse that it must be laid to rest.

In some sense, then, the model of anxiety-production as semiosis emerges again *out of* the trauma-explanation of anxiety. Like *Finnegans Wake*, *Bleak House* does not allow us to separate cause and effect, or the mind and the forces that produce it. That is to say, it is not possible for us to assign blame without recognizing that the determining fathers are themselves behaving according to some complex but hidden coercion that manifests itself in legalistic rigidity and a dogmatism from which no one in the narrative really escapes. Any supposedly initiating primal scene is also a sign of a prior traumatization; a post-structuralist cliché, this conclusion also sadly holds true for the multidimensioned psychohistory that Dickens was recomposing in his novel—a real historical past, real individual pain. Nonetheless, when, in the final pages of Dickens's story, Esther asserts that from the day on which she became the mistress of her own Bleak House the wind never again blew out of the east, we are not surprised, given that the narrative has neatly resolved many of its problems. That activity of shutting down the anxiogenic infinite regress of personal and social faultfinding is the novel's (and Chancery's) reason for being. Nonetheless, although the wind has ceased to shift, the first change that Esther and Alan make in their new home is to add "a little Growlery" (664) for Jarndyce; the sign of anxiety is reestablished even though the confusions and resentments which produced that anxiety have been shifted to other spheres, pushed outside the narrative back into history.

Anxiety and Resentment

I have noted in passing the complex interrelations between anxiety and resentment in Dickens, Joyce, and Barthelme partly because a reader like Fredric Jameson has found nineteenth-century fiction to be definitively marked by what, following Nietzsche, he calls *"ressentiment."* In *The Political Unconscious,* Jameson argues that *ressentiment* be regarded as a fundamental ideological component in Victorian literature (Jameson 201–5). Using Gissing as his major illustration, Jameson also discovers in Dickens the presentation of a class-based resentment that the fiction transforms in various ways into a moral system; this system *contains* the resentment of the privileged felt by the disfranchised by, for instance, encoding philanthropy as a moral duty. Thus the underprivileged work their revenge not in outright rebellion but by writing part of the script by which the upper class lives. They delegate some of their negative feelings in ways that reap instant reward from a guilty system that does not entirely know itself and hence can be manipulated.

Nietzsche's deeply cynical and psychologically on-target commentary on *ressentiment,* which is scattered throughout *The Genealogy of Morals* and *The Will to Power,* is part of his critique of Christianity. In the notebook jottings of 1887 and 1888, Nietzsche wrote about what he called *"the psychological problem of Christianity.*—The driving force is: *ressentiment,* the popular uprising, the revolt of the underprivileged" (Nietzsche 108). But this force, he speculates, has been suppressed. "A doctrine and religion of 'love' suppresses feelings of rivalry, of *ressentiment,* of envy—the all too natural feelings of the underprivileged—it even deifies a life of slavery, subjection, poverty, sickness, and inferiority for them under the ideal of humility and obedience. This explains why the ruling classes . . . have at all times upheld the cult of selflessness" (Nietzsche 201), which thus becomes a mask for its opposite. One thinks of Harold Skimpole's published journal, in which he labels Jarndyce "the Incarnation of Selfishness" (629). Esther's (read Jarndyce's) outrage over this assessment aside, Nietzsche provides for us the lens through which Jarndyce's self*less*ness is more accurately seen as a form of self*ish*ness. As the unreflective proponent of a system of personal charity that sustains his own class dominance, Jarndyce is the alter ego of Scrooge, who resented demands that he be charitable until his own anxiety about death and dispossession convinced him to embrace a doctrine of love. The Dead Father insists that he never wanted to take up the burden of authority appropriate to his role; he did so, he says, "for the good of all." In a sense, he is right, for the laws he claims to have written finally produce his own displacement. The son who serves the Dead Father suppresses his resentment and by doing so controls him, at least for a time.

Similarly, in *Finnegans Wake,* we find the resentments shared by all the family members reflected in the encounters that the dream presents (Mookse and Gripes, Archdruid and St. Patrick, and so on). These contests, often explicitly representing the class tensions that both Dickens and Joyce witnessed, generate much of the dis-ease of the characters and much of the anxious power of the work. I think that the reader of the *Wake* often experiences anxiety partly because many of these conflicts are never resolved but only displaced, from family life to international relations, from historical "period" to historical "period," from nineteenth-century fiction to twentieth-century representation; surely this readerly situation may be found in heightened as well as highly masked ways in the reactions of critics in Joyce's own time. Enhancing this anxiogenic effect is the language of the *Wake,* which makes it impossible for the reader to determine who is speaking, what the speaker wants, when and where the action is taking place, and what it all means: like a tortured analysand struggling to get free from inexplicable symptoms, the reader repeatedly asserts interpretations that fall short of creating ultimate clarity. I have more than once heard major Joyceans acknowledge that after tackling the *Wake* for perhaps twenty years, they had decided to give up, at least for a time, to sustain themselves against the endless vortex of disappointment that follows each foray into the narrative. This response seems to me quite understandable, even though the same critics also speak eloquently about the joys of *Wake*an language and wit. Anxiety and resentment, whether experienced or merely represented and appreciated at a distance, are not incompatible with pleasure; if they were, there would be no literature at all.

Exploring the emotional models that establish a significant continuity between nineteenth- and twentieth-century writing helps, among other things, to explain or at least position Joyce's rapid changes between the voices of children and the voice of the parent, the fluctuation of highfalutin tones and working-class rhythms, the puzzling consistency with which historical and socioeconomic issues intrude into the world of "personal" dream and desire. To try to understand the *Wake*—as we often do—mostly by reference to the formal experimentations of high modernism, rules out before we begin a needful attention to the nineteenth-century, male-centered conception of consciousness and personality that Joyce wove in and around the figures populating the narrative. So it is that the stuttering HCE, an anxious product of his resentment-marked society and the progenitor of the Dead Father, is remarkably like John Jarndyce, his very name a stammer in the text of culture. So it is that the mixture of anxiety and resentment surfaces in the works of Dickens, Joyce, and Barthelme as they respond to the specific *fatherings,* both literary and historical, that produced their works.

One insistent psychological interpreter of the phenomena I am tracing in literary terms is the neo-Freudian, Harry Stack Sullivan, who provided in the 1940s a model of the social production of anxiety that reformulates Nietzsche's insight into the mechanism of *ressentiment*. Another reason to turn to Sullivan at this point in my essay is that his 1948 article, "The Meaning of Anxiety in Psychiatry and Life," specifically comments on the lack of clarity and other inadequacies in Freud's *The Problem of Anxiety*. As Sullivan interprets Freud, anxiety is produced interpersonally, not, strictly speaking, by the passive viewing of a primal scene: "In extreme abstract, the theory holds that we come into being as persons as a consequence of unnumbered interpersonal fields of force, and that we manifest intelligible human processes only in such interpersonal fields. Like any mammalian creature, man is endowed with the potentialities for undergoing *fear*, but in almost complete contradistinction to infrahuman creatures, man in the process of becoming a person always develops a great variety of processes directly related to the undergoing of *anxiety*" (234).

Anxiety produces personality, so to speak, by restricting the free play of emotion within a "selfsystem" that often paradoxically learns not to seek relief from tension-producing conditions. Sullivan observes that tiny infants will exhibit behavioral distress "when they are in contact with the person who mothers them *and that person is anxious, angry, or otherwise disquieted*. Something which develops without a break into the tension state which we have discriminated on the basis of its specific differences from fear can be *induced* in the infant by *interpersonal influence*" (238).[4] Sullivan goes so far as to suggest that anxiety directly calls up the memory of the *evil mother*—not, we must note, the lost mother or the mother of the primal scene but that component of the mother's experience that produced in the child a discrimination among the states of being labeled *good-me, bad-me,* and *not-me;* "Bad-me is constructed from experience with anxiety-fraught situation *in which the anxiety was not severe enough to preclude observation and analysis*. Not-me grows out of the mostly retrospective analysis of observed precursors to the paralysis of referential processes which is always associated with sudden severe anxiety" (248–49). The complex and multiply paralyzing resentments in the postwar world that Sullivan anguishes over mostly include anxiety—an evasive element that often "cannot 'be known' " (250–52). Certainly Sullivan's framing of his argument in terms of a pervasive but determining *nondit* as well as in terms of referential failure makes his theory immediately compelling to post-structuralist readers of literature, perhaps even more effectively because the theory itself is rendered in an elliptical, cynical, and yet passionate rhetoric.

Essentially, projecting onto interpersonal exchanges one's childhood responses to the evil mother—and notably to her own possibly masked but nonetheless communicated anxiety—aggressively reproduces both resentments and anxieties in day-to-day life. Sullivan's line of reasoning seems to me to provide some necessary elements to the interpretation at hand. Granting, then, the interpersonal nature of anxiety-production and of self-production, we might reobserve that there seems to be no way to separate the primal scene as it takes place in individual bedrooms from the more public traumas contributing to the semiotic flowering of anxiety in a wide variety of important interactions and as a persistent preoccupation of literary representation. My argument thus far has traced some of the relations among such portrayal, literary fathering, the psychological primal scene, and literary surrogates of such unspoken scenes. The line of connection among these elements finds emphasis in the eloquent argument of Ned Lukacher that Dickens's fictional corpus is, in fact, a parenting foundation for Freud's own conception of the primal scene (Lukacher 330–36). Sullivan adds to this line of primogeniture—Dickens, Freud, Joyce, Barthelme—attention to the social elements downplayed by Freud but theorized by Nietzsche.

What is missing in this rich body of theory is, of course, women's voices and women's experience (as opposed to abstract evocations such as "maternal plenitude" or "the evil mother"). Hence it is instructive to consider a demonstrable anxiety of influence as well as the representation of anxiety in a writer in the direct line of descent, a writer who is, like Barthelme, occasionally obsessed by Joyce's fiction, the French feminist Hélène Cixous. In the remainder of this essay I look at Cixous's novel *Angst,* which moves into the foreground the subtext of anxiety. To complement Cixous's fictional response to Joyce's fathering, I turn first to the fragmentary story of Joyce's biological daughter Lucia, whose artistic talents succumbed to the pressures of insanity, a situation attesting repeatedly to the enormous task of self-creation faced by a woman deprived of personal power, historical space, and social nurturing. It seems to me important to emphasize, through the experiences of these two women, that the determinants of anxiety are enormously complex, dialectical, linguistic, and interpersonal. The fact of being born and growing up assures some measure of anxiety in our culture for everyone, male and female. Reading novels partly assures that this anxiety takes certain social forms. The hope is that coming to terms with fiction that interrogates the prevailing masculinist models of behavior, experience, and response may produce alternative patterns of interaction and hence paths for personal and social development. Such feminist paths might sidetrack the obvious fill-in-the-blank model of male structures—as in the multiply substitutive role of Jarndyce and the all-consuming assimilative qualities of the Dead Father—in favor of a tolerance of emptiness as the site at which something new may begin to take shape.

Righting the Father: Lucia Joyce

One of the encouraging phenomena of the past few years in the Joyce industry has been critical attention to the women, like Sylvia Beach, who formed part of Joyce's community in exile. Biographical work, both completed and in progress, on Joyce's wife Nora is especially provocative,[5] given the many myths that have long hovered around the Joyce marriage—that Nora was the earth mother who ballasted the intellectual Joyce, that (as he claimed) she made Joyce "a man," that she did not and could not appreciate his writing. No doubt the myths have some basis in experience, but certainly Nora was an extraordinary woman in her own right, and we do not as yet know enough about the integrity and significance of her life except as a reflex of Joyce's needs and drives. But an even more glaring absence of interpretation confronts us when we attempt to consider the life of Joyce's daughter, Lucia Anna. I want to suggest here that like Joyce's literary descendants, Lucia voiced many of her father's concerns; articulating his anxieties about being understood and valued apart from his work, she ultimately forfeited the ability to speak for herself and passed most of her life in a mental institution. Culturally, Lucia's story has been assimilated to her parent's so thoroughly that it is rare to find any but the most offhanded comment about her in the critical literature; Richard Ellmann's biography of Joyce provides a good deal of information, which I rely on below, but because of its focus on the father, as well as its perhaps necessary adoption of a paternal point of view, it does not draw the conclusions about Lucia that I pursue here. Hence, sadly but logically, the best published source of information about her anxieties and about Joyce's influence on her remains his letters.[6] My reading of these residues of Lucia's life works not only out of the Freudo-Nietzschean materials organized above but also from two additional points of reference—Alice Miller's studies on child-rearing (*The Drama of the Gifted Child, Thou Shalt Not Be Aware,* and *For Your Own Good*) and the psychology of family dynamics.

What strikes a reader right away in Ellmann's discussion of Lucia's birth is the symbolic compensatory function of her name:[7] "It was St. Anne's day, and so, since Anne was also the name of Nora's mother, they added

Anna to the first name of Lucia, the patron sight of eyesight, which Joyce had decided on earlier" (Ellmann, *James Joyce* 262). Throughout her life, this child, who suffered both emotionally and physically from a correctable strabismus, appears to have choreographed her breakdowns to keep time with Joyce's own repeated eye crises and surgeries. This evidence of identification between father and daughter—an identification that Joyce encouraged and that the sensitive, intelligent Lucia emotionally deformed herself in order to satisfy—might seem coincidental at best. But it must be borne in mind that Joyce was himself obsessed with coincidences and valued them highly enough to entertain the notion that another writer born on his birthday could complete *Finnegans Wake* for him should he die prematurely. How could such a worldview not attract a gifted child's attention? How should she remain unaware that the construction of coincidences enabled some kind of complex gratification in her beloved parent and produced as a by-product the respect and attention of that parent? Hence, it comes as little surprise that during her serious adult breakdowns Lucia's timing also responded to Joyce's compositional needs. When he was suffering deeply from the writing of *Work in Progress,* when he felt himself abandoned by his literal and spiritual patrons, when he seemed to have lost touch with his complex project, Lucia also suffered.

It is moving indeed to recall that Joyce spoke of his writing in both *Ulysses* and the *Wake* as close to madness. One suspects that he feared insanity—and what gifted person reared in a repressive environment would not worry about the extent to which he was misunderstood?—as much as he feared cancer. Perhaps the demented mother in "Eveline," the mad nun in *Portrait,* and the wandering Dennis Breen in *Ulysses* express a deep-seated personal fear that Joyce controlled by portraying these crazed victims. But objective representation of Lucia was never possible for Joyce, so intensely did he identify with her. As he remarked in a letter to Harriet Shaw Weaver in 1935, after she had visited with Lucia in England, "What I would like to know if you are writing to me is whether you liked Lucia or not. . . . She may be mad, of course, as all the doctors say but I do not like you to mention her in the same breath with my cousin or sister or anybody else [by whom Joyce had been rejected]. If she should be so mentioned then it is I who am mad" (Ellmann, *Selected Letters* 377). In the same letter, he summarizes the view of Lucia that his friends, according to Ellmann's report, despaired over: "I am in a minority of one in my opinion as everybody else apparently thinks she is crazy. She behaves like a fool very often but her mind is as clear and as unsparing as the lightning. She is a fantastic being speaking a curious abbreviated language of her own. I understand it or most of it" (376). Joyce's loving delusion about the degree of Lucia's psychosis reveals his identification with her; the child who was conceived in a compensatory interpretive matrix—as an offering to the gods, if you will—has become someone of whom the father speaks as though she were his version of himself, a misbehaved, foolish, fantastic, Dedalian artificer communicating in playful code. Is it possible that Joyce not only misread her conduct as benign but also produced that behavior in his child to air for him the fears that he could not interpret or resolve despite his frequent epistolary references to them? Afraid of but also deeply attracted to ambiguous mental states, Joyce delegated to Lucia the expression of his ambivalence and terror. He also allowed her behavior to challenge the patience and tolerance of those around him, as a way of testing his sense that the people who helped him may not actually have liked him.

I find it important that while writing to Harriet Weaver Joyce seems to have cried about Lucia's plight. He tells her that his eyes are tired because "the writing of this epistle was punctuated with lachyrmal stops" (377). Ellmann remarks on this fact as a sign of Joyce's deep concern, given that Joyce had not "wept in a letter" since 1909, when he wrote to Nora his passionate, pornographic epistles (684). For me, Joyce's emotion throws light on the family tensions that served as the matrix of Lucia's anxieties. I suspect that if Alice Miller were presented with the materials I am using, she would conclude that Lucia, a gifted child, was also an abused child. I do not mean to be inflammatory, simply to assert the fact that even though relatively little physical and emotional violence may be evident in the received standard narrative of Lucia's childhood, rather little overt violence is required to deform a sensitive and gifted child. Miller's compassionate campaign to attune parents to the unintentional damage caused by well-meaning punishments and rules makes this fact more obvious today than it was in Joyce's time. In any event, Lucia's familial situation forced her to construct a false self modeled on Joyce's own. In part, I think, this identification served not only to provide a safety-valve enactment of Joyce's fears but also to draw the attention of Lucia's remote mother. Certainly Nora's importance in the Joyce family cannot be disputed. She provided for the writer the empathic acceptance that he needed in order to be creatively productive. But she also failed to value sufficiently for Joyce's desires the productions themselves, and one can thus tentatively conclude that she was not the ideally accepting mother for a potentially creative child like her actual daughter. For one thing, Lucia's closeness to Joyce and her apparent ability to appreciate his aesthetic accomplishments enough to try her own hand at various arts probably alienated Nora, who was, at least as projected by the 1909 letters, one of the few forces in the world strong enough to produce real tears in their protean author. Was Lucia a threat to Nora's dominance over Joyce's emotions? So it would seem, given Joyce's portrayal of Nora in his later letters. In the one to Harriet Shaw Weaver from which I have been quoting, Joyce on the one hand mentions indulgently that he had to force Nora to write to Lucia and on the other hand avers fervently that Nora "personally is probably worth both of her children rolled together and multiplied by three" (376). The multiplier, three, appears to signify the two children and Joyce himself—that is, all three of Nora's "children" who sought her approval, like the feuding Shem, Shaun, and Issy of the *Wake*.

What were the manifestations of Lucia's feuding with Nora, of Nora's aggressive responses to her daughter? In addition to the fact that both parents would routinely leave the children while they attended the theater (Ellmann, *James Joyce* 412), we have Ellmann's report that although Joyce "tended to spoil" his daughter, "Nora attempted to rear her more severely, and did not hesitate to spank Lucia . . . when necessary" (434). Anyone who has read Miller's *For Your Own Good* will detect in this well-meaning report the signs of what Miller calls "poisonous pedagogy," which includes the notion that severity in child-rearing, particularly corporal punishment, is "necessary" and useful. Ellmann notes Joyce's own resistance to pandying when he was at Clongowes, but he seems not to take seriously the importance of Joyce's having dissociated himself from such violence. The Stephen Dedalus who does not defend himself against a beating in Nighttown conveys his creator's commitment to and expertise at many forms of passive resistance. But Joyce was also a person of his times, and he does not appear to have expected Nora to share his commitment.

Hence, it comes as no surprise that much of Lucia's anger is directed, during her breakdowns, toward Nora. As Ellmann tells us, on two occasions, in 1932 and again in 1934, Lucia chose the festivities for Joyce's birthday as moments in which to strike out at Nora, even going so far, in the earlier outburst, as to throw a chair at her. Perhaps Lucia's identification with her father made her feel that this was her birthday, too, and that she had a right to behave as she wished. Perhaps she played the role of jealous sister, demanding her share of attention at the favored "brother's" special celebration. The 1932 event probably also responded to Joyce's despair over his father's death a month earlier. That Giorgio's wife was only two weeks from giving birth to Joyce's grandson doubtless both increased the turmoil in Lucia's mind and enhanced her own sense of extraneousness in the family structure, as did the fact that in July of 1931 Lucia's parents, after thirty years of virtual wedlock, were married. Ellmann notes, "In August, Lucia was acting strangely; she had been much put out by her parents' marriage . . . and now she . . . crossed the Channel without them to stay with George and Helen. Her indulgent parents accepted this behavior as girlish, and did not follow her until the end of September" (*James Joyce* 641). Both the language in which this behavior is narrated to us and the conduct itself are disturbing, the former because it might encourage the reader not to consider the Joyces' "indulgence" as self-serving and the latter because Lucia's flight could only betoken her sense of being cut loose from the ground of her constructed, false self. Again, Nora's severity, inflicted upon a sensitive child, contributed, I think, to the difficulties of the troubled adult. According to Sullivan's neo-Freudian argument, Lucia appears to have projected onto those around her the responses she had to the "evil mother" (which may very well not have been Nora per se but Lucia's perception of Nora) and hence suffered anxiety, resentment, and personality disintegration as part of those interactions.

As Ellmann tells it, and he tells it very well, Lucia's anxieties were exacerbated by some extrafamilial experiences. First, she fell in love with Samuel Beckett. Given Beckett's own identification with Joyce and Joyce's tolerance of Beckett's admiration, his presence seems destined to have caused trouble for Lucia. When he ultimately rejected the daughter's advances, Nora convinced Joyce to ban Beckett from their home, and Lucia "irrationally blamed her mother for the break-up." She herself told William Bird that she was "sex-starved." When another young man, Alex Ponisovsky, proposed to Lucia, she expressed her feelings about the marriage by becoming literally catatonic after her engagement party. Ellmann states that "Nora maternally spoke of a suit for breach of promise" (*James Joyce* 649, 650). It would seem that the efforts of her family to project Lucia out of their conflicted embrace into a world in which she would have to take on a separate self produced a sign—inertness, emptiness—that there was no true self there to be called upon. The primary space for her sense of identity was the aesthetic-emotional sphere in which she had been forced to feed from her father's trough and to enact his own ambivalence and compulsions. In 1933, Lucia became "obsessed with fear about the supposed conflicts between her parents" (665), a fact that suggests a good deal of unspoken hostility even in this very outspoken family.

The other arena in which Lucia attempted to make some progress was in her choice of a career. She wrote poetry, painted *lettrines* to illustrate some work of Chaucer's and of her father's, and had a brief stint in the world of dance. The writing and drawing stirred up significant problems. When she was analyzed by Jung, he found her writing to be in Joyce's mode but without direction and purpose. Because Joyce engineered the publication of her *lettrines,* which were obviously subordinate to the works they embellished, the drawing, too, appears to have been overshadowed by the father's presence. The anxiety that Joyce produced in Lucia finds witness in a moving letter that she wrote to him in 1934 during her brief treatment by Jung: "Father, if ever I take a fancy to anybody I swear to you on the head of Jesus that it will not be because I am not fond of you. Do not forget that. I don't really know what I am writing Father. At Prangins I saw a number of artists, especially women, who seemed to me all very hysterical. Am I to turn out like them?" (Ellmann, *James Joyce* 676). Certainly, the issue of writing is here conflated with her anxieties about the artistic life, insanity, filial obligation, desire, and a refusal to know the full message of her words, this last a sign that Lucia had been encouraged not to be aware of her needs and separateness during the years when she should have been maturing emotionally. It seems fair to speculate that the daughter had never been allowed, or allowed herself, to confront her negative feelings for her father and that her insanity partly constituted a denial of her unspoken resentments.[8]

In contrast to Lucia's efforts in verse and paint, her dancing was a success. In fact, from 1926 through 1929 she worked hard at her dancing and had begun to be noticed for her skill. We are told, "Her last performance was on May 28, 1929, at an international competition at the Bal Bullier; here she appeared in a shimmering silver fish costume she had designed herself, and though she did not win the prize, she won many of the audience, who shouted, 'Nous reclamons l'irlandaise,' to the great pleasure of her father. But she now made another turnabout; she decided, with her father's approval, that she did not have the physical stamina to be a dancer, and in October and November gave up this career with 'a month's tears' " (Ellmann, *James Joyce* 612). It is, of course, only too easy to overgeneralize from a small parcel of evidence, but it seems to me that either Lucia became frightened by this separate acclaim, this movement away from her narcissistic rootedness in her father, or she responded to Joyce's masked disapproval of her venture beyond the space in which he could sustain the illusion of controlling her. Certainly, if she had become a successful dancer, she would have been articulating concerns other than or additional to his own, and perhaps the family could not deal with this loss of the spokesperson for its distress. Then, too, it was her father who was becoming frail and old before his time, not Lucia. In any event, Lucia's tears should not be viewed as less significant than her father's.

This question of tears, however, and of mourning in general is of the greatest interest in this exploration of a biological daughter's anxious response to her famous father's co-optation of her identity. As Miller eloquently and convincingly argues, such behavior speaks to a parent's real compulsions and needs—to biographical material that the parent is often unaware of and cannot control without going through an extended period of mourning for his or her own coercion in childhood. I would venture that part of Joyce's fathering can be illuminated by his own portrayal of mourning in *Ulysses*. Leopold Bloom, after all, is a man who has lost his infant son and who has chosen not to risk further efforts at procreation. This same Bloom finds constant reminders in Dublin of his sorrow. Not only does he recall his father's suicide, but he has to attend the funeral of Paddy Dignam and spends time in a cemetery meditating on death. Finally, his attention to the dissolute son of Simon Dedalus becomes conflated with his own mourning for the dead Rudy. Bloom's reaction suggests an emotional arrest; he does not regress, but he does not go forward either. He lives in a world of blasted hopes and disappointment, and his mourning has not worked through to a satisfying resolution. In contrast, his wife does seem to have made the decision to move forward into an uncharted future, even though she does so absurdly, by taking Blazes Boylan for her lover.

Joyce portrays Molly Bloom as having cried bitterly over Rudy's death but having come to terms with it in some final way, as having integrated her sorrow and worked through any personal guilt. Hence, Joyce's dream of Molly Bloom, which he wrote out for Herbert Gorman while he was planning to write *Finnegans Wake,* provides important information in this matter of mourning. Standing on a hill, dream-Molly picked up "from the grass a child's black coffin" and threw it at Bloom, saying, "I've done with you." Joyce was "indignant" and explained to her emotionally and at length what her episode in *Ulysses* was all about. In response, Molly smiled and "picked up a tiny snuffbox, in the form of a little black coffin, and tossed it towards me, saying, 'And I have done with you, too, Mr. Joyce.' " Joyce's report adds that he "had a snuffbox like the one she tossed to me when I was at Clongowes Wood College" (Ellmann, *James Joyce* 549). What interests me here is that Joyce's tiny coffin might easily be taken as the sign of another dead child, the part of Joyce that was killed off, as it were, when he had to make the abrupt and traumatizing move from his parents' home to the world of a Jesuit boarding school. Molly's repeated action of tossing the coffin (*at,* not *to,* as Joyce's gloss would have it) equates Bloom's deferred resolution of mourning with Joyce's own efforts to make up for that loss of self. The action also speaks to Joyce's sense that Molly, often perceived by him as the voice of the female principle, is an autonomous being, an independent woman beyond his control. That Joyce produced a parody of his dream, in a song which Ellmann quotes, suggests the degree of uneasiness about the dream and his need to diffuse its emotional power. The final stanza presents Molly as "Ireland's gamest daughter," whose endless lovers make the speaker want to cry. He asks, finally, "if I cling like a child to the clouds that are your petticoats, / O Molly, handsome Molly, sure you won't let me die?" (549, 550).

In all of this material, a dead child is the point of attention: Rudy, Lucia, Joyce. One could say that the murder of some aspect of childish authenticity in the young Joyce was reproduced in the co-optation of Lucia's voice and in the nonbeing of Bloom's son. Hovering in the background of these scenes is a threatening mother, who allows her son to be sent to school, who hurts her daughter. None of these actions was performed from mean spiritedness, but their repercussions register in Joyce's writing, in his family, in his daily acute anxieties. A final piece of evidence for this interpretation is Joyce's total affirmation of what he saw as Lucia's mad clairvoyance. Ellmann tells us in a footnote that when "Lucia showed Lucie Leon a picture of a coffin with the rubric, 'This is Jim,' Mme Leon assumed the reference was to her brother James, who died not long afterwards. But Lucia must have had another Jim in mind" (678). Indeed, the text of Lucia's anxiety is part of the motif of coffins, the fact of mourning, and the resistance to mourning in Joyce's work and life. And we cannot avoid making the connection between Joyce's evident fear of Molly's power, his openly expressed distrust of intellectual women, and Lucia's own projected power. Her ultimately uncured schizophrenia communicates, among other things, her withdrawal from her own creativity except in the kinds of clairvoyance that Joyce could approve without feeling threatened by them. Long before Lucia's breakdowns, Joyce wrote out in *Dubliners, Portrait,* and *Ulysses* the terms of his dilemma. These fictional terms were also the frame of her internalized childhood world. I wonder what this woman could have accomplished had she been able to battle the father's anxieties within her and break through to a truly creative, independent identity? What kinds of aesthetic losses might we not be mourning for in this kind of inquiry?[9]

Upping the Ante: Cixous

Although Joyce seems to have produced a substantially detrimental effect in his daughter, Hélène Cixous's work has found in Joyce's influence varieties of enabling. A recent issue of the *James Joyce Broadsheet* includes a retrospective view of Cixous's long biographical-critical study entitled *The Exile of James Joyce.* This review positions Cixous, in 1968, just before the impact of Lacan's interpolation into the text of Freud refashioned the shape of French psychoanalytic thought. *Angst* bears testimony that in the intervening decade (the French edition of the novel has a publication date of 1977) Cixous had both come to terms with one of her fictional fathers, James Joyce, and found a place for Lacanian psychoanalysis within her own theorizing about female subjectivity. In some sense, *Angst* develops from the traditional *Bildungsroman* formula; its protagonist moves from the intense anxieties experienced by the woman-as-child to the complex decathexis that results in her self-actualizing maturation. What Cixous attempts is a fictional escape from the chain of influence that breeds anxiety—or at least a feminist intervention that refuses mere passive acceptance of the Father's Name and authority. Her narrative constantly bears witness to Joyce's presence—for example, in its use of dreams, in its conflation of genders, in its obsession with letters and forgery—but the narrative also insists on its own agenda of meanings, some shared with the parent-text but not present in Cixous in a primarily reactive way. In particular, Cixous asks us to consider the absolutes of unity and separation as convenient fictions; she asks us to imagine that the anguish of maternal loss (objective and subjective genitive) and the subsequent repetition compulsion to replace the mother, which both is and produces anxiety behavior, can be placed under erasure by refiguring the terms of intimate relationality (parent-child, woman-lover).

By way of accomplishing this reformulation of human relations, *Angst* explores not only the anxiety of influence but also the anxiety of interpretation; the novel is a note to the protagonist, written by that woman, in a language that she cannot interpret or even own, so that the language is merely a vehicle for emotions that she is exploring in another space. Hence, she tries to position herself in relation to the following dichotomy: either the mother/man will come or s/he will not come. (The attendant subtext here is that either the writer will become James Joyce/Sigmund Freud/Charles Dickens, or she will not.) In actuality the protagonist can never choose one place or another—the mother's arms, the lover's embrace, the language of Joyce—but must occupy the space between (and possibly beyond) these points. Her coming to terms with this ambiguous reality, full of projected dread and inevitable disappointments, is the substance of the narrative—though not its total meaning, which involves more fully the effort to write or position oneself outside of this language, which creates, through its dichotomies and foregone conclusions, the anxiety that Cixous equates with patriarchy. Cixous, that is, shows us the primal scene in all of its mutually relevant tropings, as birth trauma, as alienated copulation, as the loss of a lover, and as the place of writing. The success of Cixous's endeavor, as well as its exploratory nature, finds witness in the book's epigraph: "to the Vital woman, to whom this text did not know it would lead . . ." I am reminded of Miller's dictum that the opposite of depression (which Miller, using Winnicott's terms, links directly to the subject's not knowing his or her "true self") is not "gaiety" per se but rather "vitality: the freedom to experience spontaneous feelings" (57). The Vital woman, as Cixous would have it, finds her true self beyond the words—or at least in the emptiness between the last one written and the word that will follow. She is able to project *some* things outside the burdensome and obviously patriarchal traditions of canonical literature.

Cixous's revision of the terms of human relationality is enabled in part because although *Angst* refers as extensively as *The Dead Father* to HCE (both Barthelme and Cixous asserting their indebtedness to Joyce), a more privileged reference point for Cixous's reader is the *Dubliners* character Eveline. "Eveline" obliquely depicts a female consciousness hovering between joyful identification with a suspiciously absent, or at least mostly offstage, lover and the silence in which Eveline's life has passed. Joyce ends the story by showing what is often called "dehumanization" but which appears to be, more specifically, an anxiety attack: "She felt her cheek pale and cold and, out of a maze of distress, she prayed to God to direct her, to show her what was her duty. . . . Her distress awoke a nausea in her body and she kept moving her lips in silent fervent prayer. A bell clanged upon her heart. . . . All the seas of the world tumbled about her heart. . . . Her hands clutched the iron in frenzy. Amid the seas she sent a cry of anguish!" (41).

Among other things, Cixous glosses this passage when she presents a woman confined and paralyzed by her obvious inability to make the mother return, and to control her relationship with her lover by making it into a game of *Fort! Da!*. Her narrative begins where Eveline's ends:

> The worst is upon me. This is it: the scene of Great Suffering. During this scene the impossible takes place: my death attacks me, life panics and splits in two. . . .
> Suddenly you know: all is lost. Everything. Suddenly all is known. No more scene, yet no end. Cut. You say I. And I bleed. I am outside. Bleeding. Yet formless, helpless, almost bodiless. In and out of my body. In pain. Here, I no longer have what I once had; you no longer know what you once knew. You're not there any more. Outside, frozen. Motionless. (7)

The intense suffering of the protagonist, much of it unavailable to her except in the paradoxically logical terms of the unseen and impossible replaying of the primal scene, draws the reader in its wake. Her attempt to *register* panic—to say it and thus control it—creates havoc with the idea that some single primal scene, whether recollected or mnemonically inaccessible, might be the sufficient cause of such distress. Rather, as the narrative unfolds, the focus shifts to the mechanism of anguish-reproduction, which at once is capable of collapsing all losses into one loss and of displacing that gap so that it stands at the center of every relationship.

In contrast to the response of Barthelme to Joyce's *Wake*, in which the Father is so tangible a character, in Cixous the father, apparently constrained by conflicts that he cannot admit or speak, is simply not there, not part of the narrative. Only his peculiarly reflexive, self-orienting language remains to coerce the child into paralysis. In contrast to the portrayals of Jarndyce, HCE, and the Dead Father, in which the structure of society empowers a paralyzed nonentity whose children play out, in disguise and without satisfying his or their needs, the parent's desires and fantasies, Cixous's story-without-a-father shows us a daughter who insists on saying it all, on speaking all of the fantasies promulgated by her manipulative/manipulated mother, her disappointing/disappearing lover, and her overwhelming/absent progenitor.

What seems to me significant to this discussion of *Angst* is the father's utter absence and the utterance that replaces him. Culture is thus rewritten from the daughter's point of view as she extricates herself from the fictive father's assumed gaze. Her potentially freed subjectivity is, as yet, rendered mostly through silence, but this quietness stands in contrast to Eveline's anguished inability to communicate her terror. Rather, the implicit silences of Cixous's protagonist stand for a release from the prison house of a patriarchal language and gestural repertoire. In the absence of the father, after all, there can be no ultimate primal scene, and the loss of self occasioned by the interaction of female readers and patriarchal texts transforms identity into a state beyond a language that has become, for these readers, synonymous with suffering and anxiety. It is true that Cixous's protagonist tries to fill the emptiness of her experience with frenetic, anxious speech, but she learns to create herself in a place beyond the rational, reified structures of socially imposed subjectivity. Hence, she tells us:

Suddenly, no more steps, no more walls, I am before memory's room; no more door, suddenly no more past, no memory, I haven't *returned*, I was on the point of *arriving*, I thought: "Oh you, who made yourself invisible before my eyes, I am coming," the moment is approaching, I was going to look him in the face, at last, I would see him, I was going to see him—disappear. That will be the time to look him in the face. He was lying down, his face so strangely dear to me; I was frightened, I admired his calm, he was exposed, his right eye staring into my left eye unblinking. I didn't take my right eye off the black hymen that covered his left eye. He wasn't hiding, he let me contemplate the truth, his appearance, he let my eyes caress such a tranquil absence, I would never know him, it would be him, I would never have understood him, my ignorance would increase, I revelled in it. I loved him as never before. Then I love him: mad, unknown— gone. (218)

The textual finale which follows amply repays the closest attention, for it charts the transformation of panic into a paean. The protagonist's intense love for this dead lover-turned-father recurs in a new note, not as suffering but as acceptance and transcendence. She loves, she says, the "way he was resting there eternally, on the bed which would never be a marriage bed; letting a smile flicker over his face and fade away, the expression of an unshakeable, absolutely indifferent wisdom; so certain. I am not needed." True, like the man, she is expendable, according to the terms laid out by the Man with the Smile himself. But she also metaphorically remakes the Symbolic register by seeing it from differing viewpoints. She sees herself from her deficit position as well as "Through the eyes of the mad god." Of "That vision at point blank range" she says:

Laughter tore me apart. I sat down on the top step, absolutely alone. I was escaping, anguish pouring out of my throat, I am losing, letting myself go, it was a new kind of anguish, a keen joy, I was casting off my body; I must have laughed for hours, ruinous laughter ravaging my flesh. I began to spit blood. I spewed up my story from the very first moment. That joyful laughter is clearing me out, wiping my heart clean. Relieved me.

I got rid of god. I finally threw up love. . . . There is no one left. And that certainly inspires an acute delight, a twinge of anguish that excites you, that touch of terror that makes the heart start beating again when you have just died. I didn't love any more, I didn't have to love any-body. It was love loving; whom I love.

Emphasizing the essentially comedic vision that joins the enterprises of Dickens, Joyce, and Barthelme, Cixous's protagonist identifies the love-ideology with patriarchy and lives to laugh about it. This purgation by laughter asserts that what the novel labels love takes place "out there" and is not person-specific; love for the mother, the father, and the man with the smile constitutes a discourse that she can resist, abstain from, or identify with on her own terms and in her own place. The final phrase, "whom I love," suggests a possible equation of its three words that, importantly, does not insist on becoming an assertion. A fragmentary statement, then, becomes the modality of the protagonist's self-expression, one that embraces a new kind of anguish, a suffering that delights because it is, insofar as is possible, self-generated. Further, this suffering takes place in a meditative mode, without the panic and flight of anxiety behavior, beyond the resentments of society as we know it and thus imaginatively outside a received filial frame of reference and subjectivity.

For my purposes, the critical point to be made here is that the father surfaces in Cixous in the moment of his demise. Like Barthelme *and* Joyce, Cixous represents the dead parent, larger than life, part of the landscape, unavoidable, and yet ultimately impotent. For the male writers, however, the father's death and the reasons for it both occasion the fiction and are its obsession. In contrast, for Cixous this subtextual concern surfaces at the end of her protagonist's anxiety-ridden reflections as a by-product of the more compelling search for her true self. Knowing the father stands revealed as a traditionally sanctioned but ultimately unsatisfying goal; it is not the end of the journey but only a point along the way. Hence, while Joyce reports a putative cultural totality through the dreams of a person who is (or, if s/he is not, might as well be) HCE,[10] and while Barthelme identifies the cultural whole with the Father's manufactures, Cixous reaches beyond this obsession with the hegemonies of Western civilization. As a result, she evokes an antitotalizing explanation of anxiety and of subjectivity as her protagonist seeks the space outside the patrix. And although there is no word or gesture to prove it, I believe that she actually arrives there, "one of those who have gone astray and come out on the other side" (215).

Notes

1. This issue takes an interesting shape, for example, in Plottel 122–23.
2. Cf. Werner 98–102 on *The Dead Father* and Barthelme's debt to Joyce. His citing of Joycean material in *The Dead Father* substantially agrees with my sense of that influence.
3. Bloom's discussion of "dependent heirs" like Keats and Wallace Stevens is apropos here (33).
4. Cf. Benjamin, whose conceptions of women's reality as "intersubjective" bears comparison with Sullivan's own socially committed theorizing as well as, obviously, with Marxist and post-structuralist emphases on relationality.

5. In addition to Brenda Maddox's forthcoming biography of Nora Joyce, we have interpretations of Nora's life by Padraic O Laoi (*Nora Barnacle Joyce: A Portrait* [Galway: Kenny's Bookshops, 1982]) and Edna O'Brien (*James and Nora: Portrait of Joyce's Marriage* [Northridge, Calif.: Lord John Press, 1981]).

6. There are, of course, firsthand materials about Lucia's life in her letters and other papers housed at the University of Buffalo. I have not yet been fortunate enough to spend time in Buffalo's Sylvia Beach Collection, but Bonnie Kime Scott's excellent discussion of Lucia's life draws on these papers. Scott's narration of Lucia's life (74–84) does not indicate that those materials cast light on the etiology of Lucia's mental disorder. It is worth mentioning, however, Scott's position on Nora's relationship to Lucia; whereas below I argue for a detrimental quality, however unintentional, in Nora's parenting of her gifted daughter, Scott emphasizes Nora's certainly heroic caring for Lucia during the daughter's schizophrenic outbursts, and she notes Lucia's adult memory (which I would view as not out of keeping with even a severely abused child's needs to idealize her or his parents) that Nora treated her with unvarying empathy and kindness: "She was like a sister to me and we were the best of friends. She never scolded me and . . . wanted me to be happy and have a good time" (quoted in Scott 73). Lucia's adult statements on her childhood appear to require a good deal of active psychological interpretation

   See also David Hayman's "The Papers of Lucia Joyce," in *James Joyce: The Centennial Symposium,* ed. Morris Beja, Phillip Herring, Maurice Harmon, and David Norris (Urbana: University of Illinois Press, 1986), which reports on relevant materials held at the University of Texas at Austin. Further, see Ira Nadel's discussion of the Lucia Joyce papers at University College, London, in the *James Joyce Quarterly* 22 (1985), 397–404.

7. Philip Kuberski makes a similar observation in "The Joycean Gaze: Lucia in the I of the Father," *Substance* 46 (1985), 19–66. Kuberski's essay came to my attention after my drafting of this article was completed. I find myself in partial agreement with his evocative analysis of the relationship between Lucia's schizophrenia and Joyce's narcissistic, incestuous desires; he rightly analyzes the identification between father and daughter and theorizes the genesis of the *Wake* from this identification. However, I remain troubled by the emphasis of Kuberski's piece. He focuses on Joyce-the-Wri*ting* over Lucia-the-Person, assimilating Lucia to the body of Joyce's work. As a result, Lucia emerges as less important than discourse. See also John Gordon's *Notes on Issy* (Colchester: A Wake Newslitter Press, 1982), where he discusses the effects on *Finnegans Wake* of Lucia's birth at the time of Joyce's first major eye crises.

8. At the Milwaukee Joyce symposium held in June of 1987, Ellie Ragland-Sullivan reported on untranslated Lacan materials, mostly from 1976 and 1977, in which Lacan responded to Joyce's life and work in ways that reinforce my speculations here. In particular, Lacan felt that Joyce projected his symptom onto Lucia in a kind of telepathy, and Lacan, too, notes that Lucia's name relates to the father's gaze. Looking at Lucia's letters, Lacan says that her condition constituted a way to avoid incest through her own "fragilization."

9. In the final years of his life, Joyce's suicidal behavior, especially his incongruous (for someone who spent so much time in doctors' offices) avoidance of medical aid at moments when it was obviously necessary, speaks to a degree of childhood narcissistic wounding that is consistent with Lucia's own. This dimension of Joyce's behavior bears substantial rethinking in the future in any assessment of the aims and methods of his writing. On the question of dead children, John Gordon suggested to me also considering the son born to Joyce's parents before him and Nora's stillborn son.

10. I am aware that a strong case can be and has been made (by, for instance, Julia Kristeva and Bonnie Kime Scott) for Joyce as a feminist writer and for Joyce as a writer who tries to let the repressed mother speak in his texts. For certain arguments, I would take this position myself, but it seems to me undeniable that Cixous's project seeks extrication from the horizon of the Joycean text and from a situation that Joyce himself represents without pointing to a possibility of escape. On *Angst* as "both a detachment and an arrival" that "moves away from a masculine writing scene and toward a feminine one," see Conley 94.

Works Cited

Barthelme, Donald. *The Dead Father*. New York: Pocket Books, 1975.

Barthes, Roland. *A Lover's Discourse: Fragments*. Trans. Richard Howard. New York: Hill and Wang, 1978.

Bellamy, Joe David, ed. *The New Fiction: Interviews with Innovative American Writers*. Urbana: University of Illinois Press, 1974.

Benjamin, Jessica. "A Desire of One's Own: Psychoanalytic Feminism and Intersubjective Space." In *Feminist Studies / Critical Studies*. Ed. Teresa de Lauretis. Bloomington: Indiana University Press, 1986. 78–102.

Bloom, Harold. *The Anxiety of Influence: A Theory of Poetry*. New York: Oxford University Press, 1973.

Conley, Verena Andermatt. *Hélène Cixous: Writing the Feminine*. Lincoln: University of Nebraska Press, 1984.

Cixous, Hélène. *Angst*. Trans. Jo Levy. New York: Riverrun, 1985.

Davis, Robert Con. "Post-Modern Paternity: Donald Barthelme's *The Dead Father*." In *The Fictional Father: Lacanian Readings of the Text,* ed. Robert Con Davis. Amherst: University of Massachusetts Press, 1981.

Dickens, Charles. *Bleak House*. Boston: Riverside-Houghton Mifflin, 1956.

Ellmann, Richard. *James Joyce*. New and rev. ed. New York: Oxford University Press, 1982.

Ellmann, Richard, ed. *Selected Letters of James Joyce*. New York: Viking, 1966.

Freud, Sigmund. *The Problem of Anxiety*. In *The Standard Edition of the Complete Psychological Works of Sigmund Freud*. Trans. James Strachey et al. London: Hogarth, 1953–74. Vol. 20.

Glasheen, Adaline. *Third Census of* Finnegans Wake: *An Index of the Characters and Their Roles.* Berkeley: University of California Press, 1977.

Gordon, John. *Notes on Issy.* Colchester: A Wake Newslitter Press, 1982.

Jameson, Fredric. *The Political Unconscious: Narrative as a Socially Symbolic Act.* Ithaca: Cornell University Press, 1981.

Joyce, James. *Dubliners.* New York: Penguin, 1967.

———. *Finnegans Wake.* New York: Viking, 1967.

Lernout, Geert. "Geert Lernout Reconsiders Hélène Cixous's *L'Exil de James Joyce* in the Light of Post-structuralism." *James Joyce Broadsheet* (June 1986): 3.

Lukacher, Ned. *Primal Scenes: Literature, Philosophy, Psychoanalysis.* Ithaca: Cornell University Press, 1986.

McHugh, Roland. *Annotations to* Finnegans Wake. Baltimore: The Johns Hopkins University Press, 1980.

———. *The Sigla of* Finnegans Wake. Austin: University of Texas Press, 1976.

Miller, Alice. *The Drama of the Gifted Child.* Trans. Ruth Ward. New York: Basic, 1981.

Nietzsche, Friedrich. *The Will to Power.* Trans. Walter Kaufmann and R. J. Hollingdale, ed. Walter Kaufmann. New York: Vintage, 1967.

Norris, Margot. *The Decentered Universe of* Finnegans Wake: *A Structuralist Analysis.* Baltimore: The Johns Hopkins University Press, 1974.

Plottel, Jeanine Parisier. "Surrealist Archives of Anxiety." *Yale French Studies* [special issue: "The Anxiety of Anticipation"] (1984): 121–34.

Scott, Bonnie Kime. *Joyce and Feminism.* Bloomington: Indiana University Press, 1984.

Spilka, Mark. "Leopold Bloom as Jewish Pickwick: A Neo-Dickensian Perspective." *Novel* 13 (1979): 121–46.

Sullivan, Harry Stack. "The Meaning of Anxiety in Psychiatry and in Life." *The Fusion of Psychiatry and Social Science.* New York: Norton, 1964.

Werner, Craig Hansen. *Paradoxical Resolutions: American Fiction Since James Joyce.* Urbana: University of Illinois Press, 1982.

Dora and the Name-of-the-Father:
The Structure of Hysteria

ELLIE RAGLAND-SULLIVAN

Dora's Case: Freud, Lacan, and Feminist Critique

The collection of essays *In Dora's Case:*[1] *Freud—Hysteria—Feminism* (1985)[2] does not put hysteria in parentheses as does the American psychiatric document, DSM-III, a new diagnostic manual.[3] Charles Bernheimer describes Dora's analysis thus: "The productive failure of this therapeutic effort is a symptomatic narrative that invites us to read Dora as an overdetermined figure in Freud's unconscious, the name for those gaps in his self-knowledge whose intriguing hermeneutic, rhetorical and psychosexual functions are teaching us to read anew" (*In Dora's Case*, p. 18). That is, Freud sees Dora's narrative as disjunctive and incoherent while his own is one of dominance and mastery. In *In Dora's Case* most essayists ask in various ways what Freud wanted of Dora. The authors then analyze what we can learn from Dora about the relationship of women to discourse, transference, sexuality, patriarchy, literature, interpretation, and so on.

Although Erik Erikson asked in a 1961 article what Dora wanted *of Freud*, no one has put the question in Lacanian terms. *What did Dora want?* Perhaps such a glaring absence in this "masterful" collection can be chalked up to the current tendencies to "read" (i.e., interpret) texts in light of deconstructive philosophy and method; or in terms of the feminist equation of psychoanalysis with a "master" (according to Derrida, phallocentric) discourse whose aim is to further oppress Woman through narrative strategies of mystification, seduction, or reduction. What strikes me in the various essays—both literary and analytic—is the tendency to lose sight of one very sad little girl who becomes a sad and bitter old woman named Ida Bauer. The story that is repressed, I shall argue, is not the story of Woman, but the story of Ida/Dora whose suffering and symptoms are somehow cleaned up, fictionalized, rationalized, tropized, and readied for the American marketplace where neurosis itself remains a disturbing word.

I propose to take up Lacan's idea that psychoanalysis has as its object of study the specific and unique unconscious of an individual speaking subject. Moreover, the unconscious treasury of signifiers (unconscious memories) is neither metaphor, myth, fiction, adjective, nor narrative. It is, Lacan taught, a Real place and a moment in present time. Freud gave us the picture of psychoanalysis as a theory and practice that evolves stories. When written up these become case studies, psychoanalytic paradigms, texts. Lacan's Dora is, by contrast, neither a story, a figural discursive, nor a political figure. She is a question mark: an enigma. Unlike the Freudian analyst, the Lacanian one has no knowledge to bring to Dora's implicit question; her who am I? Only Dora held that answer in a knowledge beyond everyday language, a knowledge on the side of apparent essence that Lacan named the Imaginary order. In a Lacanian "reading" Dora's cure would only be effected through a dismantling of her own particular fantasies (idealizations, misrecognitions) as they give body to symptoms. The catch-22 addressed in the Lacanian clinic lies in the idea that suffering patients cling to symptoms in order to evade the Oedipal truths that appear when Imaginary myths are shattered. Subjects protect such myths, sometimes at the cost of their own lives.

Lacan taught for decades that psychoanalytic "truth" resides in a subjective local specific, but is not knowable through induction (the positive sciences) or through generalized deductions. Lacan did, however, postulate two ways to recognize neurosis as a category—a "set" of relations—among knowledge, desire, sexuality and suffering. But the *structure* at issue in Lacan's concept of a hysterical structure is in no way related to linguistic structuralism. Rather, structure points to an ordering that infers a meaning between fundamental fantasies (unconscious ones); the lack at the center of Being-as-becoming that marks human animals; and the substitute "things" by which this lack is continually filled up in order that it not seem one. Dora's conversion symptoms bring her body into play as an Imaginary signifier. Her aphonia becomes a representational statement—the body written upon—about power, about the denial of the unconscious Real. Loss of voice is loss of a link to the social world. And the voice is, for Lacan, one of the primordial objects of desire; a palpable matrix of meaning and affect throughout life. Dora's bed-wetting is another symptom of loss of power (control)—a loss that also points to her female sex organs.

For Lacan the slits, openings, surfaces of the body, are all susceptible of eroticization during the first years of life, when opaque meanings begin to constitute themselves in pleasure/pain ensembles of memory long before biological organs play any "meaningful" or symptomatic role in an evolving life drama. But once a language system (spoken or written) is acquired, language puts forth propositions against which other words (or responses) oppose themselves, or to which they are relative. Yet, paradoxically, language works with being and body to simulate a unity. Lacan taught that repressed memories give the lie to this fake unity of being and language, but the unconscious is usually obscured by perception and grammar. It is only palpable (or observable) when it traverses discourse, body, or being in symptoms, dreams, and in the death drive (as well as in the mechanisms Freud delineated). The theory that the unconscious "speaks" us lies behind Lacan's declaration that the unconscious concerns ethics, not ontology or epistemology. Put another way, the death drive, reconceptualized by Lacan, is not innate, but is what we suffer from as speaking beings. In this sense the death drive is always with us because we use a language—at first alien to us, but to which we are gradually obliged to submit. Its presence is that of the desire of the Other which is also ours because we must accept this mortification in order to ex-ist. Seen in this light the death "drive" (or signifier) is the *contrary* of the end of life. It *is* existence.[4] The unconscious is ethical, then, because its first *cause* is human vitality (life or death), and not being.[5]

Lacan taught his interlocutors that no analyst would direct a patient in becoming free of her or his symptoms as long as analysts clung to Freud's view of psychoanalysis as a positive science based on experience.[6] Moreover, since language itself cannot signify the whole of even one person's "experience," no psychoanalysis can find its roots in a reification of linguistics. Rather, language can only determine or harden into a signifier (followed by another); that is, into singular referents. With this teaching we are far away from Saussure's structuralist universals or Freud's literalist view of dreams, memories, or fantasies.[7] Freud thought an understanding of the narrative could cure. Lacan offered, instead, the possibility of helping an analysand create a new desire, since, clearly, the analysand cannot create (re-create) an original text/scene. In opposition to Saussure's sign—the model for contradictions—Lacan proffered his signifier as the model for distinctions. Using a logic of the signifier the analyst works with the analysand from the singularity of one case (*experimentum crucis*) toward mastery of a "crisis" (*crucis*). But the enabling principle here is the *experimentum mentis*.[8] Put another way, the symptoms that bring individuals to psychoanalytic clinics are singular, as in Bertrand Russell's sense where contradiction proves the case of "one." For Lacan symptoms are the singular facts that interpret structure, *structure* defined here to mean the effects of Oedipal ordering that produce a paradigm/case/class: *experimentum mentis* (a case of the mind).

By reading Lacan as if he were Freud (an identitarian error), many post-structuralist critics have missed a point Lacan made throughout his decades of teaching. All "cases" or stories move continually from the singularity of a story to minimal universals in structural cause. The difference between the sometimes unbearable or extreme suffering that sets neurotics apart from relatively untroubled normative subjects is the difference between the master discourse spoken with certainty by normative subjects—one based on repression—and the neurotic discourse of confusion. While "masters" know the difference between the particular and the universal, their neurotic brothers and sisters do not. One might define neurosis as the linguistic error (mental habit) of taking a crucial singular issue to be a universal proposition. The "mental" error frames the person's life with an aura of the inescapable, the unavoidable, the impossible: Antigone's tomb or the Marquis de Sade's jail. Lacan wrote S_2 to denote the determination of any subject in the retroaction of the "other" (next) signifier that substitutes again and again for primordially lost objects. But I do not mean to equate objects with things (like a breast, etc.). Lacan emphasized that the primordial objects of desire—breast, feces, the voice, the gaze— become powerful centers or matrices of meaning *because* loss itself is the prior condition necessary to establishing value for what follows. Because a primary sense of void and chaos lies at the beginning of life, Lacan (after Freud) postulated a dialectic of memory, language, and desire that winds and threads through grammar and being in a paradoxical attempt to complete a lack to which it simultaneously refers. Lacan argued that such movement is caused by what Freud called the lost continent of the unconscious.

In light of these comments, one concludes that we will never know Dora's fuller story. But we can study the *structure* to which her symptoms refer, symptoms as carefully recorded by Freud as any historical documenter might do. Lacan, like Freud, takes the symptoms to be metaphors; indicative of something else. It is not surprising that this "something else" is what has set the cat among the pigeons. Dora has doubtless become the feminist/literary/psychoanalytic whodunit of our day. In her conclusion to a review of *In Dora's Case*, Kate Mele credits the editors for ending with a four-page bibliography, thereby wisely suggesting that "there is no conclusion to Freud's story of Dora."[9]

If we accept Neil Hertz's latest words on Dora, we would agree that we can never know what Dora wanted (or wanted of Freud) because Freud wrote over her speech, thus distorting her case forever.[10] If we agree with Hélène Cixous and Catherine Clément writing *La jeune née* in 1975, then we more or less know Dora's story anyway. Her silent protest is a feminine protest against male power.[11] The American psychiatric establishment, meanwhile, cares little for what Neil Hertz or Cixous/Clément have said (if they even know their work at all). For that establishment has ceased altogether to write about hysteria as a nosographic entity. Having discarded Freud's view of hysteria as a disease caused by sexual trauma, or extreme forgetting, the clinical overview is that hysteria is not a noun but an adjective to be applied to emotional outbursts or loss of "self"-control. While Jeffrey Masson has won some support for his literalist claim that hysterics were actual incest victims—which is probably true as far as it goes—the typical American clinician takes an equally reductionist and simple sociohistorical view of hysteria.[12] Hysterics were victims of sexual repression in the unliberated, unenlightened era of Freud.

What the American psychiatric/analytic establishment has in common with contemporary feminist and literary theory is the belief that hysteria is not a neurosis. Some feminists think hysteria was never a neurosis and some analysts say it is no longer one. The clinic has new "pathologies" to worry about: anorexia, bulimia, depression, borderline personalities, multiple ones, and so on. Essentialist feminists and literary theorists, on the other hand, have cleaned up the word *hysteria*; have equated it with Woman, with moral and biological superiority over the male sex; or with the personal, the confessional, with talking. And the awkward little word *neurosis*—ever so reminiscent of the 1950s—has been pushed off-stage. Like Sylvia Plath and Luce Irigaray, Dora has become a martyr to the oppressions of patriarchy. I would like to propose a third point of view: one that would combine both the feminist attention to Dora's plight—reminiscent of woman's lot—and one that would take up the issue of the clinic as a place where individual, singular, suffering persons go with some degree of hope that psychic pain can be attenuated there. My scrutiny of Dora as a troubled girl, young woman, adult, and old woman, will take us rather far afield from the biological cum sexual Dora Neil Hertz described at the New York MLA (1986): a Dora taken out of the hands of men who urged her not to fear vaginal penetration and placed in the hands of women who point to her repressed lesbian desires as the source of her suffering.

In my argument the parties would not be psychoanalysts versus feminists, nor psychoanalysis and feminism, but the psychoanalytic feminist dialectic itself. I propose that while sexual desire is always at issue in any story of suffering, its role is symptomatic, not causative. But symptomatic of what? Jeffrey Masson's book *A Dark Science* stresses what feminists have long emphasized and what Lacan concluded in *Séminaire* XX. Woman is man's symptom.[13] Yet the issue of what constitutes cure or even symptoms is itself problematic. Whether one condemns past and present atrocities practiced on women, or simply the "therapeutic" injunction to women to find cure in accepting their sexual and maternal "destinies," one must continually challenge the theories and practices that propose "cure" through sexology or at the level of behaviorally induced adaptation to cultural norms. In my understanding, Lacan advanced the theory and practice of psychoanalysis by insisting on the ethical dimension in analysis and in being. He asked repeatedly what constitutes the "good" of an individual life? Conversely, he asked what "evil"—what symptoms—suffering points to? In Lacan's context feminist claims that Dora's suffering equals the universal woes of Woman would constitute an appropriation of a very specific desire and mistake the nature of one human's suffering for sociological oppression of all. That is, by demarginalizing Dora, by making her fashionable, how do feminist identifications with her symptoms help women unless, indeed, their symptoms are hers?

In his consideration of what constitutes a symptom, Lacan said it can only (re)-produce itself by occulting an unconscious truth/desire. At an ontological/epistemological level there is no symptom, then, unless a person believes in "it" (*ça/quod*), believes the symptom has something vital to tell him or her. The symptom, in this purview, is something that dallies with the unconscious and with the Real side of *jouissance* where *jouissance* is linked to alienation and death rather than to pleasure and eros. I would suggest that by ignoring the scope of Lacan's theories and the precision of their formulation, and by blaming psychoanalysis and patriarchy for Dora's plight (her symptoms), certain feminist arguments miss the larger issue. Every person's life struggle can only be confronted as a singular, internal dialectic. Freud and Lacan (for all their masculinist biases) recognized that hysterical suffering is a kind of pure pain where an unconscious message—an alien discourse—traverses an individual's narrative, and vitality as well. But on a more general level, perhaps feminists who identify with Dora have understood what Lacan came to theorize in 1972 and 1973: that repression mythologizes a harmony between the sexes when misunderstandings and battles are more truly representative of "relations." "Ça ne va pas entre les hommes et les femmes," Lacan said in *Encore*.

What Lacan recognized (that Freud did not) is that culture itself contains the lack or *malaise* that feminists have equated with patriarchy. Lacan described this *malaise* as an uneasiness that emanates from patriarchal repression and plays around the Name-of-the-father. The reason such male identification with culture might itself cause a social *malaise* could well derive from the paradigmatic way in which a boy learns the incest taboo. That is, males are usually separated/differentiated from their mother's bodies and being in a way females are not. The impact of an early injunction to difference pushes males in the direction of introjecting an identification with law or morality ("No") while "girls" more typically deal with the pleasure and pain of feeling too little difference. Perhaps the place where Lacan's brand of psychoanalysis can meet with feminism is not only in a cultural critique but also in a consciousness of the specificity of these Oedipal effects on every subject. Far from returning women to a repressed place, Lacan urged that repressions be lifted both in the clinic (praxis) and in the culture (theory) so that any individual might have the freedom of creating a desire beyond the fixedness of destructive family myths and unconscious assignments of position.

Lacan argued, then, that just as hysteria is not particular only to women, neither do men have a monopoly on mastery (repression denied). Indeed, why do some contemporary feminists compare their lives to Dora's when many of their situations more closely resemble her brother's life? Otto Bauer was a labor leader, a public spokesperson, a successful human being, an esteemed individual. Dora spent her life going from doctor to doctor to be told over and over that there was no physiological basis to her endless chain of aches and woes.[14] Indeed, I am more intrigued by the degree to which Dora's hysteria was a success than I am by rehashing the reasons Freud's treatment was such a failure. Clearly, he did not have the answers or techniques to help Ida Bauer. Lacan taught that in hysteria the analysand (and analyst) is confronted with an unconscious decision made by the subject of desire (usually female) to cling to her suffering in order to assure the Other of its predominance. In order to guarantee herself that she *is* . . . Lacan delineated the structure of hysteria as a placing of oneself in the Other *in order to* make oneself the object of alien desire. Not only is a certain repetitive ego unity of fantasies and ideals ensured, but sick family games are also authorized and accepted. Being-for-oneself is sacrificed to the insatiable power requirements of an Other—whose *savoir* is ordered by related sets of memories—for whom/which a subject is willing to risk her or his life. Deleuze and Guattari valorized the machinelike, inhuman quality of this Other in their *Anti-Oedipe*.[15] But they erred by finding freedom in this place of slavery. Lacan did not find neurosis funny. Nor, I would argue, did Dora.

Hysterical suffering is, in Lacan's view, the quintessence—the Ur-type—of neurosis, for the structure depends on guaranteeing the Other of its continuing authority. A hysterical subject is defined, then, as one whose complicitous slavery frames her (his) life. One thinks of sayings such as: "You are your own worst enemy"; "A house clearly divided." But our interest here is in one case of the particular: a suffering girl whose brothers are the Wolfman, the Ratman, and Little Hans. Freud clearly did not think women had a patent on psychoanalysis or neurosis, although some feminists have argued that psychoanalysis rightfully belongs to Woman. But as Claire Kahane points out, Dora's privileged status within psychoanalytic history and feminist theory lies in the fact that Freud's account of her unwittingly puts the finger on gender differences as the key to the unnatural way in which identity is constituted by the cultural rather than by the animal natural (instincts and sexual stages) to which Freud reduced his discoveries.

American feminist readings of Dora remain somewhat faithful to Freud's one-on-one phenomenological concept of subject/object relations. Dora remains the victim of Freud, her father, Herr K., etc. In a Lacanian reading Dora becomes the objectal victim of her own unconscious desire, a player within a circular quadrature. Lacan's emphasis on the sexual impasse between men and women goes in quite another direction from Freud's asymmetrical thinking about males and females. For Lacan this impasse is itself the *cause* (or condition) of a structural asymmetry at the heart of being: the creation of lack (as desire) caused by separation(s) initiated in reference to Name(s)-of-the-father. If Lacan is correct in saying that gender and desire emanate from an unconscious *savoir*, then gender and desire are not natural (or initially biological) effects to be interpreted, but mysterious relations susceptible of decoding because and only because a piece of meaning is missing.

But we live in a climate in the United States where the most advanced readings of Lacan claim to be "ontological" (Steven Melville) rather than "epistemological" (Barbara Johnson).[16] Throughout his long life Lacan taught that psychoanalysis treats troubled beings; unraveled egos that may unravel further. Thus, both analyst and analysand confront issues of judgment and ethics ("Kant avec Sade"). For Lacan the unconscious itself is concerned with desire/ethics more fundamentally than with ontics (ego stuff) or epistemology (mind stuff).[17] With this theory Lacan takes us back to the dilemma Freud never solved. How do we talk about the clinic—the singular—within an academic discourse of the plural? How are we to understand the Lacanian goal of trying to deflect a letter from reaching its destination, from trying to stop the endless circulation of ignorant "self" repeatings? Lacan's departure from Freudian biological determinism lies partly in his pursuing Freud's idea that a treatment could be directed (even though the cure is not coincidental with the *guérisson* that either occurs, or not, outside the clinic and within an analysand's own time/timing). But *guérisson* of symptoms lies *hors sens*, on the slope of transforming desire where desire becomes creative, reconstructive, and enactive.

In my reading of Dora, the case is a paradigm of *unreconstructed* desire. The way she signifies herself—represents herself as a subject for other signifiers—never changes. Throughout her life she remains victim and martyr, martyrdom being the face-saving side of victimhood. What is at stake in Dora's case is an unconscious position, I would argue; a position sometimes occupied by a man (particularly in the past by male mystics). But to argue this way, I must follow Lacan and Jacques-Alain Miller (after him) in the kind of retroactive deductive reasoning that finds a *raison d'être* in a logic of the signifier; joined to a theory of the topology of the subject that accounts for overlappings of the Imaginary, Symbolic, and Real knotted by the agent of the Name(s)-of-the-father. In tandem these theories help an analyst—or a listener/reader who knows how to scan discourse—pay heed to the Oedipal effects of a particular life story. By pushing my arguments in this direction I have tried to bring analysis eye-to-eye with interpretation. On one level it can be argued that the clinic can be talked about—not only as productive of texts or case studies, but also as analogous to the isolated singularity of writing, reading, or viewing. But, then, what would one do with the clinical "story"?

Many Anglo-American readings of Dora use interpretive strategies similar to those Freud used in his efforts to cure: to give cohesive meaning to a life by uncovering a whole story. The whole of a life story can never be recovered within a Lacanian purview; indeed never exists in "full" form at any time or in any place. In Freud's clinic the analyst's interpretation was decisive, however, because *his* role was that of Seer/Interpreter. In this context interpretation sought autoconsistency, coherence, and comprehensibility.[18] In the Lacanian clinic the analyst is neither the Interpreter nor the One-Who-Knows. The interpreter is, instead, the subject's own desire and discourse. Although desire (as lack) resides metonymically on the side of the Real, it shows up metaphorically in bodily and other symptoms. A physical symptom speaks a repressed "word" that cannot be enunciated without damage to the analysand's belief system (of idealizations and enshrined myths). Put another way, the symptom tells secrets in an only *apparently* mute language. The Lacanian analyst works at dissolving symptoms and traversing Imaginary (ego) fantasies, and thus aims askew of the analysand's "story." Implicitly urging the analysand to say who wants/wanted what, what he or she *might* want now, such an analyst resembles no one more than Perry Mason as he relentlessly sets about unmasking hidden desires to bring out the truth behind a given crime.[19]

Finally, there are no literal characters to blame, no discursive figures. There are only mechanistic, archaic, dead, and often lethal, letters.[20]

The unconscious speaks from an Other place, but in present time, Lacan said, suggesting that even the Bible can be read as an encoding of Other messages, not the reverse.[21] Does psychoanalysis reverse theology? Does the death drive show up as the absoluteness of the Other in statements such as: "I am a jealous God. Thou shalt have no other gods before me"?[22] Beyond the seeming cohesiveness of grammar, memories, and fantasies—personal or cultural—lie memory effects and ensembles whose order(ing) refers to a subject's (or group's) *jouissance*. Paradoxically the order is both fixed in terms of primordiality and particular effects, and random in relation to initial structuring and to the variables that will trigger responses (what Lacan called meetings or *rencontres*).

But psychoanalysis has been on trial for decades. Indeed, one must agree with the American feminist readings of Freud in the 1950s, with their accusations of sexism and Victorian modalities, and with the repetitions of these accusations by contemporary American feminists echoing their French sisters in the 1960s and 1970s. But something is lost in stopping here. Juliet Mitchell reminded us that Freud was not all bad, nor all wrong.[23] Lacan has reminded us that, whatever his imperfections, Freud's goal was to cure suffering people. He wanted to stop their misery. In looking at Dora's case we also see that Freud took seriously a woman's words about her innocence in a sex story. Now we have to admit that such would not have been the typical Viennese male's reaction at the beginning of this century. With these reminders, perhaps we can say yet one more thing about Dora by accepting that we will never know what Freud's unconscious desires were regarding this young woman, nor hers regarding him. We need not look beyond Kant, Peirce, Lacan, and Derrida, among others, to be reminded that we cannot recuperate the primordial in any literalist way.

What do we know about what Dora wanted? We do not even know if she had a *demande d'analyse*. Her father took her to Freud because she threatened suicide at age eighteen. An exchange was made between two men with the same goal: to make her well. Her father and Freud had different reasons, of course. Herr Bauer wanted Ida/Dora out of his affairs while Freud wanted to see if psychoanalysis worked. But what did Dora want? Some feminists have tried to answer this question at the level of the bisexuality attributed to Dora (and other hysterics) by both Freud and Lacan. In the same breath some feminist readings accuse Freud and Lacan of occulting the feminine. By aligning themselves with Luce Irigaray's indictment of Lacan such feminists place Lacan on the same side as Freud:

a phallocrat. One wonders if it has not yet become clear from Lacan's own texts that his concept of a phallus refers to a signifier for the language imposed on any subject with the purpose of giving that subject an identity? The resulting identity is paradoxically one of mental alienation. And insofar as identity is gendered and erotic (heterosexual, homosexual, bisexual, transsexual) the effect of the phallic signifier does link up with sexual organs.[24] But the primary functions of the phallic signifier involve the learning of separation where the demand links up to "drive" to create limits and boundaries: the acquisition of a place within the Symbolic (cultural) order. The positionings and fictions that accompany these divisions map the path of a subject's sexuality from a *jouissance* that exceeds language.

My Lacanian reading of Dora takes into account his reconceptualization of the unconscious as a primal scene of Other *jouissance* that is a Real hole in the fabric of being and knowing. To drive this point home, Lacan described the human body as a torus—a doughnut—not a sphere.[25] The torus turns into another name for a void against which all identity issues are to be measured. Put another way, Lacan declared that metaphor (a doubleness in meaning and in "selfhood") is only ever possible in reference to structure or metonymy: the ordering that precedes it, even if the order includes a seemingly consistent surface.[26] If we take into account Lacan's ideas of the symptom as a metaphor, desire as a metonymy, and the ego as the metonymy of desire, then how are we to interpret Dora's symptoms except through one more version of the endless chain of ego stories that abound? I can see no way out of this interpretive bind except through arguing from structure; and from one more reading of Dora's dreams (keeping in mind Freud's opinion that dreaming is a universal phenomenon, common to all humans, the normal prototype of pathological phenomena).[27]

If there is, as Lacan opined, a structuration that one can label hysteria, then any analysis thereof would do better now to consider an analysand's symptoms than, for example, Freud's narrative strategies. Symptoms, Lacan taught, are wed to the ego/object, to myths and idealizations, to conscious denials. Symptoms take part in the denial of unconscious truths that cannot be faced. Neurotic structure tells the story of a being whose body and soul are sacrificed to repressed memories and desires of a dead family novel whose "letters" remain active, nonetheless, as glowing embers. In Dora's case, we might come to another view of matters if we credit Lacan with understanding Freud's discovery, and going beyond it in effecting cure. In this spirit Lacan redefined Freud's reading of hysteria. In Lacan's hands hysteria becomes a masochism that drives a subject with the unconscious goal of remaining unsatisfied as the necessary condition of "being." Lacan's analytic aim was to smash the hysteric's fantasy that her being equals an Other desire and to replace this fantasy with creative desire that works at producing substitutions and displacements outside the family novel.

The precondition for considering a Lacanian view of hysteria is that one toy with the idea of a Real and palpable ontological lack at the heart of human existence; with the idea that there is a *malaise*—an uneasiness—fundamental to the human condition; with the idea that the precondition of having/being a "self" rests on a negation of the possibility of that precondition.[28] The dignity that Lacan accords the neurotic—over a normative subject—is that the structure defines itself as taking paradox into account.[29] A normative (or master) structure—based on the denial of any division inherent to being or knowing—eschews paradox. Put in other terms, *méconnaissance* operates the subject's path in conscious life while desire—positioned toward lack—lies in a shadow zone behind ego certainties. Lacan concluded that there is an overlap of conscious and unconscious realms that shows up in thinking and being as a split whose "proof" is a certain anxiety regarding one's own *savoir*.[30] Even though Lacan always followed this trail of an unconscious that keeps us from saying it all, grasping the essence, pinning it down, knowing for sure, he did not, as have contemporary deconstructionists, draw the (only apparently) obvious conclusion: that one must remain on the side of ambiguity, opacity, or undecidability.

Lacan taught that structure can be reconstructed but cannot be deconstructed. Since the signifying chain is fundamentally unconscious, not directly visible, it can only be interpreted through its effects. Moreover, insofar as structure derives from the coexistence of same and different/other (being oneself and not being oneself), as the contradictory condition for subjecthood, it follows that the language of desire can only ever be investigated along circuitous and paradoxical paths. A Derridean play of letters, anagrams, traces, or tropes will not, in this purview, lead to any knowledge of an unconscious signifying order. But Freud himself fell into the deconstructionist trap, a trap of literalizing the meaning of unconscious meaning. The consequence, according to Lacanian psychoanalysts, is that Dora could reject Freud Imaginarily by incorporating him as part of her own fantasy worldview. As long as Freud was far away from her unconscious *sens*—attributing Dora's symptoms to masturbation, etc.—she was free to continue seeing him. But once the Real of her trauma was addressed, the Real crux of her pain exposed, Dora fled.[31]

In a Lacanian context Freud failed in his analysis of Dora, in part, because he did not understand that love/hate or life/death conflicts are not between the analyst and analysand but between the patient's own ego ideals and fantasies and her unconscious desires. Lacan pointed out in his 1953 essay on the transference that not only did Freud make himself an active player in Dora's fantasy (Imaginary) system but, furthermore, was duped by his own literalist view of sexuality—to the point that in 1923 Freud would dismiss the unconscious as a signifying place in favor of a topography based on animal (biological) and mechanistic (physics) models of conflict and explosion. But in 1901 when Freud tried to smash Dora's rationalizations and explanations, Lacan argued, he was on the track of seeing (knowing) that the Real power of unconscious meaning is an enemy of conscious rationalizations/misrecognitions.[32]

While Derrida has been the prime mover in dismissing issues of origins as having any determinative impact on knowledge or truth, Lacan taught that the constitutive path of a given subject's sexuality is inseparable from the constitution of her or his identity and mentality. But since the mythic and objectal origins of being are radically lost, unconscious, it is hard to accept the idea that the ego has the structure of a symptom *because* it hides our own secrets from us. Thus, the ego does not recognize transference as a global "acting-out" of recognition demands (the Imaginary order). Nor are anxiety and doubt thought to be indicative of a Real void beyond apparent certainties (the Other order of desire as *savoir*). Nor do people see the role language plays in constituting a subject who has a certain set of beliefs and intentions that persist over and beyond any ability to map syntax (Chomsky), deconstruct grammar (Derrida), idealize self and other, or describe the world.

Throughout his decades of teaching Lacan continually referred to Dora. In "The Direction of Treatment and Principles of Its Power" (1958), for example, he argues that hysterics generally remain captives of purely imaginary identification because their fantasies imply its ensnarement.[33] In "Intervention on the Transference" (1953) Lacan had already opened the door to a reconsideration of what he has termed the ego blockage or *méconnaissance* that hindered Freud as well as Dora and hastened the end of Dora's three-month analysis.[34] In essays such as these Lacan emphasized the suturing role played by any analysand's ego in analysis. But he stressed the even more crucial issue: that an analyst's ego resistance joined to ignorance of his or her own desire can block the analysand's progress toward finding (then refashioning) the truth of her or his desire into a new "truth."

Because Freud did not understand that the unconscious is the residual outcome or effect of language on being, he did not understand how to help Dora help herself. His head-on attack had none of the subtlety required by an analysis where words, names, or sounds are seen as nodal points between conscious and unconscious meaning systems. Nor did it approach the idea of a relation between structure and symptoms whose logic lies in a metaphorical/metonymic functioning of desire. In my reading, then, Freud lacked the tool of adequate theory (although his intentions were for the good); so Dora had no one to help her reframe her desire. Like Freud a Lacanian analyst might confront Dora with the challenge to unravel the certainty of her "self"-myths, with the difference that the Lacanian analyst views such work as death work whose only *raison d'être* lies in the direction of freeing the analysand from the stultifying effects of the family novel. Such a challenge is treated with utmost care. In this purview Dora's question would be rephrased a few times. *Was will das Weib* is not *Dora's* question, but Freud's. What did Dora want? What has Dora lost? What question does Dora not want to ask herself in order not to see herself seeing herself as lacking?

The Quadrature of the Subject

I will try to answer some of these questions by first taking the issue of ego closure onto the Lacanian field where each subject exists as a "self"-contradictory quadrature. Second, I will reconsider the signifiers in Dora's two dreams in light of Lacan's idea that Freud's attention to detail in dreams shows us that one can never say everything about one's unconscious truth cum *savoir*. But one can look into a fading of the subject where unconscious terrain asserts itself in conscious life.

In "The Direction of Treatment and Principles of Its Power" Lacan pointed out that until Freud wrote "Group Psychology and the Analysis of the Ego" in 1921, he had not yet conceptualized any mode of "identification" apart from the two-body pair of subject and chosen other (the latter an object of identificatory love/hate or so on). In the Dora case, examples would be Dora and Herr K., Frau K., Dora's father, and so on. In Lacan's view, in Freud's chapter on identification he "clearly distinguished this third mode of identification that is conditioned by its function of sustaining desire and which is therefore specified by the indifference of its object" (Sheridan, *Ecrits*, p. 274). The third mode is the ideal ego, formulated by Lacan as the a' or *moi* in his Schéma L. In Lacan's theory the ideal ego's relationship to desire is a contiguous or metonymic one.

Although it is Lacan who insisted on a separation between ego ideals (others) and the ideal ego, Lacan argued that Freud discovered the distinction but did not have the theoretical apparatus to develop or maintain the concept.

The fact that Freud once spoke about the ideal ego is crucial to Lacan's idea that this concept brings us back again to Freud the clinician who intuited the connection of the ego to death, a Freud who was "so firmly tied to mundane suffering, [who] has questioned life as to its meaning . . . to say that it has only one meaning, that in which desire is borne by death. A man of desire, of a desire that he followed against his will into ways in which he saw himself reflected in feeling, domination and knowledge, but of which he, unaided, succeeded in unveiling . . . the unparalleled signifier . . . that phallus of which the receiving and giving are equally impossible for the neurotic, . . . because . . . his desire is elsewhere" (Sheridan, *Ecrits*, p. 277). Here the phallus is both an object of a desire—a desire without flow, a desire subjected to stasis—and a chain of alienated signifiers to which subjects are unconsciously identified or attached. In conscious life, the phallus marks lack.

In Dora's case the "elsewhere" of desire shows up as unconscious *jouissance* writing itself on her body in the language of symptoms. What do her symptoms mean? What does Dora believe? That is, what ideal ego (Imaginary) image does she have of who she is/would like to be? Dora seems to have imagined herself to be a good daughter, a good baby-sitter, and, perhaps, a sexually attractive young woman as well. Whatever she eventually felt about Herr K., it seems she had seen herself "through his eyes" as worthy of attention and affection for many years. But Freud rather quickly saw through her life games, arguing that they were death games, games where her complicity led to a contemplation of suicide. It is this aspect of the Dora case that Lacan linked to what he calls the structure of hysteria, structure here referring to an unconscious positioning of the ideal ego whose referent is the Other's desire. Thus, both desire and narcissism are engaged in an internal power dialectical struggle. Put another way, how does a subject represent her/himself to another signifier who is a subject in an endless chain of deadly games whose stakes are power, narcissism, desire, and *jouissance*?

Lacan has argued that sublimation (or *méconnaissance*) leaves conscious terrain vulnerable to the death drives of the superego (a set of repressed dicta and words that Lacan has described as "féroce et obscène").[35] Symptoms, for Lacan, emanate from the Real, the unsymbolized yet concrete real of unconscious *jouissance* and are, thus, on the side of structure and metonymy whose equivalence with topology—the logic of position—is a literal one.[36] When unconscious *jouissance* produces symptoms, Lacan "read" a secret satisfaction that attaches a subject to his suffering wherein the suffering—voice of the Other—does not want the good of the subject.[37] In "The Direction of Treatment" Lacan asks: "But has anyone observed, in criticizing Freud's approach ... that what strikes us as preconceived doctrine is due simply to the fact that he proceeds in inverse order? Namely, that he begins by introducing the patient to an initial mapping of his position in the real, even if the real involves a precipitation—I would even go so far as to say a systematization—of the symptoms" (Sheridan, *Ecrits*, p. 236).

Freud did not hesitate to point out that Dora's body spoke the words she repressed. Beyond the physical symptoms Freud pointed out that Dora's slap (of Herr K.) meant more than she was saying. Moreover, Lacan goes on, Freud made Dora realize that she was not merely a bit player in the disorder of her father's world; indeed, she was the mainspring of this disorder, her misery giving the lie to family fictions. Furthermore, her disinterest and complacency regarding her own fate were not acceptable to Freud. Lacan's interest in Dora is not in the pros and cons of Freud's strategies. In matters of strategy Lacan always taught his students that as analysts they had to find myriad ways to aim askew of a patient's symptoms. Lacan saw the Dora case as paradigmatic for reasons other than Freud's mishandling of it.

"I [Lacan] have long stressed the Hegelian procedures at work in this reversal of the *belle âme* in relation to the reality that it accuses. It is hardly a question of adapting to it, but to show it that it is only too well adapted, since it assists in the construction of that very reality" (Sheridan, *Ecrits*, pp. 235–36). As we know, the Hegelian *belle âme* has such a positive view of her/himself that such a person—like Molière's Alceste—cannot imagine that he or she can inflict any pain on anyone else. The *belle âme* is the quintessential victim of others (the martyr/saint figure). Lacan's point is that any analyst who buys into a *belle âme* set of fantasies can only lose on all fronts. Not only does the analysand remain imprisoned in a strait-jacket of imagined victimization, the analyst can only ever finally fall into the trap of being just one more bad guy. Lacan pinpointed such a structure as particular to the kinds of fantasies projected by hysterics to support a fragile, and paradoxically rigid, ideal ego.

In Dora's case Lacan adds that Freud's bold conception of interpretation has also not been given its "full mantic meaning," its power of prophecy. Although he mapped the real of unconscious symptoms, then proceeded to discover transference identifications, Freud still failed to realize that the conscious ego of perception—both his and the patient's—is a unifying agent of exclusion that lies about the unconscious by occulting subjective structure. By constantly shuffling the cards of his evidence faceup, Freud gave Lacan the evidence with which to answer some of Freud's own doubts. Although he never decided how identification truly worked, Freud left behind a relatively consistent picture of what the ego was. Lacan argued that Freud did not, however, understand the ego any better than he did the complexities of identificatory processes because he failed to see the idealizing, compensatory functions of the ego. Still, Lacan reads the Dora case as highly instructive—not so much because Freud discovered transference here but because Freud did not understand that the great power of transference lay in *his not using it* (Sheridan, *Ecrits*, p. 236). Indeed, when Freud uses his power to interpret, to demand a little truth, a little love, he drives Dora away.

Lacan taught that the neurotic subject saves narcissistic face by not recognizing the vagaries of unconscious desires, nor its connection to the death signifier when suffering is involved. Who wants to admit they have been duped by intimates? In Lacanian terms, when the structure of alienation imprisons a person behind the bars of neurosis or psychosis, key signifiers always point beyond the fixity of ego identity themes to particular lacks in the unconscious Real. In *Freud et le désir du psychanalyste* Serge Cottet argues as did Lacan himself that the ego has the structure of the symptom insofar as it is enigmatic or unreadable to itself.[38] Lacanian analysts decipher symptoms as meaningful texts that refer opaquely to structure and to an unconscious signifying chain. But, insofar as signifiers are encoded for meaning and point to the *sens* behind a seemingly objective *signification* rather than to sexual energy per se, Lacan would necessarily take Freud to task for his theory that biological energy always lay behind sexual (desiring) drives in a literal one-to-one causative sense. When Freud exposed a drive, what he called *Trieb*, Lacan points out that we fail to see that *Trieb* (quite different from an instinct) implies in and of itself the advent of a signifier (Sheridan, *Ecrits*, p. 236): a meaning (*sens*) beyond meaning (*signification*).

Perhaps we can break out of the phenomenological bind by looking retrospectively at Dora's symptoms to deduce something about her ideal ego (a'), if we take her demands in a structural sense. Put another way, the particular of Dora's unconscious may yield some meaning at the level of the universal as Lacan interpreted it. That is, metaphor runs into metonymy in a place where metonymy equals structure, and structure refers to the function of the Name(s)-of-the-father in binding the Imaginary, Symbolic, and Real orders. The effect of the father's Name(s) refers to what Lacan called the phallic signifier: that which has no signified. He depicted the hysterical structure this way: Φ to D. That is, the hysteric's demand (for love) is that she remain lacking.[39] Dora's overt demands are that she be recognized (loved) as a dutiful and caring daughter, one who nursed her ill father and takes care of the children of Frau and Herr K. She also asks that her parents believe her story about Herr K.'s sexual proposition proffered beside the lake. When they believed him, Dora left her parents a suicide note, argued with her father, fainted, and Herr Bauer took his daughter to Freud. The good doctor was *supposed* to convince the recalcitrant girl to believe the bourgeois family fiction regarding the father's gratitude-filled friendship with Frau K. Sleeping dogs (should) lie.

But Freud did not respect the family lies. Nor did he support Dora's father, who believed Herr K.'s lie and attributed an immoral fantasy to his daughter. One might wonder why feminists have not seen Freud as Dora's rescuer then? Mostly because he committed the masculinist blunder of circumscribing her desire within a blinkered male, heterosexual framework. What interests me beyond (outside) Freud's blunders is the acuity with which he headed for the place of her secret "truth": in her dreams. There he hoped to find what *Dora* wanted. One might imagine how disconcerting all this was for Dora. On the one hand he freed her from the cruelty of her family's insults, from the indignity of being thought a bad girl because she had mentioned the taboo word: *sex*. On the other hand, Freud did something even more unbearable. He tried to go beyond Dora's ego fantasies into the place Lacan has called the Real of unconscious desire.

The problem Lacan finds in hysteria is a structural one of identificatory nature: an unconscious desire to reify desire in conscious life as lack. Castration is linked to the demand for love. In this way the unconscious *jouissance* of an Other's desire can run roughshod over an individual's potential freedom. In Lacan's view it was this radically absent—at the level of conscious admission—Other that Freud interrogated. Why did Dora dismiss Herr K.? Why did Dora not want to marry a nice boy? Why did Dora remain within the equivocal scene of her family's impossible sexual games? Why did Herr K.'s sexual proposition finally tip the scales? In my estimation his offer had the effect of tearing a veil from Dora's eyes regarding what she was worth on the sexual merry-go-round. In *Séminaire III* Lacan tells us Herr K. *was* her ego. A glimpse of this *savoir* revealed what already victimized or objecti-fied her in an unconscious drama of sexual masters and slaves.[40] Put another way, the link between the signifier (Dora's symptoms) and the referent (the meaning or *sens* of her desire) is sliced by the blade of Dora's unconscious intentionality. She can only sustain her sense of being an "ideal" by remaining a wronged and suffering "object," also attesting to her anger at Herr K.'s devaluation of his wife (Frau K.) with whom she identifies unconsciously.

If Lacan is right in arguing that certain men and women resist dropping deadly family games in order to free up their *own* desire—the desire to be cured creating the cure—because their ideal ego myths are too fragile to risk confrontation with Other *savoir*, it becomes easier to contemplate the possibility that some women participate in their own oppression. Lacan viewed the hysteric—usually a female—as one who preserves the power of the dead father (the fantasy of an ideal father) over and above the conscious admission that a denigrated imaginary father may have been impotent, minimal, mean, or simply ineffectual. For Lacan all identificatory scenarios are structured by the first relationships that determined a subject's existence in the world. In Dora's case her unconscious *savoir* gives power to a deficient family "head" who paradoxically has "everlasting life" at the expense of his daughter's freedom to exit from the family primal scene. In this context one could imagine Dora's ideal ego myth—a cherished daughter, a caring daughter—in dialectical conflict with repressed superego messages telling her to simply "get lost." In my picture of Dora her hysterical symptoms would be the Symbolic statements of an unconscious truth: you are not the beloved subject you wish to be.[41]

Eric Laurent has described Dora as trying to constitute "herself as a subject beyond desire."[42] The impasse here is obvious. How can one sustain oneself beyond desire? The answer would be through a pretense at love divorced from desire. Herr K. had seemed to *love* Dora, a stand-in father and harmless lover. But when his love revealed itself as phallic desire, Dora suddenly knew what she was worth in her family discourse: worth less than nothing, a troublesome girl in the way. What more eloquent statement of this "knowledge" than a suicide note? "I will kill myself" is yet another way of asking if they *really* want her dead. Dora's fainting in the course of an argument with her father becomes an appropriate—indeed rational—dramatization of the fading of the subject when unconscious knowledge rears an ugly and unsalutary head.

What Freud unknowingly confronted behind a mere "case of *petite hystérie*" was, I submit, the structure of hysteria itself: that is, Dora's refusal of a knowledge emanating from a barely repressed bank of memories at the cost of living a life lightly (or heavily) threaded around the death signifier.[43] In becoming identified with her symptoms, Dora accepted the dubious honor of possessing two kinds of mastery: the mastery accrued through making the guilty parties "see" their deeds and the mastery associated with *being* an ideal (saint, martyr, victim, *belle âme*). In 1986 (at the New York MLA) Gérard Pommier argued that feminine sexuality succeeds in allying itself to male sexuality—only illusorily—by Imaginarily killing the imaginary/symbolic father. Hysterics do not do this well, he said.[44] Indeed Herr K.'s proposition challenged Dora's unsymbolized *jouissance*: unless she assumes a feminine identity, she must keep her unconscious father impotent and denigrated in order to give her suffering a *raison d'être*.

Dora's Dreams

In conclusion I propose another reading of Dora's hysteria by reconsidering her two dreams through a Lacanian grid. Lacan said many things about dreams. He described them as enunciating the desire of the Other that is not fulfilled and thus states a lack. He also described dreams as statements about a subject's lack trying to reorient the relations of a specific desire to the world of objects particular to that person.[45] Given that dreams are already distortions of an individual unconscious "truth" and that Freud's recounting of Dora's dreams is a further distortion, let us, nonetheless, try to reconstruct some connection between these narratives and the hysterical symptoms characteristic of Dora's desire. If indeed interpretation can only be a distortion—elaboration of an unconscious *savoir*—Lacan argued for minimal interpretation, an interpretation that could proceed from his four little letters: S_1, S_2, $\mathbb{S}$, a.[46]

The goal of a Lacanian dream interpretation is to winnow out a meaning of the signifier that shows a dialectical conflict between desire and ego and produces a fragment (*objet a*) from the Real. In the space of tension what usually appears is an imaginary positioning toward the phallus: i.e., the conscious subject as object of desire within the context of a family myth, unconsciously positioned toward authority—authorization—within an Other meaning system. Put another way, unconscious *jouissance* (*jouissens*) is revealed. But the *jouissance* at issue "is not pleasure; it is rather closer to unpleasure; it is that secret satisfaction which, for example, is at the heart of the symptom and attaches the subject to his sickness."[47] This Lacanian meaning of *jouissance* differs markedly from the American (French) feminist interpretations, where *jouissance* usually means sexual pleasure. Steven Melville tries to pin down Lacan's meaning in his essay "Psychoanalysis and the Place of *Jouissance*," by veering away from topology or the logic of place implicit in Lacan's later teaching. Thus, Melville defines *jouissance* in Lacan's psychoanalysis as a problematic that combines the logic of pleasure with the pleasure of logic.[48] But Melville leaves out the Real that shows up in the logic of the clinic.

Neither Freud nor Lacan saw much pleasure on the side of the ana-lysand, although their own pleasures centered on inventing a psychoan-alytic "science." The question that preoccupied Lacan was this: how does an analyst help an analysand engage (or disengage) his ego in a total re-organization of the dramatics of his or her life as a subject? Since the unconscious is *not* organized like a narrative, nor does it provide an outlet to conversation, the analyst must work at staying out of the patient's ego myth (narrative), something Freud did not know.[49] One way Lacanian analysts try to avoid the obstacle presented by the transferential structure of conversation itself is by their handling of dreams, the vehicle of the Other's discourse, Freud's "royal road to the unconscious." Both systems of denial—the ego and conversation or grammar—are put aside while the analyst listens to the analysand position the signifiers of the unconscious that show up in dreams.

If one thinks of the dream as having the structure of a gaze—the dream peers into a meaning that lies *hors sens* at the same time that this Other *sens* is shown—one must ask what *shows* the dream and what the dreamer is intended to see? One problem in analyzing anyone's dreams, especially Dora's dreams distorted first by her, then by Freud's recounting *after* the session, is that such interpretation can only treat any truth-function in a mythic or narrative form. The Lacanian analyst and philosopher Willy Apollon has argued forcefully that Lacan showed us a Freud whose cases did not reveal "truth" but rather the conditions where his invention of psychoanalysis is repeated in the reporting of *a* case only after the fact—when something came to him—possibly from his unconscious.[50] Lacan went on to argue that interpretation does not mean giving a *sens* to the Other discourse, but a lifting of the signifier that supports several signifying chains of unconscious *savoir*. These chains of meaning form around a lack, a deficiency in being and knowing. In this context dream truth is simply the recognition of some meaning *outre sens*. Insofar as dreams make meaning, albeit nonsensical or enigmatic, they remain as a proof that one aspect of memory has to do with meaning (words and images) whose profound cause cannot, then, be purely biological (brain function or genetic code), but has to do with a hole in meaning itself. Dreams try to fill in the hole as do discourse and fantasy.

In Dora's first dream perhaps we can discern some meaning that *con-tradicts* her "conscious life" analytic conversations; some opening toward a meeting with the unconscious Real. Here, I am defining the Real in opposition to the Imaginary domain of narrative or *récit*. Apollon has called this discourse space a mode Freud invented where one can speak without the point being either truth or a life story; but, rather, the efficacity of lifting the repression of an unconscious desire and moving it into the domain of ethics (judgment) and action (rather than understanding or sympathy). If we take Dora's first dream about the burning house to be an effort to reorient her desire in her world of people, to rethink her relations, it makes sense that this dream would occur right after her encounter with Herr K. at the lake, when he told her a story she could not tolerate hearing. "My wife is nothing to me," he said. The meaning in suspension concerns what signifying chain will be triggered regarding her sexual desire and the issue of her desirability. If Herr K. wants Dora because his wife is nothing to him, she has been confronted with viewing herself as a sexual substitute for the woman who has "stolen" her father. Let us imagine that Dora's long fantasy regarding her friendship with Herr K. paints her as a desirable, yet chaste, girl. In such a fantasy she would have been more than his wife: a blameless virgin, rather than a shameless adulteress. In one sentence Dora is confronted with two unpalatable facts. She "owes" Herr K. some payment, perhaps on her father's account, and she is being humiliatingly favored over the K. family governess, whom he has recently abandoned ("Dora," pp. 146–47).

In *Séminaire* XI Lacan said:

> Dora's obvious complaisance in the father's adventure with the woman who is the wife of Herr K., whose attentions to herself she accepts, is precisely the game by which she must sustain the man's desire. Furthermore, the *passage à l'acte*—breaking off the relationship by striking him, as soon as Herr K. says to her not, *I am not interested in you*, but, *I am not interested in my wife*—shows that it was necessary for her that the link should be preserved with that third element that enabled her to see the desire, which in any case was unsatisfied, subsisting—both the desire of the father whom she favoured *qua* impotent and her own desire of being unable to realize herself *qua* desire of the Other. Similarly, and this once again justifies the formula I have given, the formula that originated in the experience of the hysteric, as a means of situating it at its correct level—*man's desire is the desire of the Other.*[51]

Lacan argued that "self" or ego fictions and fantasies are always complicitous with the lack(s) particular to a given subject's unconscious suppositions. If, as I have suggested, Dora's unconscious ideal ego posture is that of a cherished yet sexually untainted girl, Herr K. has challenged the fantasy by which she is complicitous with her father's disregard for her (and his family). The lack here would concern some question surrounding the dependability of the father's name as an identity anchor. Indeed, Lacan reread *Totem and Taboo* as illustrative of a strange paradox. On the one hand, the father makes himself "loved" *because* he deprives the sons of women. That is, social love of the father is based on fear of him: his castrating power. Moreover, the law that engenders guilt comes from an imbalance of superego power characteristic of the neurotic; one whose private religion—ideal ego fantasies—organizes life around the belief in an Other's power.[52] Lacan posited neurosis in the place where an individual links the Symbolic father (superego) to Imaginary fathers. Put another way, commanding dicta join hands with issues of love and narcissism. Desire weds superego law; the sacrificial object is the neurotic subject's being and/or body.

In Dora's first dream one might see her efforts to save her mother's jewel case as a dialectical identification with her own efforts to save an image she has had of herself: a precious object. Her father stops her, saying he will not let his children be burnt for the sake of a jewel case (her mother's vanity). Potential interpretations abound. The children must not be sacrificed to trivial (feminine) matters. Or, the bearer of "family jewels" (*Schmuckkästchen*)—the father in vulgar German slang—is not permitted to destroy his children merely so a mother can preserve the symbols of her prestige (her dowry). Dora's dream father was determined to protect his children from death by fire (sexual sacrifice, passion). The jewel case as well as the death by fire become Dora's passion, Dora's sexuality, that are at stake: consumption by an Other force. Dora first dreamt of the burning house after Herr K.'s sexual offer. It is difficult not to read both destruction and passion into this metaphor. But the unconscious point of the dream would regard the position of the Real father—the place of unconscious *jouissance* where pleasure and suffering are masochistically wed—in Dora's symptoms.

Let us suggest that this dream represents what Dora represses in conscious life: that her lack of a desirable position in the family myth was bearable as long as Herr K. continued to play the fatherly role of protecting and admiring her. He was, Lacan said, her substitute ego. Indeed, Dora had for all purposes been abandoned by her father—demoted from her role as special nurse—at age six, when Frau K. became his nurse. Her mother, meanwhile, preferred her brother. At that early time her parents had moved to resort town B., where Dora's physical symptoms first appeared. Insofar as Lacan saw dreams as wishes unfulfilled in the Other— a statement about lack—perhaps her efforts to take her mother's jewel case from the burning house is a question posed to her own unconscious. Am "I" worth saving? What is feminine adornment? Does Woman count? Insofar as Dora dreamt this scene while in psychoanalysis—the discourse

that interrogates Other motivational meanings than those given in conscious life—might one not see her making attempts at freedom? Does Dora
truly *want* to leave the *Autre scène* where she has installed her own
subjectivity? Does she want to smash the ego rationalizations that neurotics
wear as ironclad armor, and break the painful complicity between ego
and unconscious desire? Does she want to know that her pain comes from
her confused identifications with an "absent" mother and delinquent father? That Dora *does* identify with Frau K. in her waking life is far from
surprising. Frau K. represents sexuality and beauty ("her beautiful white
body"). Unlike Dora's mother, Frau K. is desired by more than one man.
How could she *not* serve as a feminine identity model to a young girl
trying to position herself sexually in a very sexual world? Dora desires to
be like her, and she desires her. It is logical that she slap Herr K. when
he calls his wife "nothing."

In Dora's second dream told by Freud, the paternal function is once
more "in play." In this dream, however, her own imaginary father makes
no effort to save her: he is dead. One might say that Lacanian Imaginary
and Real *jouissance* come together to portray the dead (Symbolic) father
as the Real: the key signifier around which all neuroses waltz. Although
one might see this dream as sad, from a Lacanian purview it represents a
bit of hope. If Dora unconsciously recognizes her own father's death—
his impotence—or desires it, some idea of escape from home has penetrated the prison walls of her life narrative. In Lacanian theory symptoms
arise from the Real. But while symptoms may change from moment to
moment, the Real remains intact because it is unsymbolized unless res-
tructured in analysis. In the Lacanian scenario Dora is herself a symbol
of lack; her body a flashing signal. The most Freud could do, as a latecomer
into a drama that has been playing for years before his entry on the scene,
would be to help Dora create a scenario for herself that might restructure
her Imaginary perceptions. And he tried. But by engaging in the game of
endless identifications, he entered the Imaginary order with her. If Lacan
is right, there is no exit from that "theatrical" stage unless desire is first
addressed. Otherwise there is just a circular drama where things change
minimally, if at all.

At the end of Dora's second dream she is apathetic. This apathy may
represent the victory of the Other, an unconscious caving in to the desire
of others. This interpretation would corroborate Cathérine Millot's contention that in hysteria the father is allowed to *jouir* unconsciously as long
as he remains denigrated in actual life (*Hystérie et Obsession*, p. 226). But
what does a Symbolic father have to do with an unconscious, really?
Perhaps we can shed further light on Mitchell and Rose's contention that

femininity cannot be understood outside the symbolic process by which it is constructed, if we look more closely at what Lacan meant by such a theory.[53] Insofar as society—the Symbolic order—imposes itself on biological nature (the animal *Real-Ich* of biological need) at an early stage in life, a disjunction between the physical and societal creates a void into which language enters to ac-culturate Man. Humans are, then, the only cultural animals, whose distinctive feature at the level of meaning is that they speak. When Lacan labels the Symbolic father the dead father, he means that any societal order defines human subjects and positions them in reference to lineage. The Real is linked to the Name(s)-of-the-father as they give meaning to biological parts encoded for *sens* within a context of *jouissance* specific to one person.

Now my interpretation of the Symbolic father and the Real consequences of his effect differ somewhat from the father Jane Gallop portrays in "Keys to Dora," where Gallop takes up Hélène Cixous's position of seeing women as nothing in the Symbolic, but as phallic (omniscient) in the Imaginary.[54] The idea of the Imaginary phallic mother as all-powerful is an object-relations theory concept traceable to Melanie Klein. The Imaginary mother in Lacan's scenario is, rather, the mediator of the Oedipal crisis, and thus the moderator of desire. In this purview, Dora's mother—herself demoted from a position of desirability by her husband—might well communicate a tarnished image of him to Dora. Gallop's theoretical leanings are opaque here, however, for she takes up a position popular with French Lacanians in the 1960s: that the Symbolic is politically healthy while the Imaginary is regressive. Gallop views this hierarchy as supporting the valuation of men (Symbolic) over women (Imaginary). The men in Dora's universe are worth more than she, and all are worth more than the governess who, nonetheless, hysteric-like, subverts the hierarchies. The problem I have with this reading of Dora is that she remains a generalized sociological and phenomenological subject. And neither method of thought allows for the contradictory currents that characterize desire within a singular subject.

After leaving Freud, Dora returned to him fifteen months later, in my view in order to report a revenge. She had obtained dual admissions of guilt from Herr and Frau K.: Frau K. had admitted her affair with Dora's father and Herr K. his sexual proposition to Dora. Lacan has named this time period Dora's "temps pour comprendre" the unconscious. But what has Dora understood? I suggest that Dora wanted to redress a balance; wanted to show Freud—a stand-in for her own Other—that she was indeed above suspicion of moral taint. Her correction of the record could be read as a tacit admission that she would have nothing to do with her *own* unconscious efforts to pursue her desire outside the family novel. She insisted on her identification with the Madonna in the chapel, on her saintly behavior. But paradoxically her victory seems to me a bitter one. For by identifying herself as a "wronged victim righted" she remains at the level of Imaginary awareness where defending herself means buying into the Imaginary games around her.

But Freud deduced more in Dora's return visit—and in her second dream as well—than she could bear to hear. In the second dream Dora, at age eighteen, was walking in a town she did not recognize. All the streets and squares were strange. Although Freud pinpointed some of the detail referents in village photos Dora had recently seen, could not one surmise that the sequence also represents the different "look" things had for Dora after Freud had guided her on a tour of her own unknown terrain? However opaque certain aspects of this dream, one cannot miss the element of unconscious guilt. Dora had left home without telling her parents, and her father had then fallen ill. Does this suggest that Dora's unconscious desire—imposed by her family—was to keep the family scandal to herself lest her "betrayal" of her father bring him harm? Her dream says quite clearly: If you leave home—disobey your parents—your father will die. In this Imaginary interpretation, if Dora wants her father to live she will remain at home. If she wants to remain a hysteric she will keep her denigrated father alive, unconsciously. Put another way, she will not rock the boat. Another element in the guilt—always indicative for Lacan of some damage done to an ideal ego image—could well be that Dora had failed to recognize a sexual component in her life drama over the years until Herr K.'s bold proposition forced her to see his desire, and glimpse her own. This experience gave rise to a dream where the dead father— the Real father as desiring—appears.

Both dreams produce signifying chains that have something to say about the Imaginary father: first his efforts to rescue his children and then his death. Insofar as a dream reveals unconscious positioning toward the phallus—the incarnation of lack—Dora's dreams are poignant questionings regarding what Real power she will give the Symbolic father's Name. In *L'Éthique de la psychanalyse* (*Séminaire* VII) Lacan argued that the only guilt lies finally in giving up on one's desire, in yielding to the Other's exigencies. In Dora's second dream her father passes from a state of illness to death. She embarks on a desperate search for a train station in order to get home. She asks one hundred times where the station is. In Freud's recounting she asked for the *Bahnhof*. Incidentally, I find it strange that Freud did not refer to the *Hauptbahnhof* when nineteenth-century Vienna already had its *Hauptbahnhöfe* (Ost, West, Nord, Süd). Either the "head" is missing in Freud's recollection of Dora's telling, or perhaps her use of the word is "telling" and resounds in his memory. The grounding of an adequate identity anchor is missing in the word, perhaps in the dream, and surely in Dora's life. In her dream Dora fails to find the station but finds instead a wood. Following Freud's later emendations of the Dora case—the suggestion that Dora was sexually attracted to Frau K. rather than to Herr K.—Lacan considers Dora's refusal of a man's offer to accompany her into the woods as representative of a hysteric's vacillation between identifying her sexual desire with a woman or a man.

Lacan defined the structure of hysteria as the desire to sustain the desire of the father. She supplements the father's lack as what ought *not* to lack. Thus, in her identification with women she tries to learn what a man wants/lacks. This unexpected turn in considering hysteria makes it a cognitive-desiring position whose question centers on the father—and by extension Man—as lacking! In her second dream Dora finally found the train station in the woods, but when she could not reach it she was seized by a paralyzing anxiety. In fact anxiety is the only affect Lacan privileged, and he privileged it as the telling point where ego uncertainty meets unconscious necessity (the Real as impossibility). In Dora's dream the anxiety is doubly telling. On the one hand it states her unconscious life dilemma insofar as the hysteric's identity question centers on gender and sexuality: am I a man or a woman? On the other hand, anxiety tells even more profound "truths" in a sleep state than in a waking one. In Lacanian theory dream paralysis would point to a "beyond" in unconscious knowledge as the Real souce of conscious life impasses.

Like Freud's before them, many feminist readings of Dora's second dream have centered on the literal sexuality of the scene. While Freud saw Dora rejecting a man, many feminists have seen Dora as metaphorically going to a woman, embracing the pleasures of going into a thicket. In my estimation both readings still leave something to be desired. Lacan pushes us away from interpreting the story—an act on the side of the essentializing Imaginary—and urges us to consider the possibility that sexual pleasure is not the end point in an identity quest. In this context bisexual identification would represent the ego's scanning of its own unconscious desire for answers. Who am I? Who should I be? Where can I go? What (whom) do I want? Such scanning seeks resolution on the side of peace, although such peace may never be found.

That Dora's dream solution to paralysis is to walk upstairs, once in her home, and open a large book is not surprising to me. Lacan portrayed Freud's discovery of psychoanalysis as the discovery that woman's discourse and sexuality mean something about knowledge itself. In light of this theory perhaps we could think of Dora's turning to a book as yet one more statement about a failure to create her own answers either in life or in dreams. In this context Woman is not the object of psychoanalytic study, but psychoanalysis *is* the discourse mode opened up by Lacan's idea that Woman is man's symptom. Whereas Freud thought of dreams as fulfillments of wishes, full in their meaning, Lacan thought of dreams as unconscious statements about the lacks in a conscious life. For Freud dreams were answers, while Lacan viewed them as questions. Keeping these differences in mind, one sees how a Freudian (or a feminist) interpretation of Dora's turning to the book as a replay of the pleasure found in reading sex books with Frau K. places the drama at the level of sex acts rather than at the Lacanian problematic level of a subject's sexual identity.

In *In Dora's Case* the several authors of "Questioning the Unconscious: The Dora Archive" maintain that "even though interpretation is always over-determined, even though it includes unconscious and conscious determinates, one must nonetheless interpret."[55] They conclude their essay by arguing that we can only interpret the unknown quantities by knowlege of the fact that beyond the transference lies the difference that "escapes one's grasp" (p. 242). The French philosopher and analyst François Regnault has advanced another view of the link between drive (motivation) and knowing/interpreting. Arguing from structure—topological form—Regnault says that when one goes to a book looking for answers, it means that one has not found them in love.[56] Lacan taught that each subject who speaks is a text that interprets her or his Oedipal effects as they filter into matters of *jouissance* and *savoir*. Interpretation is desire. The excess part that points "beyond" the unconscious to a *jouis-sens*—the *objet a*—is the part Lacanian analysts try to return to the subject in a dialectical interrogation of unconscious desire, to treat the Real by the Symbolic.

No doubt Dora's case will be reinterpreted far into the future, for the case is a paradigm whose value lies in the large problematic it opens. Not only is Dora symbolic of the turn Freud made in taking women's symptoms seriously, she is also representative of Lacan's argument that Woman is, moreover, man's Symptom. More specifically, I believe the progress Lacan made in his view of Dora lies in his stress on the issue of identity in constituting the subject; a progress relative to Freud's literalist sexual interpretation, as well as to those feminist arguments that reduce identity issues to biological equations of sex/gender/pleasure. Beyond matters of sexual identity Dora dramatizes the pain of identity questions. She raises the question of whether there is a fundamental difference between bisexuality and lesbianism. In her dream testimonials Dora identifies with men and women: with the memory of cigar smoke and with Frau K.'s adorable white body. One reading of these identifications would support Lacan's view of a hysterical structure as vacillating between female models and unconsciously impotent—and thereby powerful—fathers. In this purview, the hysteric is the person who dramatizes castration issues: Do I lack something or do I not? In raising the problematic of lack to such a high level the hysteric's discourse structure—her communicative link with the world—is antithetical to the master discourse that relies on denial of castration/division.

A second advance made by Lacan's consideration of hysteria is, in my opinion, his injunction to analysts to differentiate between individuals who have a *désir du savoir* and those whose position is a *défi du savoir*. Based on my interpretation of Dora's dreams, I would suggest that although she did not request analysis, Freud awakened in her some desire to know. The particular tragedy of Ida Bauer is that her supposed (on my part) "desire to know" meets with a desire to help (on Freud's part), but Freud does not know what to do. If Lacan's view of hysteria is correct, he has made an advance in knowledge and a gain in insight that will indeed show up in praxis. In this scenario the hysteric is not EVERYWOMAN. She is particular. Indeed, she is sometimes a man. Her only universal characteristic would lie in the pain of being an "abandoned" daughter, one whose *jouissance* requires that she "act out" (act out of) the paradox of being caught in the middle of an identity conflict hidden within the walls of her being. If we look at symptoms as signifiers of trauma caused in the unnatural assumption of sexuality—not correlated with gender in a biological harmony—then we can only agree with Rose that Dora's loss of voice shows an identification with her father.[57] Her voice would be an object *a*—an object that causes desire—that links any subject's *Innenwelt* of representations and memories to the world of others and experience. In Lacanian theory silence or excessive talking become similar ways to use the voice in a quest whose aim is to deny or to know one's worth (ego) and one's desire (the Other). Talking is itself a *jouissance* that fills the hole in the Other, holding at bay the "silence" of unconscious drives by retaining or releasing them. Either side of the coin points to the phallus—the mark of lack—as the agent of the subject's question: Who am I?

Hysteria would be political, then, in the sense that it points to symptoms as having a cause that must be addressed intrasubjectively before the suffering it causes can be alleviated. But the issue of "cure" raises the feminist question again. If all women are hysterics and bisexual, then all women would be the same. And all women would be neurotic. Such an identitarian error is illogical, both philosophically and psychoanalytically. How can one defend a position in which one woman's symptoms are all women's symptoms? Yet, we cannot deny that there are patterns of identification, and directions in desire that characterize "sets" (groups) of individuals. In this context the female hysteric's counterpart is the male obsessional. And beyond the stories that tell of neurotic pain lies psychosis, an unbearable state of unsaying and unbeing. A paradox that Lacan presents in his theory of structures is the idea that the only incurable structure beongs to the normative person—male or female—who need not take account of the unconscious. This relatively untroubled subject aims at a totalizing denial in the name of the reigning ideology.

If Lacan's view of hysteria is correct, then the Doras of today have the same structural problematics as the Doras of Freud's day. That is, gender identification itself is in vascillating play and symptoms cluster around that issue. But symptoms themselves are culture-specific. Today's bulimics, anorexics, and women who cannot say who they are or what they want are, in a Lacanian context, hysterics. Having theorized hysteria as a structure, Lacan gave clinicians, feminists, and others a theory and praxis, a "diagnostic" means by which to work with seemingly enigmatic symptoms. He left a way to help suffering women re-create their lives outside the displaced repetitions that keep them locked up in family novels, only "apparently" making changes through substitutions. Lacan's goal was to offer hysterics the chance to live beyond the *jouissance* that controls a life from an unconscious positioning of an archaic father's name and desire that is all too alive. Such women may create a way to be and to desire that is uniquely their own. In this scenario psychoanalysis becomes the tool of Woman, and not the reverse.

Notes

An earlier version of this paper was delivered at the first New York/Paris VIII Psychoanalytic Workshop, June 1986.

1. Sigmund Freud, *Case Histories: 'Dora' and 'Little Hans,'* trans. Alix Strachey and James Strachey, Pelican Freud Library Series, vol. 8, ed. Angela Richards (New York: Penguin, 1985).

2. *In Dora's Case: Freud—Hysteria—Feminism,* ed. Charles Bernheimer and Claire Kahane (New York: Columbia Univ. Press, 1985).

3. *Diagnostic and Statistical Manual of Mental Disorders* III, (Washington, D.C.: American Psychiatric Association, 1980).

4. Review by Gérard Pommier of Stuart Schneiderman, *Jacques Lacan: The Death of an Intellectual Hero,* in *Lacan Study Notes* (Summer 1985), trans. Thelma Sowley, p. 24.

5. Jacques Lacan, "Subversion du sujet et dialectique du désir dans l'inconscient freudien," *Écrits* (Paris: Seuil, 1966), p. 802.
6. Jacques Lacan, "Position de l'inconscient," *Écrits*, pp. 830–32.
7. Jacques Lacan, "Kant avec Sade," *Écrits*, p. 767.
8. François Regnault, "Lacan and Experience," paper presented at the colloquium "Lacan and the Human Sciences" on Nov. 20, 1986; in press.
9. Review by Kate Mele of *In Dora's Case*, "*Dora* Reopened: Who Is Speaking and What Is Being Said?" in *Literature and Psychology* 32, no. 4 (1986), 67.
10. Neil Hertz, "Teaching Freud," paper presented at the MLA convention, New York City, Dec. 28, 1986.
11. Hélène Cixous, *La jeune née* (Paris: Union Générale d'Éditions, 10/18, 1975), trans. Betsy Wing (Ithaca: Cornell Univ. Press, 1987).
12. Jeffrey M. Masson, *The Assault on Truth: Freud's Suppression of the Seduction Theory* (New York: Farrar, Straus and Giroux, 1984).
13. Jeffrey M. Masson, *A Dark Science: Women, Sexuality and Psychiatry in the Nineteenth Century* (New York: Farrar, Straus and Giroux, 1986); see also Jacques Lacan, *Le Séminaire, livre XX: Encore*, text established by Jacques-Alain Miller (Paris: Seuil, 1975).
14. An excellent article on Ida Bauer (Dora), whose name was only revealed in 1978 by Arnold A. Rogow, was written by Eric Laurent in *Hystérie et Obsession: Les structures cliniques de la névrose et la direction de la cure*, ed. La Foundation du Champ freudien (Paris: Navarin, 1985), pp. 29–42.
15. Gilles Deleuze and Félix Guattari, *Anti-Oedipus: Capitalism and Schizophrenia*, trans. Robert Hurley, Mark Seem, and Helen Lare (New York: Viking, 1977); *L'anti-oedipe* (Paris: Editions de Minuit, 1972).
16. Stephen W. Melville, "Sexuality and Convention: On the Situation of Psychoanalysis," *Sub-Stance*, no. 50 (1986), 75–76.
17. See Stuart Schneiderman, *Jacques Lacan: The Death of an Intellectual Hero* (Cambridge, Mass.: Harvard Univ. Press, 1983).
18. François Regnault, "Usages et mésusages de Lacan," *Ornicar?: Revue du Champ freudien*, no. 36 (Jan.-Mar. 1986), 131–32.
19. Cf. Jacques Lacan, "La direction de la cure et les principes de son pouvoir," *Écrits*.
20. Some American theorists read Derrida's texts as corrective of Lacan's, or at best as a fighting for turf. See Stephen Melville, "Psychoanalysis and the Place of *Jouissance*," *Critical Inquiry* 13 (Winter 1987), 367–68. See also Melville, "Sexuality and Convention," p. 81.
21. Cf. Lacan's graph 2 in "Subversion du sujet," p. 808.
22. Jacques Lacan, "Introduction to the Names-of-the-Father Seminar," (1963), text established by Jacques-Alain Miller, *October* 40 (Spring 1987), 84–85.
23. Juliet Mitchell, *Psychoanalysis and Feminism* (New York: Pantheon Books, 1974).
24. See Melville, "Sexuality and Convention," p. 80.
25. Rosine Lefort and Robert Lefort, "L'enfant: un analysant à part entière," *L'Âne: Le Magazine Freudien*, no. 16 (May–June 1984), 5.

26. For an excellent article on Lacan's work on the *écriture du réel* which shows how he used logic and topology (the torus and the chain) to work out a dimension of space connected to subject functions, cf. Michel Grun-Rehomme, "Le trou," *Ornicar?* no. 33 (Summer 1985), 99–119.

27. For an informative discussion of the structure of hysteria, delineated by Lacan in *Encore*, see the discussion of *Le Maître et le hystérique* by Gérard Wajeman in *L'Âne*, no. 7 (Winter 1982), 3–6.

28. Lacan's *Encore* treats this theme throughout. For English translations of two of the essays one might consult *Feminine Sexuality: Jacques Lacan and the école freudienne*, ed. Juliet Mitchell and Jacqueline Rose (New York: W. W. Norton, 1983). Cf. "God and the *Jouissance* of Woman" and "A Love Letter."

29. Jacques Lacan, "Direction of Treatment and Principles of Its Power," in *Ecrits: A Selection*, ed. and trans. Alan Sheridan (New York: W. W. Norton, 1977), p. 272. Hereafter cited as Sheridan, *Ecrits*.

30. Pierre Bruno, "A côté de la placque: Sur la débilité mentale," *Ornicar?* no. 37 (Apr.-June 1986), 39.

31. Serge Cottet, *Freud et le désir du psychanalyste* (Paris: Navarin/Seuil, 1982), p. 52.

32. Jacques Lacan, "The Function and Field of Speech and Language in Psychoanalysis," in Sheridan, *Ecrits*, pp. 91–92.

33. See Lacan, "Direction of Treatment," in Sheridan, *Ecrits*, pp. 226–80.

34. See Jacques Lacan, "Intervention on Transference," in *Feminine Sexuality*, ed. Mitchell and Rose and trans. Rose, pp. 61–85.

35. Lacan, "Kant avec Sade," p. 771. See also *Le Séminaire, livre* VII: *L'Éthique de la psychanalyse* (Paris: Seuil, 1986).

36. Cf. Nathalie Charraud, "La topologie freudienne," *Ornicar?* no. 36 (Spring 1986), esp. pp. 33–34.

37. Jacques Lacan, "Kant avec Sade," pp. 766–67. See also *Séminaire* VII.

38. Cottet, *Freud et le désir*, p. 142.

39. D. S. Rabinovich, "Névrose et pulsion," *Hystérie et Obsession*, p. 59.

40. Paul Lemoine and Gennie Lemoine, "Structures pathologiques et structures de discours," *Hystérie et Obsession*, p. 180; see also *Le Séminaire, livre* III: *Les psychoses*, text established by Jacques-Alain Miller (Paris: Seuil, 1981), p. 105.

41. Cathérine Millot, "Désir et jouissance chez l'hystérique," *Hystérie et Obsession*, p. 227.

42. Eric Laurent, "Lectures de Dora," *Hystérie et Obsession*, p. 31.

43. Freud, *Case Histories: 'Dora and 'Little Hans,'* p. 54.

44. Gérard Pommier, "Women's Amorality," paper presented at the MLA convention, New York City, Dec. 29, 1986.

45. Ellie Ragland-Sullivan, *Jacques Lacan and the Philosophy of Psychoanalysis* (Urbana: Univ. of Illinois Press, 1986), see Lacan, Jacques Emile Marie, interpretation of dreams, in index, p. 349.

46. Cf. Lacan, *Le Séminaire, livre* XX: "À Jakobson," pp. 19–27. Cf. also Jacques-Alain Miller, "Lacan (Jacques)," *Encyclopaedia Universalis* 18 (1980), 110–12.

47. Interview with Jacques-Alain Miller on the appearance of *Le Séminaire, livre VII: L'Éthique de la psychanalyse* in *Le Matin*, Sept. 26, 1986, *propos* collected by Jean-Paul Morel, pp. 22ff.

48. Melville, "Psychoanalysis and the Place of *Jouissance*." Here Melville calls the joint problematic one of "'enjoymeant,' combining the logic of pleasure with the pleasure of logic," p. 351.

49. Jacques Lacan, "The Neurotic's Individual Myth," trans. Martha N. Evans, *Psychoanalytic Quarterly* 48 (1979), 407.

50. Willy Apollon, "Freud: The Trap of the 'Case History,'" *Newsletter of the Freudian Field*, no. 3 (Fall 1988).

51. Lacan, *Seminar, Book XI: The Four Fundamental Concepts*, text established by Jacques-Alain Miller, trans. Alan Sheridan (New York: W. W. Norton, 1978), p. 38.

52. Serge Cottet, "Freud et la Clinique de Dieu," *L'Âne*, no. 29 (Jan.–Mar. 1987), 42.

53. Mitchell and Rose, introductory comments on "Guiding Remarks for a Congress on Feminine Sexuality," *Feminine Sexuality*, p. 86; published in French in *Écrits* (pp. 725–36).

54. Jane Gallop, "Keys to Dora," *In Dora's Case*, p. 217.

55. J. Collins et al., "Questioning the Unconscious," *In Dora's Case*, p. 245.

56. François Regnault, *Dieu est inconscient* (Paris: Navarin, 1986).

57. Jacqueline Rose, "Dora: Fragment of an Analysis," *In Dora's Case*, p. 133.

NOTES ON CONTRIBUTORS

MARLEEN S. BARR, associate professor of English at Virginia Polytechnic Institute, is the author of *Alien to Femininity: Speculative Fiction and Feminist Theory*. She has edited *Future Females: A Critical Anthology*, *Women and Utopia: Critical Interpretations*, and special issues of *Women's Studies* and *Women's Studies International Forum*. Barr is presently completing *Feminist Fabulation: Space and Postmodern Fictions*.

TERRY BROWN, a graduate student at the University of Florida, is completing her dissertation, a feminist psychoanalytic reading of contemporary American women writers.

PAMELA L. CAUGHIE is assistant professor of English at Loyola University of Chicago. She has recently completed a book-length manuscript on Virginia Woolf and postmodernism, and she has published essays on Woolf and Sir Thomas Browne and on Kafka and Roland Barthes. Her review essay of books on gender and reading appeared in a special issue of *Papers on Language and Literature*, "Gender, Text, and Meaning."

CHRISTINE DI STEFANO is assistant professor in the political science department at the University of Washington, where she teaches courses in political theory and women in politics. She has published articles in *Hypatia* and *Women & Politics* and is currently completing an interpretive study of modern political theory and gender.

RICHARD FELDSTEIN teaches English at Rhode Island College and is coeditor of the journal *Literature and Psychology*. He has published essays on twentieth-century literature and film and is coeditor of the anthology *Feminism and Psychoanalysis*, which is forthcoming from Cornell University Press. He is currently at work on a study of stream-of-consciousness representation in the modern and postmodern novel.

VICTORIA HARRIS teaches English at Illinois State University and has published articles on Robert Bly, James Wright, Gwendolyn Brooks, Sylvia Plath, and Denise Levertov. She has recently finished a full-length manuscript entitled *The Incorporative Consciousness: The Poetry of Robert Bly*.

CHERYL HERR is associate professor of English at the University of Iowa. She is the author of *Joyce's Anatomy of Culture* (University of Illinois Press, 1986). Her current work-in-progress includes an edition of Irish political melodramas and a study of spatial aesthetics called *Significant Spaces*.

ELIZABETH A. HIRSH completed her Ph.D. at the University of Wisconsin, where she wrote a dissertation entitled "Modernism Revised: Formalism and the Feminine." Since then she has lectured in the women's studies program at Madison and has published articles in *ELH* and *Literature and Psychology*.

HELENA MICHIE is assistant professor of English at Brandeis University. She is the author of articles on the Victorian novel, women's studies, and feminist theory, and *The Flesh Made Word: Female Figures and Women's Bodies* (1987).

ELLIE RAGLAND-SULLIVAN teaches English at the University of Florida, where she edits the journal *Newsletter of the Freudian Field*. She has written two books, *Jacques Lacan and the Philosophy of Psychoanalysis* (University of Illinois Press, 1986) and *Rabelais and Panurge*. She has also published articles in *SubStance, Modern Language Journal, Poetics, Ornicar?, Literature and Psychology*, and *The Journal of Higher Education*. Currently she is completing two books on Lacan: *From Freud to Lacan* and *A Lacanian Poetics*.

JUDITH ROOF is assistant professor of English at the University of Delaware and has published essays on Beckett, Pinter, and Duras. She recently coedited the anthology *Feminism and Psychoanalysis* (forthcoming from Cornell University Press), is currently completing a book, *Metaphors of Seeing in Modern Drama*, and is at work on a study of the representation of lesbian sexuality.

RUTH SALVAGGIO teaches in English, women's studies, and the humanities at Virginia Polytechnic Institute. Her recent book, *Enlightened Absence: Classical Configurations of the Feminine*, (University of Illinois Press, 1988), explores the suppression of feminine phenomena in Enlightenment science and literature.

INDEX

Abzug, Bella, 95
Alice Doesn't (de Lauretis), 35, 76
Allen, Woody: as autobiographical
  filmmaker, 76, 77; phallocentricism in
  films of, 5, 70–71, 75, 81, 84; view of
  women by, 4–5, 69–72
Alther, Lisa, 17
Androgyny, in *Orlando*, 44, 45–46, 47, 48,
  49, 51
Angst (Cixous), 9, 10, 12, 174, 200–204
Annie Hall (film, Allen), 69, 74–75, 77
"Annie Leclerc Writing a Letter, with
  Vermeer" (Gallop), 2, 19, 25–26
Antifeminists, as Other women, 17
Anti-Oedipe (Deleuze and Guattari), 214
Anxiety: of Barthelme, 181–84; in *Bleak
  House*, 184–87; of Cixous, 200–204; and
  fathers, 10, 173, 183; in *Finnegans
  Wake*, 176–81; Freud as father of, 173,
  174–76, 190; and resentment, 185–86,
  187–92; and self, 176; sexual, 176, 179,
  180–81; of women, 9, 10, 173, 183, 213.
  See also Hysteria
Anxiety of Influence, The (Bloom), 9, 173
Apollon, Willy, 228
"At Midocean" (Bly), 127
"At the Funeral of Great Aunt Mary"
  (Bly), 126
Auden, W. H., 123
Autobiography (Mill), 163
"Awakening" (Bly), 125

Balzac, Honoré de, 107
Bananas (film, Allen), 71
Barthelme, Donald, 9, 174, 176, 181–84,
  202, 204
Barthes, Roland, 16, 49, 126, 175–76
Baudry, Jean-Louis, 75
Bauer, Ida. *See* Dora
Bauer, Otto (father of Ida/Dora), 214
Baym, Nina, 30, 38–39n.3
Beach, Sylvia, 192

Beckett, Samuel, 196
"Being a Lutheran Boy-God in Minnesota"
  (Bly), 118
Bernheimer, Charles, 208
Bird, William, 196
Bleak House (Dickens), 176, 184–87, 188
Bleier, Ruth, 56
Bloom, Harold, 2, 9, 19, 173
Bly, Robert, 117, 121; mother of, 118–19;
  and phallocentrism, 120, 124–30;
  representation of women by, 5, 6, 124–
  30; and sexism, 123, 130
Bogart, Humphrey, 72
Borderline (play), 145
Boris (Yale University computer), 20
Bové, Paul, 143
Brantenberg, Gerd: and feminist humor, 4,
  87, 90, 94, 95, 96
Broadway Danny Rose (film, Allen), 79
Bruce, Lenny, 70
Burke, Carolyn, 121
Burns, George, 75

Cantos (Pound), 146, 153
Carson, Johnny, 93
Casino Royale (film), 70
Change of World, A (Rich), 123
Chodorow, Nancy, 16, 17, 32, 61, 131
Cixous, Hélène, 212; and anxiety, 176,
  200–204, and Imaginary phallic mother,
  323; and James Joyce, 11, 174, 191,
  199–204; lament about man as idol, 128;
  as neo-Lacanian, 16; poem for, 1;
  response to patriarchal language by, 9,
  10, 12, 38n.1, 121, 124, 125, 129, 202,
  203–4; and the Vital Woman, 9, 11, 201
Class differences, and otherness, 25–26
Clément, Cathérine, 87, 93, 94, 121, 132,
  212
Close-Up (film journal), 145, 155
"Come with Me" (Bly), 127

243

INDEX

244